Visual Arts Years 7 and 8

MAKING ART
CONNECTIONS

Chris Bates
Megan Booth
Sean O'Keeffe

Visual Arts Years 7 and 8

MAKING ART
CONNECTIONS

The McGraw·Hill Companies

Sydney New York San Francisco Auckland
Bangkok Bogotá Caracas Hong Kong
Kuala Lumpur Lisbon London Madrid
Mexico City Milan New Delhi San Juan
Seoul Singapore Taipei Toronto

contents

Making Art Connections

A student artwork gallery is available for each chapter.

How to use this book

Making Art Connections is a new practice-based Visual Arts text that focuses on students' own experiences creating art, while also introducing them to the concepts of Visual Arts and the diverse worlds of a range of artists.

Student artwork

Students have a natural curiosity for what is possible and what has been achieved by their peers. Throughout the book, examples of student artwork support the artmaking activities. Seeing the work of their peers in print alongside the work of established artists gives students a reference for their own artmaking.

Further inspiration is also available from artwork galleries for each chapter on the eText.

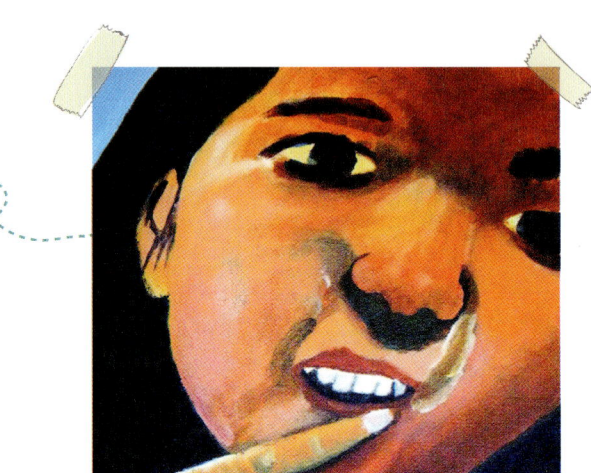

Let's make an artwork

This book represents the myriad possibilities of art. Each of the four parts of the book covers one of four major themes—people, nature, objects, and places and spaces. Each chapter focuses more specifically on aspects of the theme. Chapters are further divided into sections called 'Let's make an artwork', which guide students through making an art project, encouraging them in the use of different art forms. These are followed by in-depth studies of practising artists.

Let's make an artwork 1
Bird's-eye view

Coming up with ideas   ARTMAKING PRACTICE

Take a series of photographs based on the idea of 'a bird's-eye view'. The images can refer specifically to the life of a bird (for example, a day in the life of a school pigeon), or they can be more about the angle and perspective of a bird's-eye view.

The structures of visual arts

The language and concepts of the syllabus—Frames, Artmaking Practice and the Conceptual Framework—can be intimidating for an 11- or 12-year-old student venturing into high school visual arts for the first time. *Making Art Connections* uses creative scaffolding to promote familiarity and build confidence.

Discussion, research and planning in your visual arts diary

CONCEPTUAL FRAMEWORK	PRACTICE	FRAMES
Artist Artwork World Audience	Ideas and actions	Structural—symbolism, visual qualities and composition Subjective—feelings, spontaneity, imagination and the subconscious Cultural—identity

NG ART CONNECTIONS **CHAPTER 2**

as.

ographers).

nd them

12 and 14

subject

e people

special

of your

of the

ar scanned

TEACHER NOTE

Set up a digital photo shoot over several lessons so that the class can take a series of portrait shots of each other taking photographs (photographing photographers).

ONLINE RESOURCES

How to set up a photo shoot

Online Learning Centre

Online **Learning** Centre

WWW www.mhhe.com/au/makingartconnections

Key features of the *Making Art Connections* Online Learning Centre
- Worksheet templates using the three structures of Visual Arts (Frames, Artmaking Practice and Conceptual Framework)
- Additional information about and interviews with artists featured in the book
- Sample teaching and learning activities, as well as teaching strategies to support activities in the text

eText

The accompanying eText is a dynamic resource that creates an interactive teaching and learning environment for Visual Arts.

Key features of the eText
- A searchable PDF copy of the text book
- All artworks expand to full screen
- Galleries of student artworks, arranged by chapter
- Student worksheets
- Weblinks for additional information about featured artists

Acknowledgments

Thanks to Megan and Sean for great ideas and hard work. Thanks to the Visual Arts staff and students at Hornsby Girls' High School, Ku-ring-gai Creative Arts High School, Lithgow High School, MLC Burwood and Pennant Hills High School for allowing us to use images of the students' artmaking. Thanks to the editors at McGraw-Hill—Libby Houston, Ivy Chung and Eiko Bron—as well as the other publishing staff for their tireless behind-the-scenes work. And thanks to the artists who took the time to do interviews and give us valuable insights into their practice.

Chris Bates

Thanks to my co-authors Chris and Sean; my enthusiastic and talented students with whom I love to make art; the staff of Hornsby Girls' High School, especially the Art staff—Nicole, Margo, Margaret and Libby—who willingly share their expertise and artmaking ideas every day; and to the artists who continue to inspire us to keep creating and teaching students the value of art.

Megan Booth

Thanks to Chris and Megan for their confidence and support, to Rani, Rylee and Arlan O'Keeffe for their patience, to Lithgow High School for its quality learning environment and great students, to John Bawden for his mentorship, and to the artists.

Sean O'Keeffe

About this book

Making Art Connections is designed so that junior arts students are able to use it themselves; although ideally students will use it in partnership with their Visual Arts teacher as model and mentor. The material is suitable for both Years 7 and 8, both boys and girls, for city or country students and for students of differing abilities and skill levels.

More content is included in this book than is possible to cover in Visual Arts in Years 7 and 8. This allows students and teachers to choose from a range of themes and options in both practical artmaking and the study of the work of artists. The students' own Artmaking Practice is the starting point for each chapter. A thematic approach is used as an engaging way to introduce the basic structures of the study of Visual Arts in an active and enjoyable context.

As shown in How to use this book on pages vi–vii, *Making Art Connections* has been designed with a number of pedagogical features to assist in teaching and learning. Each chapter contains sections on both theory and practice, with in-depth studies of a range of artists and practical step-by-step guidance in artmaking. Students are also given plenty of opportunity to research and reflect in their visual arts diaries. In addition to the printed book, the accompanying eText and website make this publication more interactive than a conventional text.

The authors of *Making Art Connections* believe that:

- **Year 7 and 8 students need to enjoy their Visual Arts classes.** Making art and studying art and artists can be rewarding and enjoyable for students when presented in a dynamic fashion. It is important to make clear the connection between the students' own artmaking and their study and knowledge of other artists. This book presents a range of artmaking ideas and actions that will stimulate the imaginations and creativity of students as well as encourage them to begin developing their own practice. Some of these ideas will be familiar because students learn best when starting from what they know. To reach new knowledge and fresh, creative ways of working and thinking, the book also offers glimpses of tantalising new worlds to be explored in Visual Arts.

- **Students learn new ideas and skills more easily in the context of their own artmaking than when presented with information in a fragmented, abstract manner.** Students learn how to make art by knowing about art and seeing connections. Rather than having students rely only on personal experience, this book will show them the methods other artists use to come up with ideas and put these ideas into action, encouraging students to learn similar artmaking methods.

- **Students learn more quickly and deeply when they are exposed to best practice examples of artmaking and artworks coupled with expert guidance from their teacher.**

- **Students can become active rather than passive learners.** This can be achieved with encouragement to move beyond the boundaries of the classroom, both in their ideas (through research) and in their actions (by experiencing artmaking in different settings).

- **Students in Years 7 and 8 need the aid of simple structures, the expert guidance of their teachers and the use of a creative scaffolding of knowledge and skills to make learning about Visual Arts easier.** This book promotes this approach using regular, planned sequences that build on each other in every chapter.

About the eText

The eText accompanying this book contains a complete copy of the textbook in PDF format, as well as additional student artworks and worksheets. The PDFs are fully searchable, and bookmarked for easy navigation. As an additional feature, every artwork has been formatted to expand to full screen on the click of a mouse.

The eText also includes additional examples of student work to illustrate some of the possibilities of student achievement. The examples of student work are directly linked to the ideas and actions of the artists in the book as well as to the student activities, and are organised by chapter for easy access. This teaching and learning strategy is based on the premise that students learn more successfully if they have models on which to base their work. Suggested best practice is a combination of the modelling of skills, techniques and approaches used by artists in the book, the student works on the eText and the skills, techniques and approaches modelled by the teacher in the classroom.

Finally, each chapter in the textbook is supported by student worksheets on the eText. These worksheets have been designed to unpack the language of the syllabus, building students' skills, confidence and understanding in Visual Arts concepts such as the Conceptual Framework, each of the four Frames listed in the syllabus, and Practice: ideas and actions.

About the Online Learning Centre

Making Art Connections is supported by an Online Learning Centre (OLC) as an additional resource to assist teachers in the research and preparation of classroom activities. The OLC is designed to allow teachers to devise and develop activities and worksheets based on the needs of their students and the availability of resources. It will also furnish teachers with a more complex and richer source of ideas and knowledge about the teaching of Visual Arts, and research into forms of pedagogy.

In the course of preparing this textbook, the authors interviewed multiple artists as background for the In-depth studies and Critical and historical interpretations sections of selected chapters. The transcripts of these interviews are available on the OLC for teachers to peruse. Other resources include tips on how to organise an excursion, set up a photo shoot and use different media expressively. There is also a worksheet template that teachers can use to prepare their own worksheets.

www www.mhhe.com/au/makingartconnections

Introduction

The structures of Visual Arts

The study of Visual Arts relies on thousands of years of information, knowledge, conventions and skills. But art never stands still; it constantly evolves according to changes in society and culture, mutating and developing new forms. The traditional forms of painting, sculpture and architecture have now been joined by many new ways to make art. This book will present a variety of these to use and learn from.

The use of **three simple structures** to guide and focus the exploration of Visual Arts will assist students to learn about and make artworks without becoming confused. These three structures are all connected to each other and can be used to make the journey into Visual Arts enjoyable and exciting.

The three structures are:

1. Frames
2. Conceptual Framework
3. Artmaking Practice

Frames

The Frames are four different points of view that help us interpret artworks. We can use the **Structural**, **Cultural**, **Subjective** and **Postmodern Frames** to look at, understand the meaning of, write about and talk about artists, artworks, the world of art and the audience for artworks. Table 1 below shows what is covered by each of the Frames.

Table 1: Frames

STRUCTURAL	CULTURAL	SUBJECTIVE	POSTMODERN

Used to give artworks meaning:
• Symbols
• Materials
• Techniques
• Technologies
Used in a planned way:
• Visual qualities
• Visual codes
• Formal elements
• Composition
	• Time and place
	• Styles
	• Culture — Social
	    — Religious
	    — Political
	    — Economic
	    — Technological
	    — Scientific
	    — Philosophical
	• Identity — Personal
	    — National
	    — Gender
	    — Race
		• Emotion
		• Intuition
		• Imagination
		• Memory
		• Fantasy
		• Spontaneity
		• The subconscious
		• Dreams
		• Personal experience
			• Difference
			• Fragmentation
			• Questioning art rules
			• Scepticism
			• Borrowing
			• Paradox
			• Parody
			• Irony
			• Use of non-traditional technologies and materials
			• Use of non-traditional techniques

Conceptual Framework

The Conceptual Framework is made up of four agencies; that is, four means by which we can make connections and systematically think about, talk about and write about artworks. These four agencies are **artist**, **artwork**, **world** and **audience**. These agencies relate to each other, are shaped by the four Frames and reflect the **ideas** and **actions** of Artmaking Practice.

Table 2: Conceptual Framework

	ARTIST	ARTWORK
STRUCTURAL	Artists who work in the Structural Frame: • plan their artworks • use the formal elements in an organised way • use visual qualities that are ordered • follow rules for making art • use signs, symbols and images to suggest meaning in their artworks • use their artmaking knowledge and skills in their Artmaking Practice	Structural Frame artworks are: • planned using the formal elements • given meaning by types of materials used and the methods of construction • meant to communicate meaning by the use of signs, symbols and images • meant to represent the artist's knowledge about visual qualities and the rules of art
CULTURAL	Artists who work in the Cultural Frame: • reflect the ideas and beliefs of their society • reflect ideas about identity • make artworks that comment on society • contribute to the culture in their artmaking	Cultural Frame artworks are: • reflections of the ideas and beliefs of society • representations of the interests of society • reflections of educational and intellectual knowledge
SUBJECTIVE	Artists who work in the Subjective Frame: • use feelings, intuition, imagination and personal experiences in artmaking • respond to the world in emotional, expressive and sometimes spontaneous ways • rely on the inner world of imagination, dreams and their subconscious	Subjective Frame artworks are: • representations of the artist's personal experiences, feelings and subconscious mind • meant to cause an emotional reaction • spontaneous and expressive representations rather than planned and careful ones
POSTMODERN	Artists who work in the Postmodern Frame: • challenge ideas and ask questions about the accepted rules of art • point out inconsistencies • borrow ideas and actions from other artists • use non-traditional materials, new technologies and methods of construction	Postmodern Frame artworks are: • unconventional in their use of materials and methods • representations that borrow ideas and actions from other artists • meant to challenge the accepted rules of art

WORLD	AUDIENCE
Structural Frame artists see the world as: • logical and systematic • a place to find the signs, symbols and visual qualities they use in their artworks • a place where the rules of art are clear and understood by those educated in art	The Structural Frame audience: • knows about the structures of art • knows about the accepted rules of art • judges artworks according to how the artist works within the rules
Cultural Frame artists see the world as: • a series of agencies that promote culture (e.g. art galleries, art schools, the arts media, art critics) • a cultural place within which the artist develops and sells artworks	The Cultural Frame audience: • judges artworks by their cultural, political and economic value • values social meaning in the artworks
Subjective Frame artists see the world as: • an interior place of their subconscious mind and emotions • a place where ideas and actions for artmaking can be based on dreams, fantasies and the absurd • a place where imagination, feelings, memories and associations are valued	The Subjective Frame audience: • has an emotional response to the artworks • finds an emotional connection with the work • values the use of spontaneous and expressive representation
Postmodern Frame artists see the world as: • fragmented, full of inconsistencies and doubt • a place of clashing viewpoints and values that compete with each other • a place where ideas are not fixed but are always changing	The Postmodern Frame audience: • accepts many different viewpoints • values difference in artworks • rejects the accepted rules of art

Artmaking Practice

Artmaking Practice refers to the **ideas** artists have and the **actions** they take to produce artworks. One of the ways you can understand how this works is by connecting Artmaking Practice with the Frames (shown in Table 1) and the Conceptual Framework (shown in Table 2).

Table 3: Artmaking Practice

IDEAS	CONCEPTUAL FRAMEWORK			
	ARTIST	**ARTWORK**	**WORLD**	**AUDIENCE**
	• Has a set of beliefs about art • Works with aesthetics (i.e. ideas about beauty in art) • Has knowledge and skills • Comes up with ideas according to the Frame(s) the artist works within	• Form of artwork (e.g. painting, sculpture, print) suggests ideas • Materials and methods to be used suggest ideas • Function of the work suggests ideas	Personal world: • Values, beliefs and interests • Identity • Cultural and educational background • Own experience, memory and imagination The art world: • Customs and conventions • Art galleries, museums, art critics • Other artists The world of: • Culture • Politics • Science and technology • Religion • Mass media and communication	• How an audience is reached (e.g. galleries, or the internet) can suggest ideas • Type of audience can suggest ideas • Ways an audience can participate can suggest ideas
ACTIONS	**FRAMES**			
	STRUCTURAL	**CULTURAL**	**SUBJECTIVE**	**POSTMODERN**
	The Structural Frame artist: • makes a planned response to ideas • uses methods and materials in a controlled way • uses symbols, conventional visual qualities and formal elements to give meaning	The Cultural Frame artist: • makes a response to ideas that is culturally aware • uses methods and materials that reflect the time and culture • uses a style of artmaking that reflects the culture	The Subjective Frame artist: • has an emotional or an intuitive response to ideas • uses methods and materials in an expressive and spontaneous way • invents personal solutions to visual problems	The Postmodern Frame artist: • responds to ideas by borrowing forms from other times and other artists • uses non-traditional methods and materials • asks questions about the accepted rules of art

Part one

THE WORLD OF PEOPLE

Chapter 1

Facing the world

We are fascinated by our own face and the faces of other people. We look at each other and recognise a likeness. But we also see the character and personality behind the mask. Because of this, depictions of the face, and especially portraiture, have developed as an important aspect of artmaking.

Artmaking sequence	Form	Artists
Let's make an artwork 1 *Portrait*	Photography, collage	• *Jason Mecier* • Rembrandt van Rijn, Vincent Van Gogh, Ian Tatton, Hercilia Lopes
Let's make an artwork 2 *About face*	Painting, mask-making	• *Ben Quilty* • Barbie Kjar, Bert Simons, Arlene TextaQueen

Let's make an artwork 1
Portrait

Coming up with ideas   ARTMAKING PRACTICE

Take a series of photographs of yourself and others, and use these in your artmaking.

Discussion, research and planning in your visual arts diary

CONCEPTUAL FRAMEWORK	PRACTICE	FRAMES
Artist Artwork World Audience	Ideas and actions	Structural—symbolism, visual qualities and composition Subjective—feelings, spontaneity, imagination and the subconscious Cultural—identity

Student worksheet

Rembrandt van Rijn (1606–1669), Netherlands, *Self-Portrait as a Young Man*, 1634. Oil on canvas, 61 × 152 cm. Photo: Corbis.

Vincent Van Gogh (1853–1890), Netherlands, *Self-Portrait Before His Easel*, 1889. Oil on canvas, 65.5 × 50.5 cm. Photo: Corbis.

Ian Tatton (1973–), United Kingdom (UK), lives in Australia, *MC Radioactive*, 2006. Black and white photograph. © Ian Tatton.

Looking at the works of the three artists above, as well as the work by **Jason Mecier** further ahead in the chapter, discuss the main features of a portrait. For example:

1. emphasis on the face
2. a likeness
3. personality or character
4. the world of the portrait subject
5. use of symbolism
6. expressive use of form, methods, materials and composition.

ONLINE RESOURCES

Rembrandt van Rijn

Vincent Van Gogh

Info sheet
Why do artists paint self portraits?

In your visual arts diary:

- list the main features of a portrait
- list two important actions each artist takes to make a portrait
- list the Structural Frame qualities in the Rembrandt artwork and the Subjective Frame qualities in the Van Gogh artwork, using the Frames table in the Introduction to help you
- choose one artwork and list the symbols used, explaining what you think they tell us about the person in the portrait.

Discuss with your friends one way each artist sets out to interest the audience. Using this knowledge, list and sketch some ideas for your portrait photographs in your visual arts diary.

TEACHER NOTE

Set up a digital photo shoot over several lessons so that the class can take a series of portrait shots of each other, as well as self portraits.

ONLINE RESOURCES

How to set up a photo shoot

Taking action   ARTMAKING PRACTICE

Option 1   Photography

- Share school cameras, or use your own camera or mobile phone camera.
- Work in small groups to take a series of digital photographs of each other and yourself.
- Use a variety of different lighting conditions, such as available light from a window, light from a reading lamp or coloured spotlight, or even candlelight.
- Experiment with different facial expressions and head positions (for example, eyes averted, closed or looking directly at the camera) and different vantage points (for example, from above, looking down or face-on).
- Download the images onto a school or home computer. Use photographic editing software to enhance, adjust or add effects to capture both the likeness and personality of the portrait subject.

Option 2   Collage

- Using the artwork by Jason Mecier and Hercilia Lopes on page 6 as inspiration, make a symbolic self-portrait collage, with a photograph of yourself as the basis.
- Collect magazine cut-outs of images that represent aspects of your personality and scan them into a computer.

- Use photographic editing software to superimpose these images over your self-portrait photograph to transform it into a symbolic image. Make sure it still looks like you!

Low-tech alternative

- Use an existing printed photograph of your face, such as a school photo.
- Collect some small personal objects that can be your personal symbols.
- Glue the objects onto the photograph of your face using strong glue.

In-depth study
Jason Mecier

CRITICAL AND HISTORICAL INTERPRETATIONS

CONCEPTUAL FRAMEWORK: WORLD

The world of Jason Mecier is that of contemporary American pop culture.

ARTIST FRAMES: STRUCTURAL

Mecier lives and works as an illustrator in San Francisco. He is a self-taught artist who specialises in 3-D mosaic portraits of famous people.

ARTWORK FRAMES: STRUCTURAL

Like all Mecier's portraits, *Pink* is a one-of-a-kind, handcrafted mosaic. It has been reproduced as the poster for one of Pink's concerts in the USA (United States of America). It uses a traditional portrait pose, showing the head and shoulders of the subject, pop/rock singer Pink. The artist uses a kitsch style so that Pink is presented as an icon of popular culture.

PRACTICE: IDEAS

Mecier explores ideas about celebrity and modern 'throwaway' consumer society. Instead of using paint or a photograph, he assembles his portraits using the personal possessions of his wealthy and famous subjects. He bases the portraits on images borrowed from posters, magazines or television. The artist's raw materials are found objects—discarded junk that he collects as well as the personal rubbish donated by the stars themselves. In Pink's portrait, Mecier has put great effort into using just the right objects to express not only Pink's appearance, but also her inner world.

Jason Mecier, *Pink*. 3-D mosaic, mixed media, 61 × 89 cm. © Jason Mecier. 1969–, USA

kitsch: art considered to be in poor taste

icon: an object or image of devotion

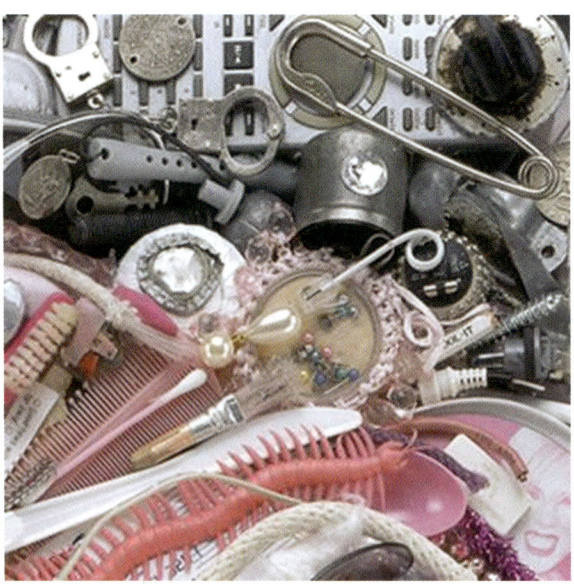

Detail of Jason Mecier's *Pink*. © Jason Mecier.

PRACTICE: ACTIONS

This portrait of Pink is assembled in a careful and detailed fashion to create an almost photographically real portrait made from objects sent to him from Pink's junk drawer. This includes pink and white hair and beauty products, ribbons and rope, plastic cutlery and cotton buds. These symbolise the softer feminine aspects of her personality. These contrast with the darker, harder qualities of the discarded metal objects—safety pins, zippers, locks, keys, coins, nuts and bolts—he also uses.

AUDIENCE

The artist's choice of celebrities as his subject matter appeals to a wide audience. His work has been exhibited internationally and printed in many publications.

WWW www.jasonmecier.com
www.theispot.com/artist/jmecier

Student worksheet

ONLINE RESOURCES

Hercilia Lopes

scanograph: a digital image captured by scanning objects on a scanner rather than using a digital camera

TEACHER NOTE

Demonstrate the use of the camera-less technique of scanography. You can find information on the internet. Some websites are listed here.

Extension

Look at the artwork by Hercilia Lopes.

WWW www.scannography.org/artists/Lopes-Hercilia.html

- Collect objects that reflect your personality.
- Arrange the objects on a flatbed scanner, or the scanner on an inkjet printer, to form your portrait.
- Make a **scanograph** by scanning the arranged objects into a computer and using photographic editing software to edit and enhance the image.
- Print your portrait as large as you can on photographic paper.

WWW http://digital-photography-school.com/how-to-use-your-flatbed-scanner-as-digital-camera
www.scanner-magic.com/scanner-tips.html
www.jpgmag.com/stories/13264

Hercilia Lopes, contemporary artist, Brazil, *Universo-Feminino-X*, 2008. Scanograph, discarded jewellery. © Hercilia Lopes.

Let's make an artwork 2
About face

Coming up with ideas   ARTMAKING PRACTICE

Draw your own portrait or a portrait of one of your friends, or create a mask working in the Cultural and Structural Frames.

Discussion, research and planning in your visual arts diary

CONCEPTUAL FRAMEWORK	PRACTICE	FRAMES
Artist Artwork World Audience	Ideas and actions	Structural—visual qualities, formal elements, symbols and planning Subjective—imagination, expression and spontaneity Cultural—reflecting the ideas and beliefs of society, identity

Student worksheet

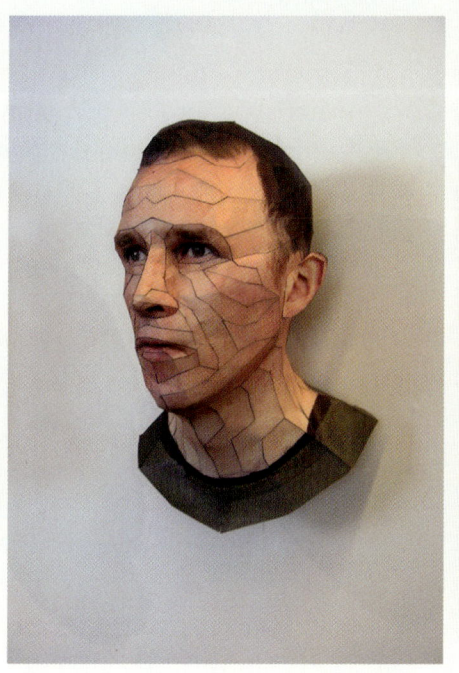

Arlene TextaQueen (1975–), Australia, *Self-portrait in Textas*, 2009. Texta on paper, 78 × 118 cm. © Annie Joscelyne.

Bert Simons (1965–), Netherlands, *Self Portrait*, 2006. Laser scan 3-D portrait, paper, life-size. © Bert Simons.

Barbie Kjar (1957–), Australia, *Bella*, 2007. Coloured drypoint etching on paper, 56 × 56 cm. Image courtesy of the artist and Bett Gallery, Hobart, Tasmania.

To help you come up with ideas for your artmaking, look at the works of the three artists on page 7, the artwork by **Ben Quilty** further ahead in the chapter and the works of the artists you looked at in 'Let's make an artwork 1'.

Revisit the notes on the main features of a portrait that you made in your visual arts diary in 'Let's make an artwork 1'.

In your visual arts diary:

- begin planning your own drawing or mask
- research and make notes on the qualities of the Structural, Cultural and Subjective Frames you will use in your artmaking, using the Frames table in the Introduction to help you.

Taking action   ARTMAKING PRACTICE
Option 1   Painting

- Make use of your self-portrait photographs from 'Let's make an artwork 1'. Use these as visual references for a painted self-portrait.
- Look at the artworks of Rembrandt and Van Gogh on page 3 for inspiration.
- Work in one of the following frames:
  - Structural Frame—use a variety of painting techniques and materials to produce a planned self-portrait, considering the formal elements, such as pose and composition; and use visual qualities that give a likeness of you and show an audience your character. (Refer to the artworks of Barbie Kjar and Arlene TextaQueen on page 7, and Ben Quilty on page 9.)
  - Subjective Frame—take an expressive, spontaneous and imaginative approach, making use of colours that express emotion rather than being realistic. (Refer to the artworks of Barbie Kjar and Arlene TextaQueen on page 7, and Ben Quilty on page 9.)
  - Cultural Frame—make reference to your identity and character. Refer to the work of Arlene TextaQueen on page 7 and Ben Quilty on page 9.

Option 2   Mask-making

- Make a mask for yourself using a theme. The theme could be based on a book, such as *Alice in Wonderland*, or it could be a simple theme such as jungle animals, artworks or the planets.
- Use books and the internet to research your theme, collecting visual ideas and recording them in your visual arts diary.
- Look at the work of Bert Simons on page 7 for inspiration.
- Make some sketches of your mask designs and choose which aspects of the Cultural and Structural Frames you will use in making your mask.
- Discuss with your teacher which methods and materials you will use, and then create your mask.

In-depth study
Ben Quilty

CRITICAL AND HISTORICAL INTERPRETATIONS

Ben Quilty, *Self portrait after Madrid*, 2008. Oil and oil bar on linen, 214 × 183 cm. Image courtesy of the artist and Grantpirrie.
1973–, Australia

CONCEPTUAL FRAMEWORK: WORLD

Ben Quilty's world is that of young Australian male culture. He grew up in the outer northern suburbs of Sydney. He chooses subjects that are local and familiar to him. Quilty sets out to represent the things that dominate so many young men's lives: their cars and the ritual of 'getting smashed'. He uses large images of Torana cars, human skulls with dangling cigarettes and heads of ugly drunken men—sometimes his friends, and sometimes even himself.

ARTIST FRAMES: SUBJECTIVE

figurative: representing or portraying things so they are recognisable

Quilty is a **figurative** artist who wants to express his feelings and personal experiences in paintings on a large scale. He applies thick oil paint onto the canvas in a way that is rapid and aggressive, but also skilful.

ARTWORK FRAMES: SUBJECTIVE

Self portrait after Madrid is a large, confronting, unflattering image of the artist's head shown against the empty background of the canvas. Light shines from underneath so that the eyes appear haunted and the mouth is open as if to cry out.

PRACTICE: IDEAS

The idea behind this self portrait was to express deep feelings. The artist had recently visited the Prado Museum in Madrid, home to many of Spain's finest artists, including Velasquez and Goya. Quilty says he was overwhelmed by the emotional depth of the works at the Prado Museum, ranging from the joy of life to horrors of war. He says he wanted to depict himself in this portrait as though he was 'gazing into the fires of hell'.

PRACTICE: ACTIONS

impasto medium: an additive put into paint to make it very thick

This image of Quilty's face is vibrant and textured. The oil paint is mixed with so much **impasto medium** that it stands up in a 3-D fashion from the surface of the canvas. The paint is applied using cake-decorating tools rather than paintbrushes. Even though he applies the paint in broad strokes, the artist can skilfully model his own likeness. Quilty says he is energised by his 'almost violent' way of painting because it allows him to get images out of his head and onto the canvas very quickly.

AUDIENCE

Ben Quilty's paintings are disturbing, and they challenge an audience with their huge scale. Up close the paint has the appearance of being slapdash, but the further back the audience stands from the works, the more realistic they become. Quilty has developed a large audience across Australia and is exhibited in major art galleries. He is also developing a more international audience, especially in Europe.

WWW www.benquilty.com
www.janmurphygallery.com.au
www.grantpirrie.com

Student worksheet

Shadow people

Chapter 2

Your shadow follows you everywhere you go, reminding you of the parts of yourself that you can see but never fully understand. Shadows have been represented in the traditions and beliefs of many cultures throughout time and have been a rich source of inspiration for artmaking.

Artmaking sequence	Form	Artists
Let's make an artwork 1 *Shooting shadows*	Photography/graphics	• *Sue Ford* • Wolfgang Sievers, Unknown artist of iPod-styled image
Let's make an artwork 2 *Passing shadows*	Painting, printmaking	• *Robert Boynes* • Rafael Lozano-Hemmer, Andy Warhol, Peter Coffin, Kara Walker
Let's make an artwork 3 *Chasing shadows*	Drawing, photography	• *Ellis Gallagher* • Christian Boltanski, Cornelia Parker

Let's make an artwork 1
Shooting shadows

Coming up with ideas ARTMAKING PRACTICE

Take a series of photographs of yourself and others. Then create an image of a dark figure set against a bright, atmospheric background.

Discussion, research and planning in your visual arts diary

Student worksheet

CONCEPTUAL FRAMEWORK	PRACTICE	FRAMES
Artist	Ideas and actions	Cultural—exploring ideas, beliefs and values through artworks
Artwork		
World		Subjective—communicating feelings and emotions through artworks
Audience		

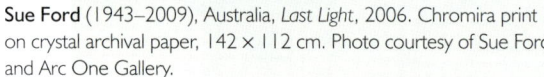

Sue Ford (1943–2009), Australia, *Last Light*, 2006. Chromira print on crystal archival paper, 142 × 112 cm. Photo courtesy of Sue Ford and Arc One Gallery.

A street view of a pedestrian passing by an iPod-styled image, artist unknown, title unknown. Digital illustration. Photo: Getty Images.

Look at the artworks of **Sue Ford** and the other artists here and examine the ways in which they have used shadows.

In your visual arts diary:

- research the symbolism of shadows
- research the symbolism of light
- collect images from different cultures in which shadows and light have been depicted in their traditions and beliefs
- make a list of some ways that shadows and light are present in your everyday world
- create a visual brainstorm of places that are special to you and make you recall particular feelings, emotions or memories relating to shadows and light.

Wolfgang Sievers (1913–2007), Australia, *Designer Gerhard Herbst holding his 'Prestige' material, Red Bluff Sandringham, Melbourne*, 1950. Gelatine silver photograph, 24 × 19 cm. National Gallery of Australia, Canberra. Gift of the artist 1988.

Taking action   ARTMAKING PRACTICE

Option 1   Photography

- Share school cameras, or use your own cameras or your mobile phone cameras.
- Take a series of photographs of people using digital cameras (photograph photographers).
- Keep the people you are photographing in shadow and the background behind them very bright so they appear as silhouettes (refer to Sue Ford's images on pages 12 and 14 as examples).
- If the lighting conditions for the photo shoot do not allow you to keep your subject in shadow, use photographic editing software to edit your images to make the people darker and alter the exposure or contrast.
- Find a book or magazine image (or bring one from home) of a place that has special meaning for you, for example the beach, a park, the bush, or even an image of your home or school.
- Scan your chosen background image into the computer.
- Use photographic editing software to cut the silhouette of a person from one of the photos you took during the photo shoot and paste the dark figure against your scanned background image.
- Digitally enhance the contrast and colours in your image to make it dreamlike.

Low-tech alternative: Collage

- Find an image of a place that is special to you and brings back feelings and memories.
- Over the image place a silhouette of a dark figure cut from black paper.
- Alternatively, if there is a figure in the original photograph, cut the figure out of the image. Mount the image, now without the figure, on black cardboard so that the shadow-form of a person remains against the background image.

Option 2   Photography

- Refer to the Apple iPod advertising image on page 12 that features black silhouettes of people dancing against brightly coloured backgrounds.
- Make an iPod-style image by taking photographs of people dancing and moving.
- Use your computer's imaging software to stylise your photographs. Shade the people in your images black and cut them out of the original image.
- Place the shadow-like figures against brightly coloured backgrounds.
- Search for 'iPod images' on the internet and you will find free tutorials with step-by-step instructions on how to digitally alter your images to create an iPod-styled shadow people artwork.

www www.photoshopsupport.com/tutorials/jennifer/ipod.html
www.photoshoplab.com/Make-Your-Own-iPod-style-Photo.html

TEACHER NOTE

Set up a digital photo shoot over several lessons so that the class can take a series of portrait shots of each other taking photographs (photographing photographers).

ONLINE RESOURCES

How to set up a photo shoot

In-depth study
Sue Ford

CRITICAL AND HISTORICAL INTERPRETATIONS

Sue Ford, *Dissolution*, 2006. Chromira print on crystal archival paper, 142 × 112 cm. Photo courtesy of Sue Ford and Arc One Gallery. 1943–2009, Australia

CONCEPTUAL FRAMEWORK: WORLD

Sue Ford's world was centred on Australian art and photography. She lived and worked by the sea and was influenced by the coastal environment and the physical beauty of nature around her. The world of technology also had a direct impact on her artmaking practice.

ARTIST FRAMES: SUBJECTIVE

Sue Ford was an artist who worked in the Subjective Frame, creating landscape images so rich in colour that they appear almost imaginary. Ford captured the beauty of everyday beach scenes and transformed them into light-filled magical landscapes. Her mystical images evoke strong feelings and memories relating to beach holidays.

ARTWORK FRAMES: CULTURAL

In *Dissolution*, Sue Ford captured the essence of Australian beach culture and the summer holiday experience. She was interested in exploring the ways that people interacted with the landscape and the way that they seemed to take snapshot images to record significant places, memories and moments in time.

PRACTICE: IDEAS

Sue Ford was interested in the way that the accessibility and wide-spread use of digital cameras enabled everyone to become a photographer. She investigated the ways that new technologies were changing peoples' attitudes to cameras and photography. Ford observed that people were beginning to use digital cameras to take photographs in a more playful way. Her ideas related to the playful nature of amateur documentary photography.

PRACTICE: ACTIONS

Sue Ford used a digital camera to capture silhouette images of people photographing beach sunsets. She digitally manipulated her images in Photoshop, layering them and adding more colour and texture to each part of the image. In the completed images the silhouettes of the dark figures stand out against the luminous (light-filled) landscape.

AUDIENCE

The artworks of Sue Ford have been shown in galleries and exhibitions throughout Australia. Audiences can appreciate the familiar coastal landscapes featured in her artworks. People respond not only to the visual qualities of Ford's artworks but also in a subjective way, to the powerful feelings and memories that the images call to mind. In *Dissolution*, Ford seduces her audience by capturing the moment at sunset when the light is at its most magical and extraordinary. Ironically, the series of images titled 'Last Light' included some of the final artworks Ford created before her death; they have become an important part of her artistic legacy.

WWW   www.arc1gallery.com/artists/sueford/FordProfile.shtm
www.wattersgallery.com/artists/ford.htm

Let's make an artwork 2
Passing shadows

Coming up with ideas   ARTMAKING PRACTICE

Create a painting or a print that captures shadow silhouettes of people in motion.

Discussion, research and planning in your visual arts diary

CONCEPTUAL FRAMEWORK	PRACTICE	FRAMES
Artist Artwork World Audience	Ideas and actions	Subjective—communicating feelings and emotions through artworks Cultural—exploring ideas, beliefs and values through artworks Structural—exploring materials and methods in artmaking

Student worksheet

Rafael Lozano-Hemmer (1967–), Spain, *Frequency and volume*, 2008. Installation view. The Curve, Barbican Art Gallery, 9 Oct–18 Jan 2009. Radio frequency projections using light and sound. Photo Eliot Wyman. Courtesy Barbican Art Gallery.

Andy Warhol (1928–1987), USA, *Shadows*, 1978. Acrylic, variously silk-screened and hand-painted on canvas. Installation view at Dia: Beacon, NY. Photo: Bill Jacobson. Collection: Dia Art Foundation. © Dia Art Foundation/Viscopy.

WWW www.lozano-hemmer.com

Examine artworks in which the artist has used shadows.

- Refer to the above artworks by Rafael Lozano-Hemmer and Andy Warhol, the artwork by **Robert Boynes** further ahead in the chapter, and the work of the artists from 'Let's make an artwork 1'. This will help you to come up with ideas for artmaking.
- Begin planning and thinking of ideas for your photographing/painting/printmaking.
- Use the Frames table in the Introduction to help you research the qualities of the Structural, Cultural and Subjective Frames that you will use in your artmaking. Record these in your visual arts diary.

Taking action   ARTMAKING PRACTICE
Option 1   Painting

- Take photographs of people in motion. Enlarge your most successful photograph.
- Ask your teacher to help you make three or four photocopies of your image, enlarged to different sizes.
- Cut the moving figures out of your photocopied images to create paper stencils.
- Hold the stencil against canvas, board or paper, and fill in the stencil with a dark paint to create people-shaped figures on the canvas/paper. Repeat your figures several times to create an interesting composition (see Robert Boynes's paintings on page 18). Allow your stencilled shadows to dry on the canvas/paper.
- Select either two warm colours (for example, yellow and red) or two cool colours (for example, blue and green) that reflect the way you feel about people moving through the urban landscape.
- Mix your paints with a little water so that they become thin and runny. Take a broad brush and apply your paints in layered washes of colour. Keep the colours light in some areas and darker in others.

- While your colour washes are still wet, rub back gently into the paint with a cloth or some paper towel in some areas of your canvas to make the texture of your image more interesting.

Option 2 Printmaking

- Collect an image of yourself or another person in motion.
- Enlarge the original image using the photocopier. Trace the outline of your figure onto black or coloured paper or card and cut out a paper silhouette.
- Trace the silhouette image onto a lino-block and use lino-cutting tools to cut away the background, leaving only the solid silhouette image.
- Using block-printing ink, print your lino-block silhouettes on white paper.
- You can also arrange your original paper-cut silhouette on white paper and frame it beside your finished print to show your artmaking process.

Extension

Look at the artworks of Kara Walker and Peter Coffin below.

www http://learn.walkerart.org/karawalker
www.saatchi-gallery.co.uk/artists/peter_coffin.htm

- Work in pairs or small groups and use your paper-cut silhouettes of moving shadow people to create a narrative or story.
- Extend your ideas by creating a shadow play, projection or stop-frame animation to tell your story. Ask your teacher for ideas about how to do this.

Kara Walker (1969–), USA, *Darkytown rebellion*, 2001. Projection, cut paper and adhesive on wall, 427 × 1144 cm. Photo: courtesy of the artist and Sikkema Jenkins & Co.

Peter Coffin (1972–), USA, *Sculpture silhouette prop (A. Giacometti 'Diego' 1960)*, 2007. Silhouette sculpture, mixed media, dimensions variable. Courtesy of the Saatchi Gallery, London. © Peter Coffin, 2009.

In-depth study
Robert Boynes

CRITICAL AND HISTORICAL INTERPRETATIONS

Robert Boynes, *The red bridge*, 2008. Acrylic on canvas, 120 × 244 cm. Photo courtesy of the artist and Brenda May Gallery, Sydney. Licensed by Viscopy.
1942– , Australia

CONCEPTUAL FRAMEWORK: WORLD

Robert Boynes's world is that of the Australian contemporary artist/photographer, where traditional painting practices and new technologies meet. Boynes's relationship with the bustling world of the city greatly influences his artmaking practice.

ARTIST FRAMES: CULTURAL/STRUCTURAL

Robert Boynes is a structural artist who documents urban chaos. He aims to capture the feeling of isolation that people can experience in a city, even when they are surrounded by people. His artworks are a direct response to the city environment, which he believes can be impersonal and unfriendly.

ARTWORK FRAMES: STRUCTURAL/SUBJECTIVE

In *The Red Bridge*, Robert Boynes works in the Subjective Frame, using dark tones to create shadow-like representations of people moving through the city. His images capture feelings and memories relating to loneliness and isolation. He creates contrast in his images by layering painterly washes of warm reds, yellows and oranges over the top of dark shadowy figures. The repetition of shadow people riding their bicycles along the street makes it appear as if they are floating through a dreamlike cityscape.

PRACTICE: IDEAS

Robert Boynes's ideas relate to his observations of people in the city and he documents his observations photographically. He produces paintings that reduce people to shadow-like representations of busy, lonely city dwellers. He wants his artworks to mirror everyday city life.

PRACTICE: ACTIONS

Robert Boynes uses photographic silk-screen printing techniques and acrylic paint to construct his artworks. After taking digital photographs, he scans them into the computer and manipulates them until he is happy with their composition He then transfers the digital image onto a large-format silk screen and prints it onto canvas. Boynes paints back into the canvas with layers of acrylic paint and then repeats the process of printing the image onto the canvas with his silkscreen, sometimes dragging it through the wet paint. He rubs back into his painting and washes away certain parts of it to reveal sections of his image that have been hidden under layers of paint. He also repaints other areas of the image with thin washes of colour.

AUDIENCE

The artworks of Robert Boynes appeal to audiences familiar with city living. You can see his paintings in art galleries, in books and online. He does not tell his audience the meaning behind his artworks, but rather wants them to reflect on the aspects of the city that, like parts of his paintings, remain hidden.

WWW www.robertboynes.com
www.nga.gov.au/TALES/Robert.cfm
www.beavergalleries.com.au/boynes.htm
www.brendamaygallery.com.au

Student worksheet

Let's make an artwork 3
Chasing shadows

Coming up with ideas   ARTMAKING PRACTICE

Create a drawing installation using chalk to trace the shadows of people and everyday objects. Document the process and finished installation by taking photographs.

Discussion, research and planning in your visual arts diary

CONCEPTUAL FRAMEWORK	PRACTICE	FRAMES
Artist Artwork World Audience	Ideas and actions	Postmodern—experimenting with new materials and methods in artmaking Structural—exploring materials and methods in artmaking

Research the work of Ellis Gallagher and one other artist who has been influenced by street art, graffiti and postmodern culture (look at the artists in Chapter 10 of this book). In your visual arts diary:

- explain how the personal and wider world of these artists may have influenced their ideas
- describe how each artist communicates meaning to their audience through their artworks
- investigate what 'street art' is and explain how it is different to the art seen in art galleries.

Ellis Gallagher (1973–), USA, *Bike chalk drawing in gallery*. Installation view Sara Tecchia Roma New York. Photo by Paola Mastrangelo.

Ellis Gallagher (1973–), USA, *Bike chalk drawing in street*. Chalk pavement drawing. Photo courtesy of the artist.

Taking action   ARTMAKING PRACTICE
Option 1   Drawing, photography

Create chalk shadow drawings in the playground by tracing the shadows of everyday objects using chalk. You may choose to:

- trace shadows directly onto concrete surfaces (only with the permission of your teacher of course!)
- take objects outside to trace such as chairs, ladders, shoes and bags
- trace objects that are site specific, such as fences, railings, buildings and signs
- trace the shadow repeatedly as it moves with the sun
- document the process of creating the chalk shadow installation by taking photographs
- document the disintegration of the chalk drawing as it washes/wears away.

Option 2   Drawing

Place large pieces of paper on the ground and trace the shadows onto paper for use in further artmaking (such as paintings or installations).

Extension

- Work in pairs or small groups to document the process of creating your chalk-drawing installations by taking many photographs in quick succession that can be made into a stop-frame animation. (You can create stop-frame animations simply by importing still images into a video-editing program.)
- Make a soundtrack for your stop-frame animation using an existing song, or use music-editing software to create an original soundtrack.

ONLINE RESOURCES

Creating shadow plays, projections and simple stop-frame animations

In-depth study
Ellis Gallagher

CRITICAL AND HISTORICAL INTERPRETATIONS

Ellis Gallagher, *Bike shadow*, 2005. Chalk pavement drawing. Photo: Chang W. Lee/*The New York Times*/Redux.
1973– , USA

....

CONCEPTUAL FRAMEWORK: WORLD

Ellis Gallagher's world is New York City and contemporary urban street art created in public spaces with the aim of getting the attention of passers by. He is well known for using chalk to trace around the shadows of everyday objects on New York streets. Originally his relationship to the art world was as an illegal graffiti artist; however, Gallagher has developed more socially acceptable ways of making art.

ARTIST FRAMES: POSTMODERN

Ellis Gallagher belongs to a generation of postmodern street artists using non-traditional materials to create street art. His artworks are site specific and last only for a short time. They are placed where everyone can see them, and they do not cause permanent damage to property or the environment. Gallagher is interested in the way that artworks and objects can change once placed somewhere unexpected. He aims to make audiences stop and question whether what they see before them is actually art. Gallagher uses his artmaking practice to blur the boundaries between art and graffiti, raising questions about the relationship between graffiti and the art world.

ARTWORK FRAMES: STRUCTURAL

In *Bike shadow*, Ellis Gallagher uses yellow **sidewalk chalk** to trace around the shadow of his bicycle on the street. He refers to his artworks as acts of 'ocular echoism', which literally means 'sight repeated'. By tracing the shadows of everyday objects, he transforms the ordinary into the extraordinary. As well as making street art, Gallagher documents his artwork, taking a photograph of each finished shadow drawing.

PRACTICE: IDEAS

Ellis Gallagher explores ideas about finding beauty in the everyday world. He creates artworks that are interactive and unexpected and make people stop and think about art and their relationship to the world around them. Since 2005, Gallagher has traced literally thousands of chalk shadows of everyday objects in and around New York City. He hopes that his artworks will inspire people to look carefully at things that they may have otherwise passed by in the street.

PRACTICE: ACTIONS

Ellis Gallagher uses sidewalk chalk to outline the shadows of common objects on the street such as signs, mailboxes, fire hydrants, parking meters, lampposts, bicycles and garbage cans. As his chalk-drawing installations disappear after rain and do not cause any damage to property, they do not come under the legal definition of graffiti; however, he was once arrested for creating a chalk installation on a New York street. Gallagher's artmaking actions are completed quickly, attracting immediate public attention. He signs every shadow drawing in chalk with '© ELLIS G.', so that people recognise that the chalk outlines are his artworks. He also exhibits photographs of his chalk drawings in art galleries.

AUDIENCE

Ellis Gallagher's artworks are created for the general public. People who encounter his chalk drawings do not have to know about or like art to appreciate his work. His audience ranges from people who pass by his installations on the street, to those who see his artworks in galleries, books and magazines or via the internet. People are surprised by their chance encounters with © ELLIS G.'s artworks, which magically appear, and then disappear without a trace. Gallagher likes his audience to interact with his artworks and experience their familiar surroundings in new ways, discovering that even the most ordinary things in life can be beautiful.

WWW www.myspace.com/ellis_gee
www.saratecchia.com/artists/ellis_gallagher/bio.php
http://www.nytimes.com/2005/12/10/nyregion/10chalk.html

Extension

Christian Boltanski (1944–), France, *Les Ombres (The Shadows)*, 2008. Installation and projection of figures cut out of oxidised copper with candles. Photo: Marian Goodman Gallery. ADAGP licensed by Viscopy.

Cornelia Parker (1956–), England, *Cold Dark Matter: An Exploded View*, 1991. A garden shed and contents blown up. Photo: courtesy the Artist and Frith Street Gallery, London.

Look at the artworks by Christian Boltanski and Cornelia Parker above.

- Create small human figures from tin foil and scraps of junk, paper and cardboard.
- Experiment with a variety of light sources such as lamps, candles or even an overhead projector to cast shadows of your objects.
- Document your shadow installation by taking photographs.

Write a paragraph in your visual arts diary explaining whether you feel it is it the shadow or the object that is your actual artwork.

TEACHER NOTE

Class debate Separate your class into two teams to debate, with logical arguments, whether it is the object or the artwork that is the actual artwork.

Chapter 3

Moving people

We are always moving. From the moment our life begins to the day it ends, human beings are constantly shifting, changing, growing, breathing, running, walking and crawling. The world we live in is fast-paced and often full of busy moving people. They are a ready source of ideas and inspiration for artists.

Artmaking sequence	Form	Artists
Let's make an artwork 1 *Art on the move*	Drawing, painting	• *Edgar Degas, Marcel Duchamp* • Jackson Pollock, Franz Kline
Let's make an artwork 2 *Follow the movement*	Photography, video, cell animation	• *Merilyn Fairskye* • Giacomo Balla, Daniel Crooks

Let's make an artwork 1

Art on the move

Coming up with ideas   ARTMAKING PRACTICE

Make a series of drawings or paintings capturing the movement of people.

Discussion, research and planning in your visual arts diary

Student
worksheet

CONCEPTUAL FRAMEWORK	PRACTICE	FRAMES
Artist Artwork World Audience	Ideas and actions	Structural—methods and materials, visual qualities, composition Subjective—spontaneous, imaginative and expressive qualities

Jackson Pollock at work. Photo: Getty Images.

Franz Kline (1910–1962), USA, *Chief*, 1950. Oil on canvas, 148.3 × 186.7 cm. Digital image, ©2010, The Museum of Modern Art, New York/Scala, Florence.

TEACHER NOTE

Discuss how, before photography, artists relied on observation and visual memory. Many artists still prefer this to working from photographs, which may not capture the feeling of the moment.

ONLINE RESOURCES

Jackson Pollock

When we think of artworks about moving people, we tend to think of images of movement being captured by artists as paintings, photographs or sculptures. Capturing movement is difficult because many art practices take time to do. Look at how movement is captured in the works of the two artists above, as well as the works by **Edgar Degas** and **Marcel Duchamp** further ahead in the chapter.

In your visual arts diary:

- discuss each artist's ideas in relation to the use of movement as subject matter, using the Artmaking Practice table in the Introduction to help you
- list two important actions each artist takes, using the Artmaking Practice table in the Introduction to help you

- describe which Frame each artist is working in and the qualities of that Frame you can see in the artworks, using the Frames table in the Introduction to help you
- list the symbols used in one of the artworks and explain what you think they tell us about the meaning of the work
- indicate how each artwork reflects the artist's world, using the Conceptual Framework table in the Introduction to help you.

The act of making art itself requires people to move. Artwork can be about recording this movement by people as they make artwork. As artists, we can record the actions of others through observation or we can record our own processes.

In your visual arts diary, borrow and sketch some ideas for photography and printmaking compositions based on the artwork discussed on page 25, and come up with some ideas of your own.

WWW www.moma.org/collection
www.nga.gov/feature/pollock/pollockhome.shtm

Taking action   ARTMAKING PRACTICE
Option 1   Drawing

- Observe people during your day at school, and on your way to and from school. Capture their movements in quick drawings in your visual arts diary, depicting any differences in how people move depending on the time of day.
- Try capturing a single movement as a quick series of drawings in sequence.
- Observe people on a weekend or away from school, and capture their movements in quick drawings in your visual arts diary. Notice how people move differently when they are away from work and school.
- Observe movements in the art room as people go about making artwork. Capture the sorts of movements people make when they work on a drawing or painting.

- Think about the evidence of these different kinds of movements you find in artworks. Can you see if a painter has made quick or slow movements in a painting just by looking at its surface? Do the lines and marks in a drawing give you an idea about how the artist moved to make them?
- Based on your observations, choose one drawing from each time period (the school day, away from school, and in the art room) and enlarge it.

Option 2   Drawing

- Using charcoal or soft lead pencil and butcher's paper, make a series of action drawings that explore your own movement.
- You may choose to put on some music and move your arm in time to the music to make marks; or, you may choose to close your eyes or draw blindfolded.
- Try doing a number of different movements with your drawing hand, such as circles and squares.
- Try working over the drawing in different colours.

Option 3   Painting

- Record the movement of making a painting in different ways to create a series of action paintings.
- Use paint mediums like impasto or modelling compounds to ensure your brushstrokes will stay thick and textured.
- Experiment with different ways to apply paint to your surface. For example, try holding the paintbrush in your mouth or in the bend of your elbow, or even making marks with your feet!
- You may choose to record the making of a painting using a video camera.

action drawing: a style of drawing where the process of drawing is itself the main subject of the work; the drawing can be scribbles, fast scratches or slow squiggles

action painting: a style of painting in which the main idea is the movement and action of splashing, dribbling or dragging the paint across the surface in a random and energetic way

In-depth study
Edgar Degas

CRITICAL AND HISTORICAL INTERPRETATIONS

CONCEPTUAL FRAMEWORK: WORLD

Edgar Degas was a painter whose world was that of the **Impressionists** and Realists of Paris. He was influenced by the work of such artists as Eugène Delacroix and Jean Auguste Dominique Ingres. He also had an extensive Japanese print collection from which he drew inspiration. Degas is considered one of the founding members of the Impressionist movement.

ARTIST FRAMES: SUBJECTIVE

Edgar Degas spent a lifetime painting moving people. His most famous works deal with people who move for a living: dancers. As an Impressionist, Degas painted the world around him as he saw it. He was effectively recording his own life and experiences. The Impressionists recorded images and events on the spot as they happened. Although Degas felt he was recording real life as an observer, the people and places he chose to paint say much about his own personal life as well.

ARTWORK FRAMES: STRUCTURAL

In *Ballet Dancers in the Wings* on page 28, Degas is able to give a sense of sequential movement by painting a number of dancers doing the same movements, but at slightly different times. The effect is that, as we look at (or 'read') the painting from left to right, each dancer takes us a little further into the movement. It's almost like looking at one person as she goes through her routine. In fact, Degas has painted each dancer with the same coloured hair so that we make the connection more easily.

Impressionists: artists who made work that responded directly to the world as they saw it, by capturing its changing qualities, such as movement, as they happened

Edgar Degas, *Ballet Dancers in the Wings*, c. 1900. Pastel drawing, 71.1 × 66 cm. Saint Louis Art Museum, Museum Purchase 24:1935.
1834–1917, France

PRACTICE: IDEAS

Degas was fascinated with the grace and beauty of dancers. Over half his paintings depicted dancers, capturing the physical detail of movement as the dancers performed and practised. At the time he worked, dance was a major form of mainstream entertainment, ranging from classical ballet to the wilder, more popular theatre-hall dances, such as the Quadrille (also known as the Cancan), which was performed at the Moulin Rouge in Paris.

PRACTICE: ACTIONS

Degas made his work through a rigorous process of drawing and observation. Although he also practised photography, he made his paintings without the aid of technology, working quickly to capture the gestures and outlines of movements as they happened. Degas had an expert understanding of human anatomy and was able to accurately capture the physical sense of movement in the dancers' bodies.

AUDIENCE

Degas continues to be very popular with a broad range of different people. His technical skill at rendering the human figure and his understanding of colour and tone make his work very popular with a wide audience, regardless of their understanding of art; however, his complex conceptual understanding of sequential movement and composition also attract a more intellectual crowd.

www www.metmuseum.org/explore/degas/html/index.html

In-depth study
Marcel Duchamp
CRITICAL AND HISTORICAL INTERPRETATIONS

CONCEPTUAL FRAMEWORK:

Marcel Duchamp's world was that of the radical artist in Europe at the start of the 20th century. His early painting experimented with elements of both Cubism and Futurism. Like Eadweard Muybridge and Doc Edgerton, Duchamp also recognised the influence of the stop-motion photography of Étienne-Jules Marey.

ARTIST FRAMES: STRUCTURAL

Marcel Duchamp is perhaps one of the most important modern artists in history. He had a systematic approach, and was always experimenting with new ideas of how to think about art and how to push the boundaries of what art could be. Many of his ideas, and works including *Nude Descending a Staircase, No. 2*, have been major influences on many of today's major artists.

ARTWORK FRAMES: STRUCTURAL

In *Nude Descending a Staircase, No. 2* Duchamp has painted a representation of a figure coming down a staircase. The materials Duchamp used—the paint and canvas—were traditional at the time, but the way that he painted the scene was not. Duchamp chose to show the movement of the figure as she descends down the staircase. He has done this with a limited range of colours, using only tones of brown. The figure is proportioned but highly abstract. It is the attempt to show the path of the figure's movement that makes this painting so radical and important. The painting shows a sort of trail of movement from the top to the bottom of the stairs, as if the figure is leaving a trail of ghost images of each previous movement.

PRACTICE: IDEAS

Duchamp responded to the world around him, recognising that changes in technology and society would change the way we look at and make art. He pioneered many new ways of making art, including the way artists show human movement in artworks.

Before the advent of photography, the only way to capture reality was to draw or paint it, and success in

Marcel Duchamp, *Nude Descending a Staircase, No. 2*, 1912. Oil on canvas, 146 × 89 cm. Photo: Philadelphia Museum of Art/licensed by Viscopy. 1887–1968, France

Cubism: a style of modern painting begun in France in the early 20th century that featured flat, fragmented and geometric representations of objects, shown from more than one view point

Futurism: an Italian art movement from 1910 to the 1920s that embraced everything new and modern and rejected the past

stop-motion: a form of animation where objects are photographed and moved slightly between each shot, giving the appearance, when the photographs are viewed quickly in succession, that the object is moving on its own

art was often measured by how realistic an image was. However, when photography was invented, artists, no matter how skilled, were no longer the most accurate image-makers. Photography could show reality with an accuracy that paintings could not. Duchamp realised that, with the invention of photography, artists would have to explore other ways of making images.

PRACTICE: ACTION

Nude Descending a Staircase, No. 2 is an attempt to capture something in human movement that a photograph cannot. A photograph generally only captures a single moment in time, and one point of view. Duchamp was trying to capture more than one moment and one view in the painting. Later, moving pictures and time lapse photography would challenge painting as the most accurate way to represent movement.

AUDIENCE

Like nearly all of his work, *Nude Descending a Staircase, No. 2* caused significant controversy when it was first exhibited. Even today, a hundred years later, the painting can still provoke heated discussion and strong reactions from an audience.

 Student worksheet

WWW www.philamuseum.org/collections/

Let's make an artwork 2
Follow the movement
Coming up with ideas   ARTMAKING PRACTICE

Make a video artwork or a cell animation about moving people.

 Student worksheet

Discussion, research and planning in your visual arts diary

CONCEPTUAL FRAMEWORK	PRACTICE	FRAMES
Artist	Ideas and actions	Structural—materials, techniques and technologies
Artwork		Subjective—imagination and memory
World		
Audience		

Giacomo Balla (1871–1958), Italy, *Dynamism of a Dog on a Leash*, 1912. Oil on canvas, 90 × 110 cm. Photo: Albright-Knox Art Gallery NY/Bridgeman/DACS Viscopy.

Daniel Crooks (1973–), New Zealand, *Intersection No. 4 (vertical volume)*, 2008. Single channel HD digital video with sound, 4.29 minutes, edition of 3, AP1. Image: Anna Schwartz Gallery, Melbourne and Sydney.

Look at the artworks on page 30. Then read the following text and answer the questions in your visual arts diary.

- In the painting *Dynamism of a Dog on a Leash*, Balla has painted a busy little dog on its way somewhere. How has he captured the busy energy of the dog?
- Daniel Crooks, like Duchamp, explores moving people with the precision and experimentation of a scientist. Daniel makes video art that explores time and the way people move. His videos are colourful abstract images that stretch and distort the normal world into new and strange compositions. Daniel uses computer editing to cut up video images into slices which he then collages back together. How have Daniel Crooks and Balla explored similar ideas in their artworks?
- In what ways are the artworks different?

Use the internet to research and view more artistic videos about movement.

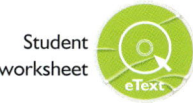

WWW www.annaschwartzgallery.com/works/artist_exhibitions

Taking action   ARTMAKING PRACTICE
Option 1 Photography

- Using a still camera with a slow **shutter speed**, photograph people moving around the playground at lunchtime. Having the camera set to a slow shutter speed and mounted on a tripod will produce images that show people blurred from one end of the shot to another, creating a trail.
- Experiment with a similar technique at night: use a long **exposure** by setting the camera to a slow shutter speed. Mount the camera on a tripod. Use glow sticks or torches to 'draw' shapes or 'write' in the air, moving the lights rapidly around in front of the camera. The camera will record the trail of light.
- Print or develop the best of your day and night movement shots.

shutter speed: the length of time a camera's shutter is open when taking a photo, affecting the amount of light exposed through the lens to light-sensitive paper or a digital image sensor

exposure: the total amount of light the shutter of a camera lets in when it is open

Option 2 Video

- Have someone sit still in the playground all lunchtime while you video them.
- Have them sit somewhere where they will be surrounded by moving people, and eat their lunch with very slow movements.
- Speed the video up. The result will look like the person is eating normally while everyone else rushes around them.
- You might also want to try filming someone as they move slowly backwards around the playground, then reverse the footage.

Option 3 Cell animation

- Make a series of drawings of a person moving in sequence.
- Copy the drawings onto clear acetate and paint them as animation cells.
- Using a digital camera, photograph the cells in sequence to make a cell animation. (You can find out more about animation in Chapter 13.)
- Download the images onto a school or home computer and use photographic editing software to create an animation by combining your still images.

In-depth study
Merilyn Fairskye
CRITICAL AND HISTORICAL INTERPRETATIONS

Merilyn Fairskye, *Connected #12*, 2002–2003, from the series *Connected*. Type C print on Duraclear, 175 × 87.5 cm. Image: the artist and Stills Gallery/Viscopy.
1950–, Australia

CONCEPTUAL FRAMEWORK: WORLD

Merilyn Fairskye is a photographer, video artist and university teacher whose world is that of contemporary art and photography. She works in the Media Arts Studio of Sydney College of the Arts, University of Sydney.

ARTIST FRAME: SUBJECTIVE

Fairskye takes photos and videos of moving people. She is interested in the way people move in public places like airports and at the beach. Her videos capture movement in unusual ways. Like Marcel Duchamp, Merilyn Fairskye tries to capture more than a still moment in her photos.

ARTWORK FRAME: STRUCTURAL

In *Connected #12* we are presented with a mysterious scene. The photograph is moody and dark. We see a figure from the back as she hurries along a busy city street at dusk. The lights of the city, cars and office windows contrast strong warm light against the cold grey of the street. Both the figure and the lights are blurry. The figure has continued to move and we as the viewer seem to be following her.

PRACTICE: IDEAS

Fairskye's photographs remind the audience of what it is like to be in a busy crowd as people rush about. *Connected #12* captures the frantic energy of a busy street around dusk as people rush about trying to get home. There is a sense of unease and even drama in the picture. By framing the subject from the back, Fairskye gives the viewer the sense they might be watching a chase, or someone being stalked. The bright light almost looks like a flash of fire heightening the tension in the image.

PRACTICE: ACTIONS

The blurry effect in *Connected #12* has been achieved by taking a photo using a slow shutter speed. The figures seem blurry because they continued to move as the photograph was taken.

AUDIENCE

Merilyn Fairskye lives in Sydney, but like many Australian artists she exhibits widely both in Australia and overseas. Because she photographs everyday people and scenes, her work has a wide appeal. Her underwater series captures the popular activity of swimming from a new and interesting perspective. Work like this that makes an audience look at itself in a new and unusual way is often popular.

Student worksheet

WWW www.fairskye.com/

Watching people

We are surrounded by people every day. We watch them come and go, passing us by as they go about their daily lives. People intrigue, inspire and entertain us. When we watch people, we become aware that we too are being watched. Our observations of people help us to make better sense of our world and our relationships. Throughout history, many artists have used their observations of people to inform their artmaking practice.

Artmaking sequence	Form	Artists
Let's make an artwork 1 *Snap-happy street style*	Photography	• *Shoichi Aoki* • Narelle Autio, Robert Billington
Let's make an artwork 2 *Peeking into private worlds*	Drawing, stop-frame animation	• *Graham Cheney, Keith Loutit* • Grace Cossington Smith, Charles Conder, Ian Pearson

Let's make an artwork 1
Snap-happy street style

Coming up with ideas   ARTMAKING PRACTICE

Take a series of photographs that document people's actions and interactions.

Discussion, research and planning in your visual arts diary

Student worksheet

CONCEPTUAL FRAMEWORK	PRACTICE	FRAMES
Artist Artwork World Audience	Ideas and actions	Cultural—exploring ideas, beliefs and values through artworks Structural—exploring materials and methods in artmaking Postmodern—experimenting with new materials and methods in artmaking

Shoichi Aoki (1955–), Untitled, Japan. Photograph from *Fresh FRUiTS*.

Robert Billington (1954–), Australia, *Cafe with Dogs*. Black and white photograph, 41 × 41 cm. Photograph by Robert Billington.

Narelle Autio (1969–), Australia, *Untitled (cat#15)*, 2002 from *Not of this Earth*. Photograph, archival inkjet prints on canvas 66 × 100 cm. © Narelle Autio. Image: Stills Gallery.

Look at the works of the artists above, as well as the additional artwork by **Shoichi Aoki** further ahead in the chapter.

In your visual arts diary:

- list two important artmaking actions each artist takes
- describe how each artist has used their observations of people to inspire their ideas for artmaking
- describe which Frame you think each artist is working in (use the Frames table in the Introduction to help you) and describe the qualities of that Frame you can see in the photographs
- choose one of the artworks and explain what the actions and interactions of the people depicted tell us about the meaning of the work
- write a paragraph about someone that you have watched today (but do not use their name), describing their actions and interactions.

Collect some images from magazines that document the actions and interactions of people.

Harajuku: the district in Tokyo where young people gathered in the 1990s to socialise, particularly on Sundays; and the place from where street-style fashion emerged.

Taking action   ARTMAKING PRACTICE
Option 1   Photography

- Bring in a range of colourful clothes, toys and props and dress up in Harajuku-style clothing.
- Share school cameras, or use your own camera or mobile phone camera.
- Take photos of yourself and others in Harajuku style. Refer to Shoichi Aoki's images on pages 34 and 37 for inspiration.
- Use the Structural Frame when making decisions about the composition of your images. Consider how the people are posing in Shoichi Aoki's photographs and ask your subjects to pose in a similar way. Position people in front of school lockers, doorways, fences or textured walls and use interesting but simple backgrounds for your photographs. Take some images of people alone and other images of people in groups.
- Experiment with a variety of viewpoints and camera angles.
- Download the images onto a school or home computer. Use photographic editing software to enhance the composition, contrast and colours in your images so that they are bright and expressive.
- Create a series of your best three photographs, choosing images that are as clear and crisp as possible.

TEACHER NOTE

Before your lesson, investigate locations around your school where students may be able to safely take photographs from an aerial perspective.

Option 2 Photography

- Find a location that allows you to safely observe people from above; for example, from a walkway, set of stairs, verandah, retaining wall or the top of a hill. Refer to Narelle Autio's image on page 34 taken from an aerial perspective for inspiration.
- Set up a photo shoot and photograph people from above. Act as the director of the photo shoot and ask your subjects to move around so that you can capture their movements.

- Make use of the Structural Frame when considering the composition of your photos and reflect on Autio's use of space and composition.
- Organise your subjects so that they look as if they are relaxing or having a picnic, and take more photos from above.
- Download the images onto a school or home computer. Use photographic editing software to enhance the composition, cropping your photos if necessary.
- Create a series of your best three photographs, choosing images that are as clear and crisp as possible.

In-depth study
Shoichi Aoki

CRITICAL AND HISTORICAL INTERPRETATIONS

CONCEPTUAL FRAMEWORK: WORLD

Shoichi Aoki's world is that of contemporary Japanese photography and popular culture. His artmaking practice is influenced by Western culture, globalisation and the mass media. Although he is based in Tokyo, he has an international audience.

ARTIST FRAMES: CULTURAL/POSTMODERN

In 1997, Aoki began creating a monthly magazine called *FRUiTS* to document the new fashion trends being worn by teenagers in Japan. He was inspired by the way that young people used fashion to counterbalance the strict values of Japanese society and express their creativity and individuality. The new-style fashions combine traditional Japanese high fashion with items borrowed from Western popular culture. Young people's outfits consist of many layers of clothing, discordant colours, jarring patterns and accessories. The fashion trends look a little crazy or, as the Japanese say, *kawai*, which means 'cute'. Aoki captures the photos for his magazine in the backstreets of Harajuku in Tokyo.

discordant: clashing, unmatching

ARTWORK FRAMES: STRUCTURAL/POSTMODERN

In *FRUiTS* magazine no. 11, Shoichi Aoki shows photographs of a teenager dressed in clothes that combine aspects of traditional Japanese kimono fashion with Postmodern Harajuku-style fashion. His subject is placed centrally in the composition and commands the audience's attention. Aoki's documentary style of fashion photography breaks many of the conventions of high fashion photography. Rather than photographing fashion models in a studio setting with props and lighting, Aoki captures images of real people in the streets of Harajuku.

PRACTICE: IDEAS

Aoki explores ideas that relate to Japanese youth street fashion and culture. He is interested in documenting the changes occurring within Japanese society that are reflected in the clothes worn by Japan's young people. His ideas also related to Western popular culture and the mass media.

PRACTICE: ACTIONS

Aoki uses a digital camera to capture his subjects on the street and does not use a structured approach. He regularly visits the places where young people are gathered and asks them if he can photograph them. His subjects enjoy being photographed and adopt cute poses that make them appear youthful or childlike.

AUDIENCE

Shoichi Aoki has a global audience, with *FRUiTS* magazine sold in Japan and many other countries throughout the world. Aoki's colourful documentary-style photographs have been shown in art galleries and museums in Japan and internationally. Western audiences are particularly captivated by the colourful and creative Japanese culture and fashion trends. The internet has provided a further forum for discussion of Aoki's artworks and a platform for the sharing of documentary-style street fashion images. Aoki has published his artworks in two books: *FRUiTS* and *Fresh FRUiTS*.

www.style-arena.jp

www.powerhousemuseum.com/exhibitions/fruits.asp

Shoichi Aoki, Untitled, 1998. Digital photograph originally published in *FRUiTS* magazine no. 11. Powerhouse Museum, Sydney.
1955–, Japan

TEACHER NOTE

Discuss with the class how the Japanese Harajuku-style fashion movement has had an impact on fashion trends and popular culture on a global scale.

Let's make an artwork 2
Peeking into private worlds

Coming up with ideas   ARTMAKING PRACTICE

Create a drawing or a stop-frame animation that is inspired by your observations of people.

Discussion, research and planning in your visual arts diary

Student worksheet

CONCEPTUAL FRAMEWORK	PRACTICE	FRAMES
Artist	Ideas and actions	Cultural—exploring ideas, beliefs and values through artworks
Artwork		Structural—exploring materials and methods in artmaking
World		Subjective—communicating feelings and emotions through artworks
Audience		

Grace Cossington Smith (1892–1984), Australia, *The Lacquer Room*, 1935–1936. Oil on paperboard on plywood, 74 × 90.8 cm. Collection Art Gallery of New South Wales, Sydney. © Estate of Grace Cossington Smith.

Charles Conder (1868–1909), England/Australia, *Departure of the Orient—Circular Quay*, 1888. Oil on canvas 45.1 × 50 cm. Purchased 1888, Art Gallery of New South Wales, Sydney. Photograph by Jenni Cater.

ONLINE RESOURCES

Ian Pearson

Ian Pearson (1951–), Australia, *Father & Daughter*, 2008. Oil on canvas, 75 × 75 cm. Courtesy of the artist and the Art Piece Gallery.

www http://keithloutit.com/

Examine artworks that the artists have based on their observations of people and events, including the artworks on page 38, the works of **Graham Cheney** and **Keith Loutit** further ahead in the chapter, and the works of the artists from 'Let's make an artwork 1'.

In your visual arts diary:

- describe how each artist has set out to engage their audience (refer to their ideas and actions)
- brainstorm your ideas for drawings, paintings or animations that you could create, using the knowledge that you have gained by looking at the artworks on page 38
- plan the qualities of the Structural, Cultural and Subjective Frames you will use in your artmaking, using the Frames table in the Introduction Chapter to help.

Taking action   ARTMAKING PRACTICE

Option 1   Drawing

- Take a photograph or find an image in a book or magazine that depicts people who are absorbed in their own private world and do not realise that they are being watched.
- Look at the artworks of Ian Pearson on page 38 and Graham Cheney on page 41 for inspiration.
- Using your chosen image as a visual reference, make a large-scale drawing based on the Structural and Cultural Frames.
- Pay particular attention to the composition of your image and the way the figures are arranged.
- Use colour, tone and contrast in a meaningful way to **unify** your composition.
- Experiment with a variety of drawing materials such as chalks, pencils, charcoals, **gesso** and inks, as well as a variety of drawing surfaces. Discuss with your teacher the most suitable media for your drawing.

Option 2   Stop-frame animation

- Look at the tilt-shift time-lapse photography and film works of Keith Loutit.
- Use the Structural Frame to record people's movements from afar. From a distance or from an aerial perspective, photograph people moving through the school playground on their way to class after the bell has rung.
- Make sure that your camera is on a tripod so that it does not move, and take your photographs in very quick succession (one after the other) to capture people's movements.
- Take as many photos as you can until all the people have disappeared and the playground is empty.
- Download the images onto a school or home computer. Use a video or animation program to animate your images and document the movements of people in the playground.

In-depth study

Graham Cheney

CRITICAL AND HISTORICAL INTERPRETATIONS

CONCEPTUAL FRAMEWORK: WORLD

Graham Cheney is an artist and art educator whose world is that of Australian contemporary visual arts. Early in his career he worked as a graphic designer, medical illustrator and art gallery director.

ARTIST FRAMES: CULTURAL/STRUCTURAL

Cheney is an artist who documents significant moments in Australian culture that might otherwise pass by unnoticed. He is particularly interested in working with subject matter that reflects the changes occurring in the dynamics of the outer City of Sydney and the cultural, economic and social world of the greater Western Sydney area.

ARTWORK FRAMES: CULTURAL/SUBJECTIVE

rendered: shaded or depicted

Pendulums is part of a series of drawings that document the construction of the monumental Westlink M7 motorway in Sydney. In the artwork, three boys are depicted playing in their secret place, a construction site under the motorway. But why are they there? Perhaps the boy standing up is reminding them that they're late getting home. This scene has only a few props: a milk crate, a watch and some swinging spheres. The story of the boys is told through their posture and interactions with one another. They resemble the illustrations of children in junior science textbooks and could even be re-enacting what Galileo first found out about pendulums and their importance to the development of clocks. The boys are rendered like classical sculptures from the age of scientific discovery and they have a worn, weathered, aged look. The concrete structure of the M7 behind them will last for centuries, just like the pyramids of ancient Egypt.

PRACTICE: IDEAS

Cheney's ideas relate to the marking of significant events, such as the construction of large monuments and buildings. He is influenced by other artists who have used their artmaking to record important events and make observations about their world, such as Grace Cossington Smith who documented the construction of the Sydney Harbour Bridge. Cheney's ideas are also inspired by science, and how the creation of bridges and structures is based on the simplest of scientific principles, which can be demonstrated using rulers, string and household items.

PRACTICE: ACTIONS

Cheney uses many layers of drawing fixed with **binder** to create his artworks. He draws back into each layer over and over again, glazes the drawing with ink washes and then hoses it down to wash away most of the new lines. Once the artwork is dry, he begins the process all over again. White gesso is applied to some areas of the drawing to bring back areas of white and strengthen negative shapes. A variety of charcoals are used to create different effects. For example, compressed charcoal is used to make broad dark strokes, sharpened charcoal pencils are used for hatching to create areas of tone or lines that indicate contour and form, and nervous, wiggly lines are created by using thin sticks of willow charcoal. Cheney's process allows him to build up a rich surface that is full of intentional marks and random objects.

Graham Cheney, *Pendulums*, 2006. Charcoal, ink and gesso on paper, 80 cm × 60 cm. © Graham Cheney. 1963–, Australia

binder: a substance added to an artwork to form a protective coating

AUDIENCE

For the audience, viewing *Pendulums* is like peering through a hole in a fence and seeing into a private world. Cheney has exhibited this and other artworks in galleries and exhibitions both locally and nationally. His most recent artworks can be seen by a global audience on his personal website, which acts as his online gallery.

 http://grahamcheney.com

Student worksheet

In-depth study
Keith Loutit

Keith Loutit, still image of *Sunbathers pictured at Tamarama from Beached I*, 2008. Time-lapse photography.
Contemporary artist, Australia

CONCEPTUAL FRAMEWORK: WORLD

Keith Loutit's world is that of the Australian contemporary artist. His world is filled with new technologies and multi-media. While he lives and works in Sydney, Australia, Loutit's artworks are viewed on the internet by an international audience.

ARTIST FRAMES: STRUCTURAL

Loutit creates documentary-style short films that feature people going about their daily routines and everyday lives. He makes his films using a combination of animation, tilt-shift and time-lapse photography. The combination of these techniques creates an illusion that makes the people and places in his films look like a miniature version of the real thing, captured in fast-forward. Loutit takes his footage in places such as the beach and the city because he wants to create artworks that transform familiar locations into films that help audiences to see their everyday world in new ways.

ARTWORK FRAMES: CULTURAL/STRUCTURAL

In *Beached I*, Loutit documents aspects of beach culture at Tamarama, a popular beach in Sydney. Due to the miniaturisation and the hyper-speed of the figures in the film the footage appears more like an illusion than reality. The beach scene is shot from an aerial perspective, which enables audience members to become passive observers of their world. Loutit invites audiences to pause and take a closer look at the actions and interactions of people in familiar places and spaces.

PRACTICE: IDEAS

Loutit's ideas relate to everyday life and are direct observations of people going about their daily routines. The relationships and interactions between the figures in his films are central to the meaning of his artworks. Loutit believes that we live in a fascinating world that deserves more careful observation. His ideas grow out of a desire to engage audiences and help them to see their world from a new perspective. The miniaturisation of the people and places in the film creates a sense of perspective and serves to remind us that, as humans, we have only a very small part to play in this world.

PRACTICE: ACTIONS

To create still images that are sharp in the foreground but blurred in the background, Loutit uses a high-quality camera lens that is tilted off its usual plane of focus. This technique is called tilt-shift photography. He also uses time-lapse photography to capture thousands of images in quick succession over a long period of time. In combination, these techniques create a sense of minaturisation and make the people and objects in the images appear smaller than they really are. Once he has captured thousands of still images, Loutit uses stop-frame animation to piece the photographs together to form a short film that speeds up the footage. It can take up to 20 000 still images to create a four minute film, however, Loutit's finished films are usually made up of between 3000 and 6000 images.

AUDIENCE

Keith Loutit's films appeal to a wide audience but they are particularly appealing to Australian audiences who have a strong connection with the places that are featured in his films. Loutit believes in creating art that everyone can see and he makes his films available online through video blogging websites, such as Vimeo. He has also been commissioned to produce commercial advertisements and video clips using his tilt-shift and time-lapse techniques. Loutit wants his audiences to connect with his artworks through their own memories and experiences of familiar locations; and he hopes that by engaging with his films, they may begin to see their world from a different perspective.

WWW http://www.keithloutit.com
http://vimeo.com/keithloutit
http://exitcreative.net/blog/2009/04/keith-loutit-tilt-shift-short-films/
www.youtube.com/watch?v=g9_dNW_3Mbc
www.youtube.com/watch?v=0xkMTi3K3tl&feature=related

Crowds + isolated people

The world can be a crowded place. We might love the feeling of being part of a crowd, but there are also times when we like to be alone. Sometimes we can be in a busy crowd and still be alone. Artists have long made art about the isolated person and the crowd.

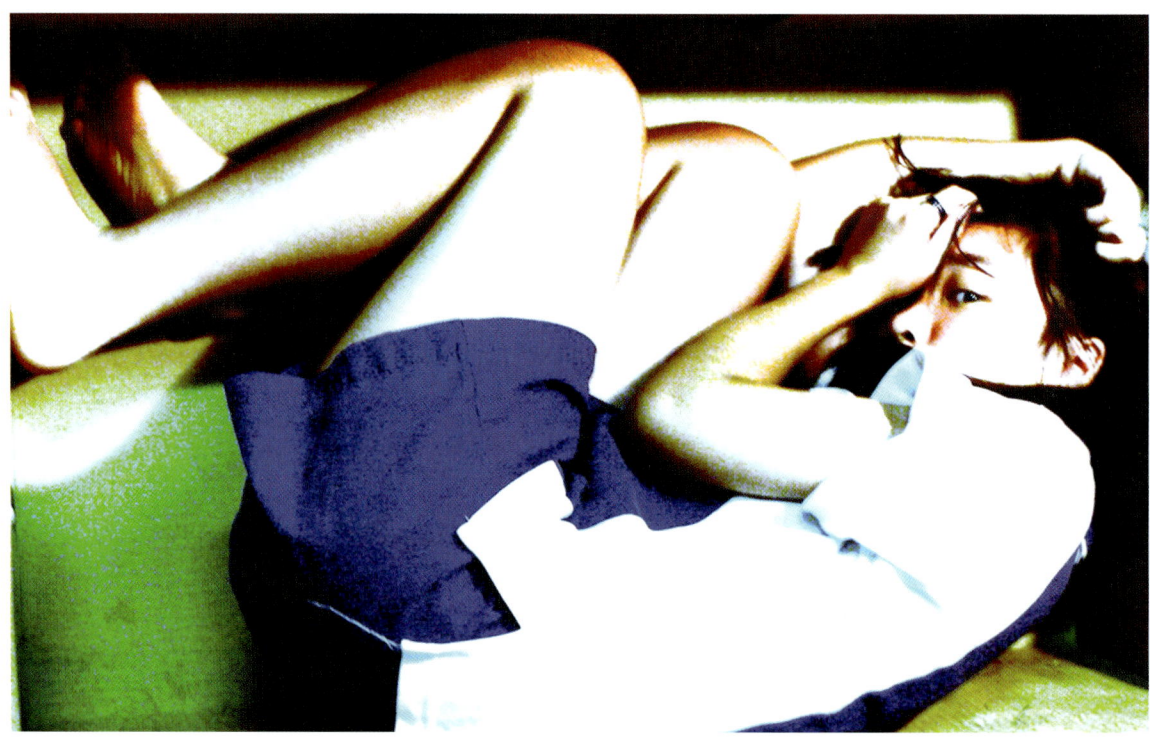

Artmaking sequence	Form	Artists
Let's make an artwork 1 *Alone*	Sculpture, flip book animation	• *Ron Mueck* • Auguste Rodin, Marvel Studios
Let's make an artwork 2 *Gathering*	Installation, animation	• *Antony Gormley* • Do-Ho Suh, Nele Azevedo
Let's make an artwork 3 *Alone in a crowd*	Photography, painting	• *Russell Drysdale, Ali Yanya* • Edward Hopper, Ross Sparks

Let's make an artwork 1
Alone

Coming up with ideas   ARTMAKING PRACTICE

Make living sculptures or design a flip book animation based on the theme of the isolated person.

Discussion, research and planning in your visual arts diary

CONCEPTUAL FRAMEWORK	PRACTICE	FRAMES
Artist Artwork World Audience	Ideas and actions	Structural—using symbolism to give meaning, visual qualities, planned composition Postmodern—borrowing ideas and actions from other artists

Student worksheet

Auguste **Rodin** (1840–1917), France, *The Thinker*, 1884. Bronze sculpture, 71.4 × 59.9 × 42.4 cm. National Gallery of Victoria, Melbourne. Felton Bequest, 1921.

Marvel Studios, BLT & Associates, *The Symbiote Spider-Man, Venom*, 2007. Poster for the movie *Spider-Man 3*. Image: Marvel/Sony Pictures/The Kobal Collection.

Look at the works of the artists above, as well as the artwork by **Ron Mueck** further ahead in the chapter.

In your visual arts diary:

* discuss each artist's ideas in depicting the human figure and telling a story, using the Artmaking Practice table in the Introduction to help you

- list two important actions each artist takes, using the Artmaking Practice table in the Introduction to help you
- describe which Frame you think each artist is working in (using the Frames table in the Introduction to help you) and describe the qualities of that Frame you can see in the artworks
- list the symbols used in one of these artworks and explain what you think they tell us about the meaning of the work
- choose the artist whose work most appeals to you and explore some aspects of the world that has affected their artmaking, using the Conceptual Framework table in the Introduction to help you
- borrow and sketch some ideas for compositions based on your study of these artworks
- indicate one way each artist sets out to catch and hold the interest of the audience.

Taking action   ARTMAKING PRACTICE

Option 1   Sculpture

- Look back at the crouching poses of the figures by Rodin and Marvel Studios on page 45, and at the figure by Ron Mueck on page 47.

  - Use the Structural Frame and make living sculptures of other students in the class placed in similar crouching poses.
  - Find a cardboard box large enough for your models to pose in.
  - Document your living sculptures by photographing them with a digital camera.
  - Download the images onto a school or home computer. Use photographic editing software to manipulate the colour and tone to further emphasise the theme of isolation.

Option 2   Flip book animation

  - Look at the flip book animation used in the bottom right-hand corner of this book—notice how if you flip quickly through the book, the images in the bottom corner blur together to look like a moving animation.
  - Use the Postmodern Frame and borrow this idea to design and make a flip book animation based on the theme of being isolated in a crowd.
  - Devise a story about isolation and create simple figures that you can use to represent a fragment of this story in animated form.
  - Use an old discarded book and draw your animation using a black felt-tip pen on the corner of each page.

In-depth study
Ron Mueck

CRITICAL AND HISTORICAL INTERPRETATIONS

Ron Mueck, *Boy*, 1999. Sculpture, fibreglass, resin, silicone, 5 m. Photo © Eric Dufour.
1958–, Australia/UK

CONCEPTUAL FRAMEWORK: WORLD

Ron Mueck was born in Melbourne but now lives and works in the United Kingdom (UK).
His professional background is in the world of children's television, animatronics for the
movie industry, and advertising, for which he made life-like puppets and figurines. In 1996,
he made the move into the world of contemporary art with his first artwork, a sculpture
titled *Dead Dad*, which was shown in the British art show *Sensations*.

ARTIST FRAMES: STRUCTURAL

Mueck works in the tradition of realism. He aims to create such an extraordinary degree of
reality in his artworks that they are often called 'hyperreal', meaning more real than real.
He achieves this realism through careful observation of models and by using his advanced
technical skills with materials and methods to replicate the human figure.

ARTWORK FRAMES: STRUCTURAL

Boy is a gigantic five-metre sculpture of a crouching boy. Mueck uses visual qualities that suggest an awkward adolescent who seems lost in his own thoughts as he stares rather uneasily over his arms into the distance.

PRACTICE: IDEAS

The artist's main idea in *Boy* is to change his audience's perceptions of reality. The sculpture of the boy, a young adolescent, is exact and real in every detail—except that he is gigantic. Although he towers over any audience and could, with the playfulness of a child, squash them like bugs, his pose and troubled gaze expose a young, vulnerable boy, an unsure and isolated figure.

PRACTICE: ACTIONS

The artist's detailed sculptures are always either miniature or monumental in size. Mueck's earlier pieces were made using fibreglass, but he now also uses silicone, which is more flexible and allows greater ease in shaping body parts and implanting hair. Mueck began

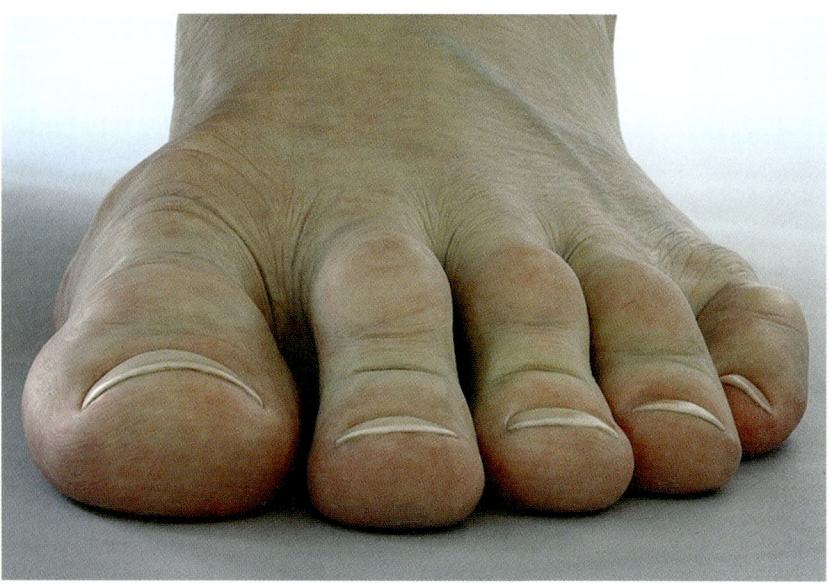

Boy by drawing a model in a series of various poses, then making small plaster sculptures to check the proportions. He then made a large sculpture to scale of modelling clay over chicken wire covered in plaster bandages. He carefully scraped and smoothed the clay surface to build up realistic details, then made a mould from the sculpture in separate sections. A layer of silicone was applied to the mould, followed by fibreglass and resin. After several hours, the mould and wet clay were removed, leaving just the fibreglass and silicone sculpture. This was coloured with resin, and acrylic paint was used to create details such as the veins, blemishes, hair follicles, moles, wrinkles and nails.

Detail of Ron Mueck's *Boy*. Photo © Eric Dufour.

AUDIENCE

Boy has been seen by an international audience—first in the UK Millennium Dome exhibition in London in 2000, then at the Venice Biennale in 2001 and later at the art museum ARoS in the city of Aarhus, Denmark. Wherever it is shown, audiences seem fascinated by this figure of a young boy who is both terrifying and vulnerable at the same time.

WWW www.brooklynmuseum.org/exhibitions/ron_mueck
www.jamescohan.com/artists/ron-mueck
www.artcyclopedia.com/artists/mueck_ron.html
http://nga.gov.au/mueck/director.cfm

Let's make an artwork 2

Gathering

Coming up with ideas   ARTMAKING PRACTICE

Make an installation or an animation using the theme of the isolated person and the crowd.

Discussion, research and planning in your visual arts diary

CONCEPTUAL FRAMEWORK	PRACTICE	FRAMES
Artist Artwork World Audience	Ideas and actions	Structural—using symbolism to give meaning, visual qualities, planned composition Cultural—the ideas and beliefs of society

Student worksheet

Do-Ho Suh (1962–), Korea, *Floor*, 1997–2000. Installation, PVC figures, glass plates, phenolic sheets and polyurethane resin, dimensions variable. Courtesy of the artist and Lehmann Maupin Gallery, New York.

Nele Azevedo, contemporary artist, Brazil, *Melting Men*, 2009, from the *Minimum Monument* project. Site-specific installation, steps of the Concert Hall, in Berlin's Gendarmenmarkt Square, 1200 ice figures. Image: John Macdougall/AFP/Getty Images.

Look at the works of the two artists above as well as the artwork of **Antony Gormley** further ahead in the chapter.

In your visual arts diary:

- discuss each artist's ideas in their artmaking about crowds, using the Artmaking Practice table in the Introduction to help you
- list two important actions each artist takes to make installations
- describe which Frame each artist is working in (use the Frames table in the Introduction to help you) and describe the qualities of that Frame you can see in the installations

- list the symbols used in one of the installations and explain what you think they tell us about the meaning of the artwork
- indicate one way each artist sets out to interest the audience, using the Conceptual Framework table in the Introduction to help you
- note the types of materials you can use in your own installations that will reflect the ideas of crowds and the isolated person, borrowing ideas from these installations
- sketch and make notes on some ideas for your own installations about crowds based on your study of these artworks.

Taking action   ARTMAKING PRACTICE
Option 1 Installation

- Bring in some stuffed toys, dolls or action figures from home to be the 'crowd' in your installation.

- Work in small groups to set up installations based on the theme of crowds. Look back at the artworks of Do-Ho Suh and Nele Azevedo on page 49, and at the artwork by Antony Gormley on page 51 for inspiration.
- Using the Structural Frame, experiment with placing the small figures in different crowd situations to create different visual qualities.
- Use a digital camera to document each installation. Experiment with different viewpoints, for example, from above, from the side and face-on.
- Download the images onto a school or home computer. Use photographic editing software to edit, enhance, adjust or add effects to capture what you want to communicate to an audience about a crowd.

Option 2 Animation

- Bring in some stuffed toys, dolls or action figures from home to be the 'crowd' in an animation.
- Use the Structural Frame (for example, planned composition, methods and materials used) to give meaning.
- Decide what you want your crowd to be doing (for example, tumbling down the stairs), and place your toys or action figures into position.

- Using a digital camera, take as many shots as possible, moving your toys or action figures slightly between each shot.
- Make sure that you put your camera on a tripod or keep it very steady so there is no camera movement and each shot is taken from exactly the same place.
- Download the images onto a school or home computer. Use photographic editing software to edit and adjust each image so they are all the same size, with the same lighting effects.
- If available, use film editing or animation software to make a short film with the images. Alternatively, print out the images separately and use them to make a flip book animation. Look at the bottom-right corner of this book, and you will see that a section of the book comprises a flip book animation.

In-depth study

Antony Gormley

CRITICAL AND HISTORICAL INTERPRETATIONS

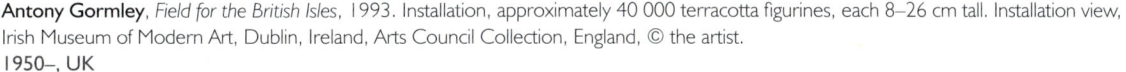

Antony Gormley, *Field for the British Isles*, 1993. Installation, approximately 40 000 terracotta figurines, each 8–26 cm tall. Installation view, Irish Museum of Modern Art, Dublin, Ireland, Arts Council Collection, England, © the artist.
1950–, UK

CONCEPTUAL FRAMEWORK: WORLD

Antony Gormley's world is that of contemporary sculpture, politics and society. He is interested in how the art world can reflect the everyday world by becoming part of it.

ARTIST FRAMES: STRUCTURAL/CULTURAL

votive: an image or sculpture dedicated to a god

Gormley is interested in the symbolism of a crowd of people rather than the single, heroic figure that is often depicted in artworks. Gormley uses small human figurines to make up the crowd in his installation *Field for the British Isles* because humans have been making idols, and **votive** and fertility figures in many different civilisations and cultures for many thousands of years and they seem important to us.

ARTWORK FRAMES: STRUCTURAL/CULTURAL

A hundred people from St Helens in Merseyside, UK, got together with the artist in 1993 and created around 40 000 little terracotta clay figures. These were arranged into the installation *Field for the British Isles*, which is now one of Gormley's best-known artworks. It is made up of a massed field of miniature terracotta figures, crudely shaped with little detail except for deep indents for eyes, all clustered together. This vast mass of figures seems to be almost bursting out of the place where it is installed. Gormley suggests by his placement of the figures that they could extend further than we can see. Some figures stand out because of their size and character, and some are darker than others; but all return our gaze, staring intently at us, in order to make us think that we are on display, not they.

Detail of Antony Gormley's *Field for the British Isles*, 1993. Installation, approximately 40 000 terracotta figurines, each 8–26 cm tall. Installation view, Irish Museum of Modern Art, Dublin, Ireland, Arts Council Collection, England, © the artist.

PRACTICE: IDEAS

In *Field for the British Isles*, Gormley uses the human figure in a crowd to explore one of the ways we as humans relate to each other and to our world. The artist's idea is to ask questions about the relationship between art, society as a whole (represented by his crowd of small clay figures) and the environment. Gormley uses the massed number of figures in this artwork to depict the crowd as like a virus or an invasion that, if we are not careful, will overwhelm the world. Another of the artist's ideas is that by using a collaborative process between himself as the artist and the communities who come together to make the clay figures, he can expand art from being just self-expression to something created by a collective consciousness that draws people together.

PRACTICE: ACTIONS

The 40 000 figurines, each between eight and 26 centimetres tall, were hand made in 1993 by more than 100 volunteers, aged from seven to 70. They were each given small balls of clay with which they shaped standing figures. Participants were asked to follow only a few instructions: the pieces were to be hand-sized and easy to hold, eyes were to be deep and closed and the head was to be in proportion with the body.

AUDIENCE

Field for the British Isles is an interactive piece: it both depicts a community, and helps to create a community by drawing people together through the artmaking process. It involves the audience with its field of small human figures staring intently. Gormley has repeated this installation many times in different locations throughout the world, always involving the local community. Gormley's work is exhibited extensively, in the UK and internationally.

interactive: involving a collaboration between the artist, the artwork and the audience

www www.antonygormley.com
www.southbankcentre.co.uk/gormley/light.html

Let's make an artwork 3
Alone in a crowd

Coming up with ideas   ARTMAKING PRACTICE

Take photographs or make a painting based on isolation in a crowd.

Discussion, research and planning in your visual arts diary

CONCEPTUAL FRAMEWORK	PRACTICE	FRAMES
Artist Artwork World Audience	Ideas and actions	Structural—using symbolism to give meaning, visual qualities, planned composition Subjective—expressive and imaginative qualities Postmodern—borrowing ideas and actions from other artists

Student worksheet

Edward Hopper (1882–1967), USA, *Nighthawks*, 1942. Oil on canvas, 84.1 cm × 152.4 cm. Friends of American Art Collection, 1942.51, The Art Institute of Chicago. Photo © The Art Institute of Chicago.

Ross Sparks (1965–), Australia, *Tokyo Restaurant*, 2007. Digital photograph, 3457 × 2267 pixels. Photography by Ross Sparks. Copyright Sparrowhawk Consulting.

Look at the artworks of the two artists on page 53, as well as the works of **Russell Drysdale** and **Ali Yanya** further ahead in the chapter. Discuss with your friends each artist's ideas about the theme of crowds and isolation, using the Artmaking Practice table in the Introduction to help you.

In your visual arts diary:

- list two important actions by each artist, using the Artmaking Practice table in the Introduction to help you
- describe which Frame each artist is working in (using the Frames table in the Introduction to help you) and describe the qualities of that Frame you can see in the artworks
- list the symbols used in one of the artworks and explain what you think they tell us about the meaning of the work
- indicate one way each artist is influenced by his world, using the Conceptual Framework table in the Introduction to help you
- sketch and make notes on some ideas for your own photographs and paintings about isolation within a crowd, based on your study of these artworks.

Taking action   ARTMAKING PRACTICE

Option 1   Photography

- Look back at the artworks of Edward Hopper and Ross Sparks on page 53. Use the Postmodern Frame and borrow some ideas about isolation within a crowd from these artworks.
- Next time you go to any fast food place at night, take a series of photographs using the theme of isolated people. Use available light only (no flash), and try different viewpoints, for example, from outside looking in, and sitting or standing amongst people.
- Download the images onto a school or home computer and use photographic editing software to manipulate the images to enhance the theme of isolation.

Option 2   Photography

- Share school cameras, or use your own camera, or mobile phone camera.
- Take a series of photos of single figures using the Subjective Frame (expressive and imaginative qualities). Look at the artworks of Russell Drysdale on page 56 and Ali Yanya on page 58 for inspiration.

- Experiment with the use of low light, shadows and silhouettes, with your models in poses that express isolation.
- Choose your best single-figure shots and download them onto a school or home computer. Use photographic editing software to manipulate the images to enhance the theme of isolation.

Option 3 Painting

- Look at the painting by Ali Yanya on page 58.
- Plan a painting of isolated people in a crowd using the Structural Frame (planned compositions and visual qualities that reflect the theme). First, take photographs of people in the street or a shopping centre going about their business—waiting for buses, shopping, at the train station, and so on—so they look as though they are unobserved. Alternatively, cut suitable photographs of people in everyday poses from magazines and use these.
- Experiment with tracing the figures from the photos onto tracing paper, cutting out the shapes and using the remaining paper outline as a stencil to paint their shapes.
- Design the composition of your painting so that the most interesting people are in the foreground. Experiment with making these figures larger in size, sharper in focus, darker in tone and richer in colour than the figures in the middle and background.
- Have the figures begin to disappear into the misty background to suggest depth and create a mood of mystery.

In-depth study
Russell Drysdale
CRITICAL AND HISTORICAL INTERPRETATIONS

Russell Drysdale, *The Drover's Wife*, 1945. Oil painting on canvas, 51.5 × 61.5 cm. National Gallery of Australia, Canberra. © Estate of Russell Drysdale.
1912–1981, Australia

CONCEPTUAL FRAMEWORK: WORLD

Russell Drysdale's world was that of an artist in the city who travelled extensively in the bush to gather ideas and visual information for his paintings. He had a deep knowledge of the bush, having worked for several years as a jackeroo and managing his father's property on the Riverina in Victoria. However, he decided he wanted to become an artist, and studied in Melbourne, London and Paris. He was influenced by the Expressionism of such artists as Van Gogh, Matisse, Picasso, Rouualt and Dufy as well as the structure of Cézanne.

ARTIST FRAMES: STRUCTURAL/SUBJECTIVE

Drysdale worked in the Structural Frame. He placed a strong emphasis on form, planned composition and drawing from life as well as the use of symbolism to give meaning to his paintings. He also worked in the Subjective Frame, with his expressive and imaginative

Expressionism: an art movement of the early 20th century that emphasised the inner feelings of the artist

use of oil paint. He often distorted his shapes, especially human figures, to communicate emotions to the audience.

ARTWORK FRAMES: STRUCTURAL/SUBJECTIVE

In the vast, empty drought-stricken landscape of *The Drover's Wife*, a woman stands, silent and still, looking directly at us as she waits for her husband to hitch the horse to the wagon that will take them away from their home. Her figure is large and solid, dominating the painting while her husband and the wagon are tiny in comparison. She is dressed in simple, shapeless, drab clothing, sensible shoes and a black hat, her only possession is a small travel bag.

PRACTICE: IDEAS

Drysdale was commissioned by the *Sydney Morning Herald* to record the effects of a drought on the environment and people in western New South Wales in a series of paintings. Drysdale knew about isolation and loneliness from living and working in the bush, and this understanding gave him an empathy with the country people he painted. In *The Drover's Wife,* Drysdale's idea was to use this isolated figure as a symbol of the hardships people were enduring during the drought and a symbol of the strength, patience and resignation of country women. He also wanted to show us the **paradox** of living in this inhospitable land. The woman is a symbol of isolation from the land, but at the same time she is connected to it emotionally; although to survive she and her husband have to leave, she doesn't want to go.

paradox: something that contradicts itself

PRACTICE: ACTIONS

Drysdale had made sketches of a drover and his wife while travelling near Deniliquin in the south-west of New South Wales, as well as taking many photographs. But rather than working from the sketches and photographs, Drysdale used his memory of the drover and his wife to produce a series of paintings, including *The Drover's Wife*, that reflect the extreme hardships and tragedies in the bush at that time. In the studio he sketched the composition on the canvas and then, working carefully and slowly, built up layers of thin oil paint as underpainting, and then over-painted with thicker paint. He made the sky so large it suggests a vast space, and the drover's wife dominates the work through her size, solid volume and dark tones. Drysdale uses colours that suggest the heat and dust of the bush, and adds to the mood of isolation of this single figure with the spindly skeletons of dead trees along the horizon.

AUDIENCE

Drysdale became widely recognised in the years immediately following World War II as the pre-eminent painter of the people and landscape of the Australian inland. He developed a unique vision of the Australian landscape and its people, challenging the way Australians saw their own land. He didn't present romantic images; instead he represented the Australian bush as a remote and alienating environment.

WWW www.ngv.vic.gov.au/drysdale/drysdale.htm

In-depth study
Ali Yanya
CRITICAL AND HISTORICAL INTERPRETATIONS

Ali Yanya, *Crowds I*, 2009. Oil painting on canvas, 40 × 50 cm. Photograph © Sandra Daniel.
1963–, Turkey/UK

CONCEPTUAL FRAMEWORK: WORLD

Surrealist: an artist who uses dreamlike images relying on imagination and fantasy

Ali Yanya knew he had to become an artist at secondary school when, during art history lessons, he felt he had something new to say in artmaking. One of his early influences was the Italian Surrealist artist Giorgio de Chirico. He admired de Chirico's innovative and mysterious imagery, such as deserted city squares, mysterious shadows, stopped clocks and sleeping statues, and believes he is trying to recreate the same atmosphere of mystery in his artmaking.

ARTIST FRAMES: STRUCTURAL

Ali Yanya is interested in asking questions about the human condition. He wants to know what symbols and what visual qualities, what lines, tones, colours, shapes and forms, he can use to communicate his ideas. He does not see his role as trying to answer philosophical, scientific or poetic questions about human existence. Instead he sees himself as an observer and recorder of what he sees and feels.

ARTWORK FRAMES: STRUCTURAL

In *Crowds I,* we see a group of everyday figures in a crowd. They seem to be emerging from an early morning mist, perhaps waiting to catch a train, and although in a crowd, each is wrapped in his or her own thoughts and actions. They are part of a crowd but still isolated from each other.

PRACTICE: IDEAS

The artist's main idea behind this group composition of shadowy figures in an unrecognisable space is to draw attention to the transient nature of human existence. He doesn't tell a full story; instead, his idea is to present a small glimpse of an everyday scene that suggests impermanence. We don't know what these figures are about and neither do they.

PRACTICE: ACTIONS

The figures in the artwork are like semi-transparent coloured silhouettes. Using oil paints, transparent washes and thicker paint, Yanya makes the shapes of each figure overlap, almost like cardboard cut-outs. He uses perspective to suggest space and depth, with those smaller figures in the background becoming mistier, and the figures closer to us painted larger and darker. He uses expressive colours, ranging from sombre blue-greys to glowing reds and browns, to evoke an emotional response in an audience rather than to record the real colours. His outlines are soft and blurred and the background is lost in pale, mysterious tones of grey.

AUDIENCE

Ali Yanya has exhibited his paintings and prints widely in the UK and is becoming increasingly well known internationally. The subtle tones and colours and the air of mystery in his paintings are what engages the interest of Ali Yanya's audience.

WWW www.aliyanya.com

Part two

THE WORLD OF NATURE

Water creatures

Creatures that live in water have evolved shapes and forms to survive and thrive in watery kingdoms of brilliant light and colour, as well as darker unknown depths. Artists have often been fascinated by the mystery of water creatures that take on the same shimmer and translucency of their watery world.

Artmaking sequence	Form	Artists
Let's make an artwork 1 *Catching fish*	Printmaking, painting	• *Wassily Kandinsky* • Ando Hiroshige, Louise Zattelman, Helle Jorgensen
Let's make an artwork 2 *Fishy business*	Sculpture	• *Katherine Taylor* • Melissa Hirsch, Miwa Koizumi, Unknown Indigenous rock artist

Let's make an artwork 1
Catching fish

Coming up with ideas   ARTMAKING PRACTICE

Take a series of photographs of water creatures and make prints or a painting based on the photographs.

Discussion, research and planning in your visual arts diary

CONCEPTUAL FRAMEWORK	PRACTICE	FRAMES
Artist Artwork World Audience	Ideas and actions	Structural—methods and materials, visual qualities, composition Subjective—spontaneous, imaginative and expressive qualities

Student worksheet
eText

Ando Hiroshige (1797–1858), Japan, *Horse-Mackerel and Prawns*, 1832, from the series *A Shoal of Fish*. Colour woodcut print on paper, 25.6 × 35 cm.

Helle Jorgensen (1958–), Denmark/Australia, *Spotty Fish*, 2005. Hand-coloured lino print, Japanese paper, 30 × 30 cm. © Helle Jorgensen.

Louise Zattelman (1959–), Australia, *Fish Eat More Fish*, 2006. Digital photograph, manipulated, 14 MB. © Louise Zattelman.

ONLINE RESOURCES

Ando Hiroshige

Helle Jorgensen

Louise Zattelman

Look at the artworks of the three artists on page 63 as well as that of **Wassily Kandinsky** further ahead in the chapter.

In your visual arts diary:

- discuss each artist's ideas in relation to the use of water creatures as subject matter, using the Artmaking Practice table in the Introduction to help you
- list two important actions each artist takes, using the Artmaking Practice table in the Introduction to help you
- describe which Frame each artist is working in (using the Frames table in the Introduction to help you) and describe the qualities of that Frame you can see in the works
- list the symbols used in one of the artworks and explain what you think they tell us about the meaning of the artwork
- sketch some ideas for printmaking and painting compositions, borrowed from these artworks, and come up with some ideas of your own.

TEACHER NOTE

Discuss with the class ways in which these artworks reflect each artist's world. Have students refer to the Conceptual Framework table in the Introduction.

TEACHER NOTE

For both Options, organise an excursion to a fish market or aquarium so students can make sketches and take photographs as visual reference. Otherwise, collect suitable images from magazines.

Taking action   ARTMAKING PRACTICE

Option 1   Printmaking

- Look back at Louise Zattelman's photograph on page 63.
- On an excursion to a fish market or aquarium, take a series of photographs focusing on some aspects of the Structural Frame (for example, the visual qualities of patterns and repetition in fish scales and fins) and the Subjective Frame (for example, expressive and imaginative visual qualities and intense colour).
- Using your photographs (or magazine images of water creatures) as visual reference, design a lino print that you will hand-colour.
- Plan the design for your print in your visual arts diary using black felt-tip pens. Look back at the prints of Ando Hiroshige and Helle Jorgensen on page 63 for inspiration.
- Use the Structural Frame to simplify your water creatures; concentrate on such visual qualities as outlines and patterns to show details.
- Use a composition that brings the creatures up close and make sure the shapes in the background are as interesting as the shapes of the creatures.
- Transfer your design to a lino block, using appropriate tools and techniques as discussed with your teacher. Print the image multiple times in black.
- When dry, hand-colour your prints using inks or gouache, so that each print is different in colour.
- Mount and exhibit the works together to make one large artwork.

Option 2   Painting

- Look at the work of Wassily Kandinsky on page 66.
- On an excursion to a fish market or aquarium, take a series of photographs focusing on some aspects of the Subjective Frame (for example, expressive and imaginative visual qualities and intense colour).
- Use the photographs (or magazine images of water creatures) and the Subjective Frame (for example, expressive colour and imaginative representation) to paint a detail of one of the water creatures (such as the tail, head or fins) to make a painting.

- Choose a detail that will make a strong visual statement with, for example, a dynamic composition, a high degree of colour, pattern or texture, or strong tonal contrasts. Make use of simplification of forms.
- Use different layers of acrylic paint, some with mediums such as impasto, and include some collaged materials, such as string, tissue paper and PVA papier-mâché to produce rich textures.

In-depth study

Wassily Kandinsky

CRITICAL AND HISTORICAL INTERPRETATIONS

CONCEPTUAL FRAMEWORK: WORLD

Wassily Kandinsky was a Russian lawyer who had turned to the study of painting at one of the most exciting times for art in the 20th century: the early Modern world. This was the age of the machine, scientific developments and rapid change to the physical and social structures of civilisation. It was a world of experiment and progress, and Kandinsky developed a new way of representing this new world.

ARTIST FRAMES: SUBJECTIVE

In *Black Lines* on page 66, Kandinsky worked in the Subjective Frame. He felt he had to express his emotional perceptions of the world in an abstract way that was not based on representing visual reality. Instead, after being impressed by the works of the Fauves and Post-Impressionists, his paintings became highly colourful and less structured. In around 1913, he began painting the first totally abstract works in Modern art, and became one of the most influential Modern artists. These paintings made no reference to real objects and instead were inspired by Kandinsky's deeply felt passion for music.

ARTWORK FRAMES: SUBJECTIVE

Black Lines is among the first of Kandinsky's abstract paintings. It is made up of expressive, lively brushstrokes. These create oval shapes in bright primary colours that seem to float in space. Kandinsky has then used thin, dark, agitated brushstrokes, almost like scribble, over the top of the colour.

Fauves: artists (in French, 'wild beasts') who belonged to an early 20th-century art movement that used pure, bright colours and simplified form

Post-Impressionists: artists who belongs to an early 20th-century art movement that used bright colour, broken and expressive brushstrokes and more structured composition than Impressionist artists

abstract: not representing reality

65

Wassily Kandinsky, *Black Lines*, 1913. Oil on canvas, 129.4 × 131.1 cm. Solomon R. Guggenheim Museum, New York. © 2009 Artists Rights Society (ARS), New York/ADAGP, Paris.
1866–1944, Russia

PRACTICE: IDEAS

Kandinsky's idea was to no longer use recognisable images to create meaning. Instead he would use carefully chosen and dynamic colour combinations, free-flowing shapes, and patterns of lines to suggest the same emotional power as a musical composition.

PRACTICE: ACTIONS

Kandinsky made use of larger canvases than usual. He sketched his composition quickly with thinned oil paint and then used layers of increasingly brighter oil paint to build up his shapes. He worked expressively, experimenting with his methods and materials as he went and attempting to produce a painting that looked fresh and spontaneous. The paint in this work is becoming transparent and has more of the qualities of watercolour than of oils. He did not use tonal modelling or shadows but tended to simplify and flatten shapes. In *Black Lines I* he applies his bright oil colours with larger brushes and the darker network of lines over the top is painted with a much thinner brush using paint with the consistency of ink.

AUDIENCE

Kandinsky believed his work should be able to be appreciated and understood by any audience. At the time they were produced, his paintings were largely misunderstood by most people, who dismissed his work as childish and unskilled. Only with time was his work accepted as revolutionary in the development of art in the Modern age.

Student worksheet

www www.guggenheim.org/
www.visual-arts-cork.com/famous-artists/kandinsky-wassily.htm

Let's make an artwork 2

Fishy business

Coming up with ideas ARTMAKING PRACTICE

Make sculptures based on water creatures.

Discussion, research and planning in your visual arts diary

CONCEPTUAL FRAMEWORK	PRACTICE	FRAMES
Artist Artwork World Audience	Ideas and actions	Structural—using symbolism to give meaning, visual qualities, planned composition Subjective—an expressive, imaginative approach Postmodern—borrowing ideas from other artists

Student
worksheet

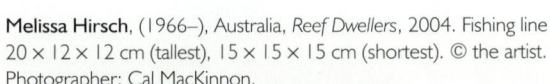

Melissa Hirsch, (1966–), Australia, *Reef Dwellers*, 2004. Fishing line
20 × 12 × 12 cm (tallest), 15 × 15 × 15 cm (shortest). © the artist.
Photographer: Cal MacKinnon.

Miwa Koizumi (1969–), Japan/USA, *PET Project*, 2005. Digital photographic
documentation of an installation, plastic water bottles in variable sizes.

Artist unknown, *Barramundi Frieze*, Indigenous
rock art, ceiling of Ubirr Rock, Kakadu,
date unknown: from as early as 20 000 BC.
Red and yellow ochre, white clay, natural
binding agents. Photograph by Reg Morrison.

ONLINE RESOURCES

Melissa Hirsch

Miwa Koizumi

Look at the artworks of the three artists on page 67 as well as that of **Katherine Taylor** further ahead in the chapter.

In your visual arts diary:

- identify the main idea in each artwork and discuss how each idea is related to the theme of water creatures, using the Artmaking Practice table in the Introduction to help you
- list two important actions each artist takes, using the Artmaking Practice table in the Introduction to help you
- describe which Frame each artist is working in (use the Frames table in the Introduction to help you) and the qualities of that Frame you can see in the artworks
- list the symbols used in one of the artworks and explain what you think they mean
- choose the artist whose work most appeals to you and explore some aspects of the world that has influenced their artwork, using the Conceptual Framework table in the Introduction to help you
- sketch some of your ideas for sculptures based on water creatures, thinking about which Frame you will work in, the composition, visual qualities, methods and materials.

Taking action   ARTMAKING PRACTICE
Option 1   Sculpture

- Choose one of your sketches or photos collected for 'Let's make an artwork 1', or collect more images of water creatures like jellyfish or anemones to use as the starting point for a sculpture using the Subjective Frame (expressive and imaginative qualities) and the Postmodern Frame (borrowing ideas from other artists).
- Look back at the water creatures created by Miwa Koizumi and the colours of Melissa Kirsch's fishing-line sculptures on page 67 for inspiration.
- Recycle discarded cardboard to make beautiful artworks, using your collected images as visual reference.
- Make hemispherical heads using papier-mâché over a balloon or ball.
- Colour and cut strips of cardboard for the tentacles and join these to the head with a glue gun.

Option 2 Sculpture

- Choose one of your sketches or photos collected for 'Let's make an artwork 1', or collect more images of water creatures to use as the basis for a stick sculpture using the Structural Frame (planned composition, linear and patterned visual qualities).
- Look at Katherine Taylor's artwork on page 70, and the X-ray style of the barramundi frieze at the Ubirr rock art site on page 67 for inspiration.
- Collect a bucket full of sticks and twigs in various lengths and thicknesses.
- Design your water creature by planning the patterns of such parts as the bones, fins and tail, and any surrounding corals or sea plants. Translate these into lines that can be created using the sticks and twigs.
- Assemble your sculpture using a glue gun to permanently fasten the sticks.
- Fill some parts of the sculpture with paper or fabric.
- Paint your sculptures, either with the colours of the water, or, for maximum impact, black.

Extension

- Choose one of your sketches or photos of water creatures from 'Let's make an artwork 1', or collect more water images as the basis for paper sculptures using the Subjective Frame.
- Look back at the X-ray style of the barramundi frieze at the Ubirr rock on page 67 and the delicate colours of Melissa Kirsch's fishing-line sculptures on page 67.
- Use these visual resources as the starting point for an expressive and imaginative drawing of the water creature on tracing paper using soft pastels in a range of colours that suggest water. Combine the pastels with touches of coloured inks and white paint to reproduce the textures and patterns of the creatures.
- Paint a layer of PVA over the crayons and paint to fix them and make the paper stiff.
- When the paper is dry, tear around the outline of your water creature.
- Bend florist wire into shapes and lines that suggest the structure, bones and patterns of the water creature and have a tail of wire long enough to fasten to a small wooden base that will anchor the paper sculpture.
- Tear another piece of tissue paper the same shape as the creature (it doesn't have to be perfect). Sandwich the wire between the two sheets and glue with PVA glue. When dry, fix to the base.

In-depth study
Katherine Taylor
CRITICAL AND HISTORICAL INTERPRETATIONS

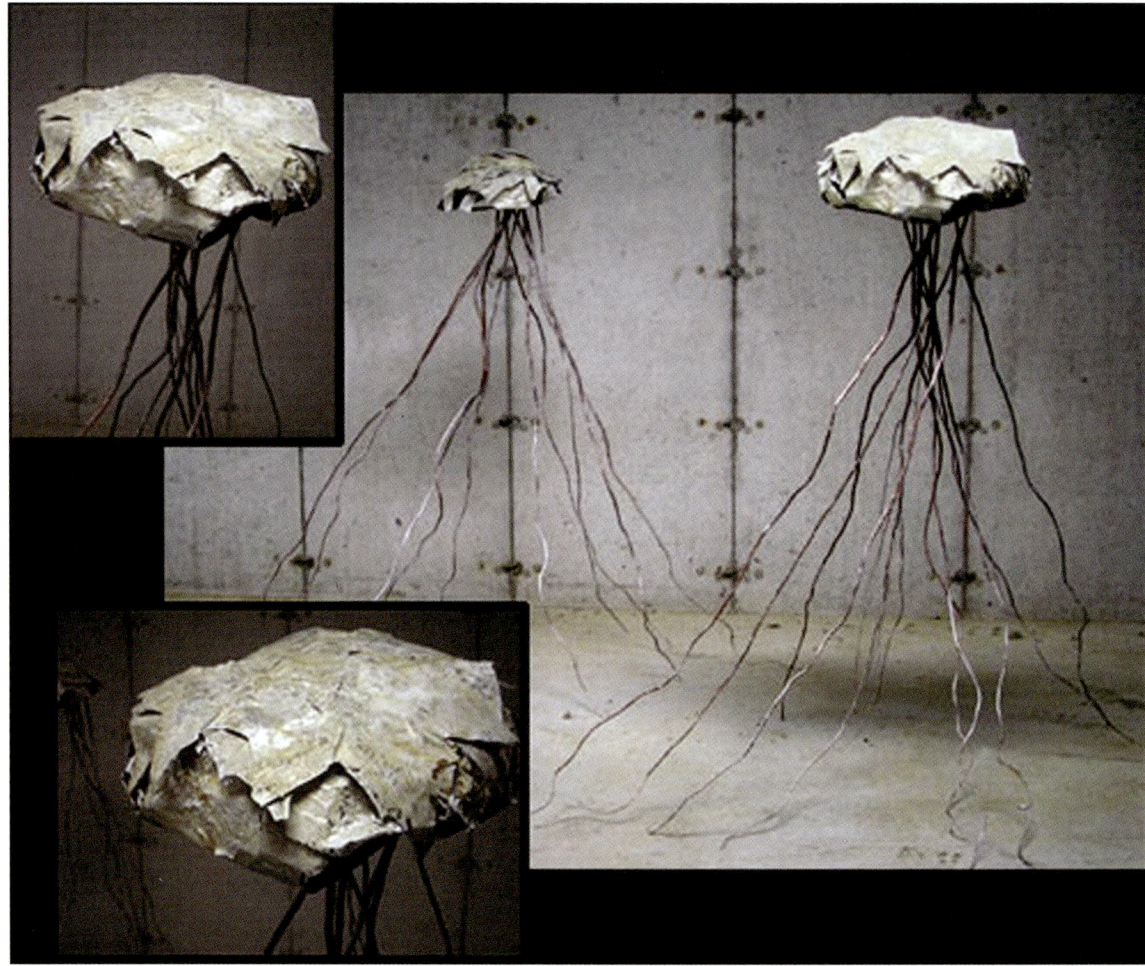

Katherine Taylor, *Weebotts*, 2006. Sculpture, sticks, leaves, cardboard, paint, 100 × 100 × 130 cm. © the artist Katherine C Taylor. 1974–, USA

CONCEPTUAL FRAMEWORK: WORLD

Katherine Taylor's world is a personal one of making art. Although she lives in the USA she completed her art studies in Melbourne. Her interest in art was first stimulated in high school along with a love of languages. She has lived and worked as an artist in both the USA and Spain.

ARTIST FRAMES: SUBJECTIVE

Katherine Taylor is an artist who works in the Subjective Frame. Her ideas and images emerge from her subconscious mind and she feels compelled to express them in her artmaking. She makes use of memory and intuition, allowing her imagination to have full reign in coming up with ideas for her sculptures.

ARTWORK FRAMES: STRUCTURAL

In *Weebotts*, fragile, spindly legs supporting flattened oval forms resemble partly organic, partly mechanical creatures that don't seem to belong in normal gravity. They could be aliens from outer space or they could belong in a watery environment; the artist doesn't say, she leaves it to us.

PRACTICE: IDEAS

The idea for this work came when Taylor was making artworks for an exhibition in the USA but was in London at the time. Because she had a small budget and the artworks had to be transported, she limited herself to lightweight found objects. She believes the image in these sculptures is a mysterious recurring one, as is the title *Weebotts*, but as yet she's not sure of the meaning.

PRACTICE: ACTIONS

The artist makes use of assemblage techniques to make the oval forms from leaves and cardboard that she then paints in neutral colours. She chooses sticks that are elongated, extending down from the oval forms in natural undulating lines resembling impossibly thin flexible legs or tentacles.

AUDIENCE

Katherine Taylor wants her audience to enjoy her work by bringing their own intuition and imagination to it. She has her own website on the internet and also shows her works through a gallery in Chicago.

WWW www.ktcreature.com/sculptures.html
www.galleriesmauricesternberg.com

Student
worksheet

The life of plants

Plants are important. They give us oxygen, affect our climate and are a vital part of ecosystems that also include humans and animals. Plants provide us with food and many medicines. We have contact with plants every day; they are our link to nature. The beauty of plants inspires many artists in their artmaking.

Artmaking sequence	Form	Artists
Let's make an artwork 1 *Leaf life*	Photography, scanography	• *Christian Staebler* • Olive Cotton, Ben Messina, Stewart Nelson
Let's make an artwork 2 *The manner of plants*	Drawing, printmaking	• *Jim Dine* • Margaret Preston, David Hockney, Angela Hayson
Let's make an artwork 3 *Florabundant*	Painting	• *Richard Dunlop, Mark Dixon* • Xia Chang, Albrecht Dürer, Emily Kame Kngwarreye

Let's make an artwork 1
Leaf life

Coming up with ideas   ARTMAKING PRACTICE

Take a series of photographs and scanographs of plants and use these in your artmaking.

Discussion, research and planning in your visual arts diary

CONCEPTUAL FRAMEWORK	PRACTICE	FRAMES
Artist Artwork World Audience	Ideas and actions	Structural—methods and materials, visual qualities and planned composition

Student worksheet

Olive Cotton (1911–2003), Australia, *Skeleton leaf*, 1964. Gelatin silver photograph, 24.7 × 19.6 cm. Art Gallery of New South Wales, Sydney.

Ben Messina (1975–), Australia, *Green Cactus*, from the series *Floral Elements*, 2009. Digital photograph, 32 × 32 cm. © Ben Messina.

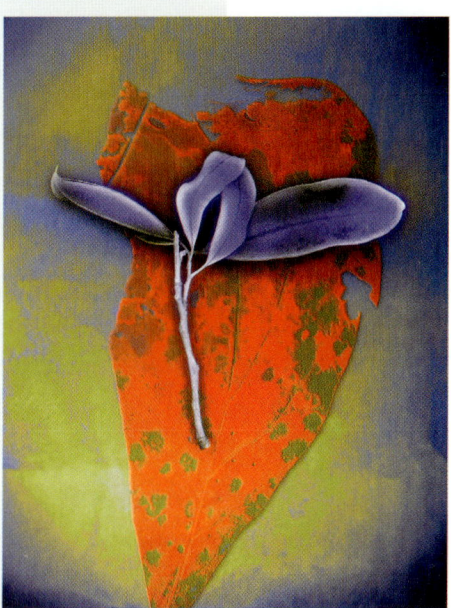

Stewart Nelson (1953–), USA, *Red Leaf, Blue Leaf*, 2008. Scanograph. © Stewart Nelson.

Looking at the works of the three artists above, as well as the work by **Christian Staebler** further ahead in the chapter, explore the ideas each artist has about plants.

In your visual arts diary:

- list two important actions each artist takes to depict plants
- list the Structural Frame qualities in each of these artworks, using the Frames table in the Introduction to help you
- choose one artwork and list the symbols used, explaining what you think they mean.

Discuss with your friends one way each artist sets out to interest the audience. Using this knowledge, list and sketch some ideas for your own plant artwork in your visual arts diary.

ONLINE RESOURCES

Stewart Nelson

Taking action   ARTMAKING PRACTICE
Option 1   Photography

- Look at the photographs of Olive Cotton and Ben Messina on page 73.
- Collect some plants or plant parts from the school grounds or from home. You can collect cuttings, or bring plants in vases or pots.
- Choose plants that are interesting visually, such as plants with an interesting structure, highly coloured plants, dead or dying plants, those with patterned and textured surfaces (in other words, plants with some distinguishing formal aspects that will make strong visual statements).
- Using the Structural Frame (structured visual qualities and planned composition), take a series of very close-up photographs of the plants using SLR cameras or digital cameras.
- Try using a variety of camera shots, angles and framing devices to effectively enhance the patterns of light and shade, textures, details of plant structures and colour.
- Use a variety of lighting angles to emphasise the three-dimensional qualities of the plants.
- Experiment with devices such as different coloured lights, natural light, use of shadows or water sprayed onto the plants.
- Download the images onto a school or home computer. Use photographic editing software to manipulate your images to achieve particular effects and to reflect and emphasise your theme. Try techniques such as cropping; sharpening or softening the focus; changing exposure, brightness and contrast; adjusting colour levels, temperature and tint; retouching; going to black and white or sepia; layering or duplicating your images or cutting and pasting parts of an image with other images to create a photomontage or overlay.

SLR camera: single-lens reflex camera, which uses an automatic moving mirror system that allows the photographer to see exactly what will be captured on film

framing device: a way of drawing attention to the subject of your image by blocking other parts of the image with something in the scene, leading the eye to the focal point

Option 2   Scanography

- Collect some plants or plant parts from the school grounds or from home. You can collect cuttings, or bring plants in vases or pots. Select plants of various different shapes, colours and textures.
- Look at the scanographs of Stewart Nelson on page 73 and Christian Staebler on page 75 for ideas. Using the Structural Frame, consider how their plants are arranged on the page.
- Lay your plants out on a flatbed scanner, or the scanner on an inkjet printer. You can choose to place them in a symmetrical composition overlap them so they form a natural composition.
- Make a scanograph by scanning the arrangement of plants into a computer.
- Use photographic editing software to manipulate your images so the colours are bright and unreal.

In-depth study
Christian Staebler

CRITICAL AND HISTORICAL INTERPRETATIONS

Christian Staebler, *Bryony*, 2005. Digital scanograph, 3543 × 4961 pixels. © Christian Staebler. 1958–, France

CONCEPTUAL FRAMEWORK: WORLD

Christian Staebler's world is that of book, magazine and packaging design and illustration. The natural world is important to him and this can be seen in his photography and scanographs. He is influenced by the artworks of Dürer and Escher because they mix reality with more altered views of the world.

ARTIST FRAMES: STRUCTURAL

Staebler sees himself as a 'maker' who tries to put order and logic into the plants he depicts so they become beautiful and communicate their natural beauty to an audience through both visual qualities and symbolism.

ARTWORK FRAMES: STRUCTURAL

Bryony shows the leaves, tendrils and white flowers of the white bryony, a European wild flower that has been used by herbalists for hundreds of years as both a medicinal plant and a poison. The artist carefully arranges the plants on the bed of the scanner and overlays them with grass stems producing a small green world where the delicate bryony is the star.

PRACTICE: IDEAS

herbarium: collection of dried plants

The artist keeps visual traces of what grows in his garden and includes them in a book project that acts like a herbarium. He discovered the bryony while clearing his fence and had to get very close to see its tiny flowers. He sees the plant as more than just a weed (as it is usually thought of), recognising it for its beauty and fragility and as an integral part of nature. This small plant is like a microcosm of the larger world of nature.

microcosm: small version of something larger

PRACTICE: ACTIONS

Staebler discovered how to use a computer scanner as a photographic tool in 1997. He places his chosen plants on the bed of the scanner, arranging them carefully and covering them with other bits of nature, in this case grass stems. This produces an image that has little perspective—it is almost flat. He concentrates on visual qualities that communicate his theme of natural beauty. In this image he creates clear details, curved shapes and line patterns contrasting with the vertical lines of the grass stems. The greenness of the image symbolises growth and life.

AUDIENCE

The artist believes anyone interested in either nature or scanography would be an interested audience for his work. He has exhibited his work in galleries in France and he has an international audience for his work via the internet.

Student worksheet

WWW www.chris-staebler.com
www.scannography.org

Let's make an artwork 2
The manner of plants

Coming up with ideas   ARTMAKING PRACTICE

Make a series of drawings or prints using plants as your subject.

Discussion, research and planning in your visual arts diary

Student worksheet

CONCEPTUAL FRAMEWORK	PRACTICE	FRAMES
Artist	Ideas and actions	Structural—methods and materials, visual qualities and composition
Artwork		
World		Subjective—spontaneous and expressive qualities
Audience		

Margaret Preston (1875–1963), Australia, *Rock Lily*, c. 1933. Hand-coloured woodcut on paper, 46.5 × 47 cm. Queensland Art Gallery/© Margaret Preston, c. 1933. Image licensed by Viscopy.

David Hockney (1937–), UK, *Cactus and Wall*, 2000. Charcoal on paper, 76 × 57 cm. © David Hockney. Photograph by Richard Schmidt.

Angela Hayson (1956–), Australia, *Solitary Communion*, 2005. Woodcut print, 121 × 86 cm. Image licensed by Viscopy.

Look at the works of the three artists above, as well as that of **Jim Dine** further ahead in the chapter.

> ONLINE RESOURCES
>
> Angela Hayson

In your visual arts diary:

- explore the different ideas each artist has about drawing plants
- describe the actions of each artist, referring to their use of materials and the drawing and printmaking methods and styles they use in their artworks
- list the Structural Frame or Subjective Frame qualities in each work, using the Frames table in the Introduction to help you
- list the visual qualities each artist has used to interest the audience.

www www.howcast.com/categories/18-Drawing-Techniques

Taking action ARTMAKING PRACTICE

Option 1 Drawing

- Use direct observation to do a series of small thumbnail sketches in your visual arts diary of plants, such as leaves on the ground, weeds, grass between the cracks of concrete or any other plants in the school grounds. Alternatively, take a series of photographs of plants to work from.
- Use a variety of different drawing materials (such as felt-tip pens, graphite pencils and conté crayons) and methods (including contour lines, hatching, crosshatching and shading) to develop your sketches (or draw the plants you have photographed).
- Choose the most interesting composition and make a large detailed drawing of these plants using both the Structural and Subjective Frames. Use graphite pencils (2B–6B)

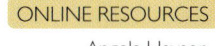

or charcoal and white chalk and an eraser. Make use of such devices as shading and hatching to give volume to the plant shapes, dark shadows contrasted with much lighter areas, or an expressive style of drawing that emphasises both the textures and patterns of the plants.

Option 2 Printmaking

- Use direct observation to do a series of small thumbnail sketches in your visual arts diary of plants, such as leaves on the ground, weeds, grass between the cracks of concrete or any other plants in the school grounds.
- Look at the prints of Margaret Preston and Angela Hayson on page 77.
- Make a series of prints using paper etching plates. Base these on your plant drawings, but choose a tiny fragment of your sketches to represent.
- Use the Structural Frame (for example, lines, tones and colours chosen; planned composition and printing method used) to give meaning. Plan your composition to look natural, with simplification and slight abstraction of shapes, very dark tones contrasted with light tones and an emphasis on pattern and texture, rather than lines. Choose colours that reflect the original plants.
- Use a variety of methods to prepare the paper or acetate plate, and in your printing technique.

In-depth study
Jim Dine

CRITICAL AND HISTORICAL INTERPRETATIONS

CONCEPTUAL FRAMEWORK: WORLD

Jim Dine became famous as one of the pop artists of the 1960s and 1970s in the USA. He is still a dynamic participant in the art world. His work has been influenced by such artists as Vincent Van Gogh, Edvard Munch, Henry Matisse and Pablo Picasso.

ARTIST FRAMES: STRUCTURAL/SUBJECTIVE

As a pop artist, Jim Dine began to make mixed-media assemblages, works that incorporated store-bought objects such as tools. He has also produced many paintings, drawings and prints with themes that have included the human figure, symbolic images such as a human heart, skulls, outstretched hands and many works based on nature.

Jim Dine, *Sun on the Paloose*, 2004. Drawing, charcoal, watercolour, pastel and spray paint on paper, 120.6 × 156.2 cm. Photograph by Kerry Ryan McFate, courtesy of Pace Wildenstein, New York. Licensed by ARS/Viscopy.
1935–, USA

ARTWORK FRAMES: STRUCTURAL/SUBJECTIVE

This large, expressive drawing shows a row of sunflowers seen by the artist in the Paloose, a region in Northwestern USA. The sunflower has long been used by artists as a symbol of great significance. Much of its meaning stems from its namesake, the sun itself. Sunflowers always turn their faces towards the sun; and this unique behaviour has appeared in many ancient myths and is viewed as a symbol of loyalty and constancy. Their physical resemblance to the sun has also influenced their meanings. The sunflower's petals have been likened to bright yellow rays of sunshine, which evoke feelings of life, warmth and happiness. But when an artist depicts sunflowers in various stages of decay, as Jim Dine does in *Sun on the Paloose*, the drawings of these flowers express feelings about the cycle of life and death.

PRACTICE: IDEAS

Dine is an artist who chooses images that appeal to him, such as the natural world, and then takes great pleasure in the act of drawing them. In this work his idea is to draw particular plants, sunflowers, to reflect his love of nature and to symbolise the rhythms of life and death in nature. Jim Dine has said of his work:

The reason I've made plant drawings all my life is because I'm in love with the plant. I draw, and it's a way of expressing my feelings at that moment, and also a way to express my feelings about the plant.

PRACTICE: ACTIONS

Dine makes use of a variety of different materials (charcoal, graphite, watercolour, pastel, acrylic, shellac, and screw heads) and an intense, expressive and imaginative technique of drawing where he continually erases and reworks the lines and shapes. He combines this with direct observation of the plants and his skills as a draughtsman. He carefully constructs the composition so that the sunflowers are arranged across the paper and silhouetted against the sky. He uses these images and symbols to give his work meaning.

draughtsman: someone who draws with skill

AUDIENCE

Jim Dine is an artist whose work is known the world over. He exhibits at many international galleries. He sets out to interest and inspire his audience with the large scale of the drawing, his deeply felt love of nature and his drawing skills.

WWW www.bobbiegreenfieldgallery.com
www.novakart.com
www.lesliesacks.com
www.nga.gov/exhibitions/2004/dine/dine_ss12.shtm
www.pacewildenstein.com

Let's make an artwork 3
Florabundant

Coming up with ideas   ARTMAKING PRACTICE

Make a series of paintings using plants and the natural world.

Discussion, research and planning in your visual arts diary

Student worksheets

CONCEPTUAL FRAMEWORK	PRACTICE	FRAMES
Artist	Ideas and actions	Structural—using symbolism to give meaning, visual qualities, planned composition
Artwork		
World		Subjective—expressive, imaginative approach
Audience		Postmodern—borrowing ideas from other artists

Look at the three artworks on page 81 as well as the paintings of **Richard Dunlop** and **Mark Dixon** further ahead in the chapter.

In your visual arts diary:

- explore each artist's ideas in relation to plants and the natural world, referring to each artist's world and culture
- list two important actions each artist takes to depict plants
- list the Structural Frame or Subjective Frame qualities in each work, using the Frames table in the Introduction to help you
- choose one of these artworks and list the symbols used, explaining what you think they tell us about the artist's attitude to the natural world.

Albrecht Dürer (1471–1528), Germany, *The Great Piece of Turf*, 1503. Watercolour and gouache on paper, 40.3 × 31.1 cm. © Erich Lessing.

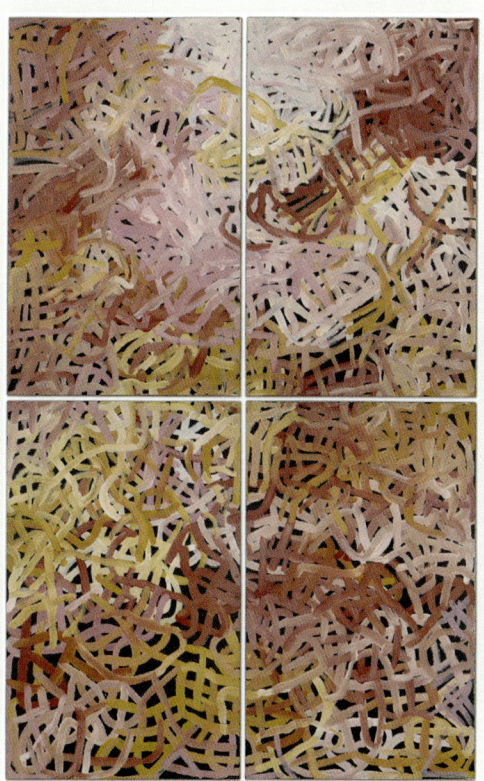

Emily Kame Kngwarreye (c. 1910–1996), Australia, *Anwerlarr angerr, Big yam*, 1996. Synthetic polymer paint on canvas, 401 × 245 cm. National Gallery of Victoria, Melbourne.

Xia Chang (1388–1470), China, *Bamboo in Wind*, Ming Dynasty, c. 1460. Hanging scroll, ink on paper, 203.4 × 59.7 cm. © The Metropolitan Museum of Art/Art Resource, NY, USA.

Discuss with your friends the visual qualities each artist has used to interest the audience. Using this knowledge and your drawings or photographs from 'Let's make an artwork 1' or 'Let's make an artwork 2', list and sketch some ideas for painting plants in your visual arts diary.

Taking action   ARTMAKING PRACTICE
Option 1   Painting

- Choose one of your sketches or photos of plants from 'Let's make an artwork 1' or 'Let's make an artwork 2' that shows the plant in great detail.
- Use this as the starting point for a small, square painting in acrylic paint of a fragment of the natural world, for example a large, interesting leaf or a small collection of twigs and bark.
- Look at the way Dürer, above, paints details of plants using direct observation.
- Reproduce the forms as accurately as possible by continually looking and experimenting with different painting techniques.
- Make use of correct proportions, realistic textures, patterns, colours, shadows and tonal modelling to give the illusion of reality.
- Now use your small painting as the starting point for a large, expressive painting in acrylic paint of the natural world. Look at the way Richard Dunlop and Mark Dixon's paintings do this (see further ahead in the chapter).

- Paint quickly and expressively using a variety of painting mediums and additives such as sand, and experiment with painting techniques that are bold and expressive rather than totally realistic. You may wish to borrow the idea of a silhouette from Mark Dixon.
- Combine the small, detailed painting with the larger, more abstract and expressive painting. Move the smaller painting over the larger work until you find where it will look best.
- Use PVA glue and some weights to glue the works together.

Option 2 Painting

- Use some of your sketches or photos of plants from 'Let's make an artwork 1' or 'Let's make an artwork 2' as the starting point for a painting.
- Use the Subjective Frame (an expressive and imaginative approach). Look at the way Richard Dunlop and Mark Dixon's paintings do this. You may wish to borrow the idea of a silhouette from Mark Dixon (see further ahead in the chapter).
- Also, use the Postmodern Frame and borrow the abstract way that Xia Chang and Emily Kame Kngwarreye on page 81 paint plants.
- Use a combination of methods and materials that are expressive. For example:
  - paint the composition expressively with PVA glue and pour sand over to create textured line patterns
  - use impasto or modelling compound to build up a sculptural, textured surface
  - use tissue paper dipped in PVA glue that is wrinkled and modelled to form shapes and lines and
  - choose a colour scheme that is realistic, or abstract and unrealistic.

In-depth study

Richard Dunlop

CRITICAL AND HISTORICAL INTERPRETATIONS

CONCEPTUAL FRAMEWORK: WORLD

Richard Dunlop's world is that of Australian art and nature. He is interested in the cycles of nature and sees them as mysterious and poetic but also vulnerable. Because of this his artmaking is full of subtle environmental themes.

ARTIST FRAMES: STRUCTURAL/SUBJECTIVE

Dunlop is both an expressive and imaginative artist as well as one who uses symbols and painting methods and materials to give his paintings meaning.

ARTWORK FRAMES: STRUCTURAL/SUBJECTIVE

Against a blue sky swirl leaves of the ginkgo tree, and other less recognisable leaves and plants. There are stems and tendrils of vines and shadows and silhouettes of other plants

Richard Dunlop, *Cabinet of Natural Curiosities*, 2006. Oil on canvas, 120 × 120 cm. Image and copyright courtesy of Richard Dunlop/ Tim Olsen Gallery Sydney.
1960–, Australia

and flowers, some looking as if they are moving naturally in the breeze, others placed in rows as if they are in a cabinet of curiosities and all are seen from different viewpoints.

PRACTICE: IDEAS

Richard Dunlop explores ideas about the beauty and fragility of nature. He plays with the idea that botanical illustration does not have to be serious, unadventurous and exact. Instead his idea is to paint plants in an inventive, poetic and imaginative way and to include elements of fantasy. He wants to capture the true beauty of nature which he sees as being one of organic chaos.

I think a lot of my paintings ... are about beauty and fate and the constant presence of something that could disrupt or destroy order. Richard Dunlop, quoted by Peter Buzza, www.timolsengallery.com

cabinet of curiosities: a room or a display cupboard in which are kept collections of objects of natural history, such as plant specimens

PRACTICE: ACTIONS

The artist uses many layers to produce *Cabinet of Natural Curiosities*. He uses a coloured first layer, then paints over the top of this the lines and shapes that form the plan of his composition. He often changes his mind as he works, and you can see this in the artwork, where he has erased paint or left expressive drips, smears, scratches and line variations over the painting. These disruptions to the creation of his artworks are deliberate, reflecting the random disruptions that occur in nature itself. Dunlop sometimes applies oil paint to look like watercolour and uses both the transparent and semi-transparent qualities of oil paint to build up rich layers of colour. His depiction of leaves is based on years of observation of nature, but his painted plants are invented forms painted from memory and his imagination.

AUDIENCE

Dunlop engages the interest of his audience with expressive patches of luminous colour, movement and lively paint that comes to life beside the more precise and detailed plants and other natural forms in this work.

WWW www.timolsengallery.com
www.janmurphygallery.com.au

In-depth study
Mark Dixon
CRITICAL AND HISTORICAL INTERPRETATIONS

Mark Dixon, *Untitled*, 2005. Acrylic on canvas, 60 × 60 cm. © Mark Dixon. 1971–, Canada

Mark Dixon, *Untitled*, 2005. Acrylic on board, 20 × 20 cm. © Mark Dixon.

CONCEPTUAL FRAMEWORK: WORLD

Mark Dixon's world is that of contemporary art in Canada, and increasingly he is becoming part of the international art world. Although he lives in the urban world of a city, he also sees himself as part of the natural world, especially the world of plants, and this is what he paints.

ARTIST FRAMES: STRUCTURAL

Dixon is an artist who works in the Structural Frame. He observes plants closely but is not interested in depicting them in realistic detail. Instead he uses paint to suggest the essence of the plants he paints. He plans each composition carefully and uses visual qualities that suggest nature.

ARTWORK FRAMES: STRUCTURAL

In both the paintings shown on page 84 the artist depicts the realistic shapes of clumps of plants. The edges of the plant forms are sometimes sharp and sometimes blurred. Within them there is expressive brushwork, colours suggesting the particular plants and patches of light and shade, but no detail. He uses one flat colour in the background so the plant forms are like silhouettes.

PRACTICE: IDEAS

Dixon's idea is to suggest the beauty of the plants he paints through his choice of paint, his methods of applying it and the visual qualities he uses.

PRACTICE: ACTIONS

Dixon makes drawings of plants, noting their colours, textures and tones. He paints the surface of his canvas or board in broad brushstrokes covering it with these colours, textures and tones. Referring to his drawings, he then cuts a **stencil** that blocks out the plant forms and paints in his background colour.

stencil: pattern with a cut-out design

AUDIENCE

Mark Dixon uses striking images of plants and vivid colours to communicate his interest in nature to an audience.

www www.markdixon.ca

Chapter 8

Domestic creatures

Domestic creatures are animals taken from the wild, tamed and trained to interact with people. They are dependent on us for food and survival; but sometimes we also become dependent on them. Domestic animals such as sheep, chickens and cattle are a source of food, often used in farming or for transport. Over time, domestic creatures like cats and dogs have become our protectors and friends. Domestic creatures are an important part of our culture and they are often depicted in artworks.

Artmaking sequence	Form	Artists
Let's make an artwork 1 *Transforming creatures*	Transforming found objects, photography	• *Graham Blondel, ancient Egyptian* Cat • Al Munro, Jeff Koons
Let's make an artwork 2 *Assembling creatures*	Assemblage sculpture	• *Geoff Harvey* • Peter Baka, Ian Swift, Randall Sinnamon

Let's make an artwork 1
Transforming creatures

Coming up with ideas   ARTMAKING PRACTICE

Transform a ready-made sculpture or photograph of a domestic animal to give it new meaning.

Discussion, research and planning in your visual arts diary

CONCEPTUAL FRAMEWORK	PRACTICE	FRAMES
Artist Artwork World Audience	Ideas and actions	Structural—exploring materials and methods in artmaking Cultural—exploring ideas, beliefs and values through artworks Postmodern—experimenting with new materials and methods in artmaking

Student worksheet

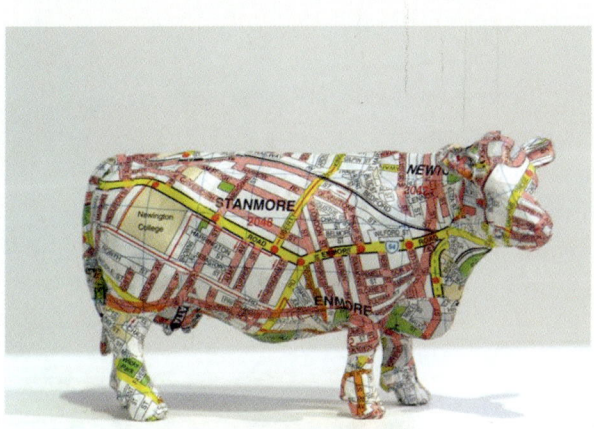

Al Munro, contemporary artist, Australia, *Future Farm 17 (Newtown)*, 2007. Found maps, polymer vinyl cast figurine, 7 × 12 × 6 cm. © Al Munro. Image: Brenda May Gallery, Sydney.

Jeff Koons (1955–), USA, *Puppy*, 1995–1996. Temporary sculpture outside the Museum of Contemporary Art, Sydney, modelled on the *White Terrier*, covered in a coat of thousands of flowering plants, approximately 12 m. © Jeff Koons. Photograph by Donald Williams.

Looking at the artworks above, as well as that of **Graham Blondel** and the ancient Egyptian *Cat* further ahead in the chapter, examine the ways that artists have used domestic animals as their inspiration for artmaking.

In your visual arts diary:

- describe which frame each artist is working in (using the Frames table in the Introduction to help you)

- list the different methods and materials used by each artist
- collect a range of images from different cultures in which animals have been represented in traditions, beliefs and aspects of people's everyday lives
- list ways that domestic animals are part of your own world, using the Conceptual Framework table in the Introduction to help you
- create a visual brainstorm of the kinds of domestic animals with which you feel a particular connection
- plan and sketch ideas for your own sculptural artwork based on your knowledge of these artworks and the works of other artists who have been inspired by animals.

Taking action   ARTMAKING PRACTICE
Option 1   Transforming found objects

- Look back at the artwork of Al Munro on page 87 and at that of Graham Blondel on page 89.
- Collect a non-precious statue or figurine of an animal that you can easily transform. *Two-dollar* shops may be a good place to source a cheap animal statue if you do not have one readily available.
- Use a variety of different methods, such as painting and collage, to transform the surface of your figurine. Use bright colours, patterns and interesting textures.
- Install your animal sculpture with a group of other animals created by your classmates and document your installation photographically.

Option 2   Photography

- Look back at the artwork of Jeff Koons on page 87.
- Find a photo of your pet or collect an image of a domestic animal from a magazine or the internet.

- Scan the image into a school or home computer. Use photographic editing software to digitally alter the picture by covering it in colourful patterns and textures.
- Crop your finished image into a square format, and print out a copy that measures 20 cm × 20 cm; or, find an image of an iconic building or site, such as the Sydney Opera House and, using editing software, cut out the image of your altered animal and place it in front of the iconic building or site.
- Alternatively, you could print out both images, cut out the animal with scissors and create a paper collage of the animal in front of the iconic building or site.

In-depth study

Graham Blondel

CRITICAL AND HISTORICAL INTERPRETATIONS

ONLINE RESOURCES

Graham Blondel

Graham Blondel, *Pack of Dogs*, 2008. Acrylic on cast resin, 30 × 38 × 15 cm. Image: Graham Blondel/licensed by Viscopy. 1949–, Australia

CONCEPTUAL FRAMEWORK: WORLD

Graham Blondel's world is that of the Australian contemporary artist. He has been an artist and art educator for more than 35 years; and, although he is based in Sydney, he has travelled and worked in many other places in Australia and overseas. He is also a director of A-Space On Cleveland, an art gallery in Surry Hills, Sydney.

ARTIST FRAMES: CULTURAL/POSTMODERN

motifs: designs

Blondel makes art to try and make sense of the world around him. He analyses information about the world and popular culture and reconstructs it in the form of collages, paintings and sculptures. He sees artmaking as a way of celebrating the complex and ridiculous aspects of everyday life. The flower **motifs** on Blondel's dog artworks also reference *Puppy*, pictured on page 87, which is a well-known artwork created by Postmodern artist Jeff Koons, featuring a gigantic puppy covered in living flowers. *Puppy* was installed outside the Museum of Contemporary Art in Sydney for a few months in 1995 and 1996.

ARTWORK FRAMES: POSTMODERN

recontextualise: take something from where it belongs and use it in a new way

In *Pack of Dogs*, Blondel **recontextualises** his decorative dog statues by grouping them together and placing them in an art gallery. Usually this kind of decorative statue might be found on a shelf in someone's home, but by taking the dogs from where they usually belong and using them in a new way, Blondel makes a comment about the place of domestic animals in our lives.

PRACTICE: IDEAS

critique: comment on something's good and bad qualities

While his idea for *Pack of Dogs* grew out of his own love of dogs, Blondel's ideas also relate to the way that domestic animals are treated in our Postmodern society. He uses his richly patterned puppies to **critique** the way that some people, such as celebrities like Paris Hilton, have turned domestic animals into decorative objects or fashion accessories that can be carried in a handbag. He is interested in the fine line between beauty and kitsch, and while his artworks are often quite humorous they also make serious statements about the absurdity of some aspects of Postmodern culture.

TEACHER NOTE

Have a class discussion about how the roles of domestic animals have changed over time and how artists have documented this. Refer to Graham Blondel, Al Munro and Jeff Koons.

intricate: detailed

PRACTICE: ACTIONS

In *Pack of Dogs*, Blondel demonstrates his love of colour and pattern by painting small resin sculptures of dachshunds, terriers and other dogs in **intricate** floral patterns and arranging them in packs or groups. Blondel arranges the dogs in groups because the repetition of shapes and patterns creates rhythm and visual interest.

TEACHER NOTE

Discuss with the class other reasons why Graham Blondel might have arranged his dogs in a pack. What symbolic meaning could this have?

AUDIENCE

Graham Blondel wants to engage and amuse his audience and make them think critically about Postmodern culture. His artworks have been shown in art galleries in Australia and overseas and images of his works are widely accessible to an internet audience via art gallery websites.

WWW www.artwhatson.com.au/a-spaceoncleveland

In-depth study
Cat

CRITICAL AND HISTORICAL INTERPRETATIONS

CONCEPTUAL FRAMEWORK: WORLD

The identity of the artist who created this ancient bronze sculpture is unknown; however, the world of the artist would have been ancient Egypt. The bronze cast cat from the Ptolemaic period was created around 330–30 BC.

ARTIST FRAMES: CULTURAL

Cats, known as *mau*, played an important role in ancient Egyptian culture. The ancient Egyptians had religious beliefs that centred on the worship of animals. Initially cats were seen as being useful for catching mice and protecting crops from being eaten by pests, but over time humans domesticated cats. The domesticated cat became a symbol of grace and dignity. The Cat goddess Bast (also known as Bastet) was a **deity** representing protection, fertility and motherhood.

ARTWORK FRAMES: STRUCTURAL

Cat is a sculpture cast from bronze. It is made of two halves that join together almost **seamlessly** to create a container for a **mummified** cat. The bronze cat is tall and sleek and is depicted as graceful, elegant, powerful and dignified.

PRACTICE: IDEAS

Cats were elevated to the position of gods and goddesses and were of great importance to Egyptian society. They were treated with great respect even after their death and some cats were even mummified, just like humans. As part of religious rituals, mummified cats were given as an offering to the goddess Bast and were buried within the surrounds of her temple.

PRACTICE: ACTIONS

Bronze cast cat sculptures often became containers for mummified cats. The technical processes of mummification are not fully known. It is thought that mummification involved similar processes to those used in embalming (a more modern process used to preserve human remains in order to prevent decay). When cats died they were often wrapped in fine linen and treated with cedar oil and spices to preserve the body for a long time. It was important to the ancient Egyptians that the external appearance of the mummified cat resembled the appearance of a living cat.

Artist unknown, 330–30 BCE, Egypt, *Cat*. Bronze cast sculpture, 28 cm. © The Metropolitan Museum of Art/ Art Resource, New York.
Ptolemaic period, c. 400–30 BC.

deity: a god, goddess, or other divine being
seamlessly: without seams or visible joins
mummified: preserved and wrapped in cloth, as was the custom in ancient Egyptian times

TEACHER NOTE

Brainstorm with the class a list of other cultures in which animals have played an important role in religious and cultural customs and beliefs.

AUDIENCE

These artworks were originally created by the people of ancient Egypt as a way of ensuring that their cats would have a smooth transition into the afterlife. They were not intended for any other audience. However, in modern times, audiences including historians, researchers, students and those people interested in art, have grown to appreciate the cultural and artistic value of these ancient artefacts.

Let's make an artwork 2
Assembling creatures

Coming up with ideas ARTMAKING PRACTICE

Create a sculpture of a domestic animal using found objects.

Discussion, research and planning in your visual arts diary

Student worksheet

ONLINE RESOURCES

Ian Swift

CONCEPTUAL FRAMEWORK	PRACTICE	FRAMES
Artist Artwork World Audience	Ideas and actions	Structural—exploring materials and methods in artmaking Cultural—exploring ideas, beliefs and values through artworks Postmodern—experimenting with new materials and methods in artmaking

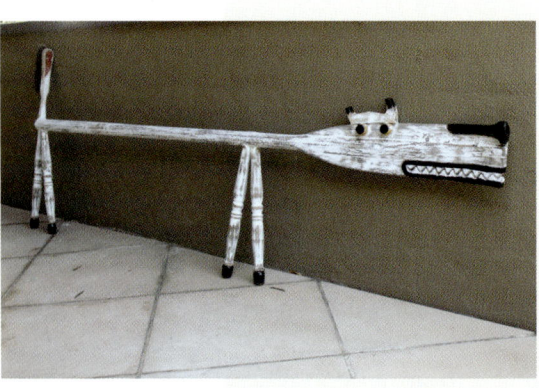

Peter Baka (1957–), Australia, *Dog*. Wooden oar, found objects and oil paint. © the artist. Image: Moonchinside Gallery.

Ian Swift (1952–), Australia, *Tex*, 2008. Found objects 51 × 22 × 52 cm. © the artist. Image: Harrison Galleries.

Randall Sinnamon (1970–), Australia, *Red Legged Scissor Headed Heron*. Steel, mangrove, casurina and teak wood, fibreglass 38 × 15 × 36 cm. © Randall Sinnamon. Image: Robin Gibson Gallery.

Look at the works of the three artists on page 92 and that of **Geoff Harvey** further ahead in the chapter.

In your visual arts diary:

- explain how the personal and wider world of these artists may have influenced their ideas (using the Conceptual Framework table in the Introduction to help you)
- describe how each artist communicates meaning to their audience through their artworks
- describe each artist's ideas, actions and material choices
- explain how each artist has captured the interest of their audience
- identify which Frame each artist uses (using the Frames table in the Introduction to help you) and describe the qualities of that Frame you can see in the artworks
- sketch some ideas for animal sculptures that you could create using everyday items
- research and list the materials and methods you might choose to use in artmaking.

Taking action   ARTMAKING PRACTICE

Option 1   Assemblage sculpture

- Collect a box of discarded everyday items that you could use to create a sculpture based on a domestic animal; for example, cutlery, cups, bits of machinery and furniture, scraps of metal and wood.
- Plan your sculpture in your visual arts diary. Look back at the artworks of Ian Swift on page 92 and Randall Sinnamon on page 92, and at the work of Geoff Harvey on page 94, for inspiration.
- Use a variety of methods to assemble your materials, such as a hammer and nails, gaffer tape, staples, PVA glue, hot glue guns or liquid nails, depending on the material you are using—but make sure that your sculpture looks visually appealing.
- You may like to paint some parts of your sculpture or leave the raw materials as they are.
- You may then like to install your finished sculpture in various places around your school or home. Think about places that you could install your sculpture that would make it seem humorous or would give the artwork added meaning. Produce a series of five photographic images that document the installation of your sculpture.

TEACHER NOTE

Collect a box of useful items for assemblage sculpture. Council clean-ups and reverse garbage (waste recyclers) are excellent places to start. Assist students in using safe, appropriate methods to construct their sculptures.

In-depth study
Geoff Harvey

CRITICAL AND HISTORICAL INTERPRETATIONS

Geoff Harvey, *Princess*. Mixed-media sculpture, life-sized. © Geoff Harvey.
1954–, Australia

CONCEPTUAL FRAMEWORK: WORLD

Geoff Harvey is an artist who lives and works in Sydney. His world is the world of
contemporary Australian art. He is a painter and sculptor best known for his sculptures
of animals, particularly dogs, made from recycled objects.

ARTIST FRAMES: STRUCTURAL/CULTURAL

Harvey makes art that reflects his observations of creatures in the world around him and
captures the playful antics of animals, their personalities and mannerisms. In 2009 he
participated in a 10 week Artist in Residence Program at Sydney's Taronga Zoo that enabled
him to get up close to the animals and observe them in their own environment. This has
greatly influenced his artmaking practice.

ARTWORK FRAMES: STRUCTURAL/CULTURAL/POSTMODERN

In *Princess*, Harvey creates two dogs made from found objects. The animals are interacting
with each other. In fact, as *Princess* sits tall and straight the other dog is checking her out
by sniffing her bottom (as all dogs identify each other through scent). This gives Harvey's
sculptures a humorous edge and highlights the animalistic behaviour of the dogs.

PRACTICE: IDEAS

Harvey's ideas are informed by his observations of, and interactions with, animals in the everyday world. Through his artworks he investigates relationships between humans and animals. He is interested in the roles that animals play in our lives, our interactions with them and their interactions with each other. Many of his sculptures have been installed in public places, bringing together the world of humans and the world of domestic creatures.

PRACTICE: ACTIONS

Harvey gathers non-traditional artmaking materials such as bits of chairs, bicycles, old pieces of wood, metal and discarded objects to create his sculptures. Using a hammer, nails and glue, he recycles objects that would otherwise have been thrown away, assembling, constructing and remaking them into animal sculptures of life-like proportions.

AUDIENCE

Harvey's artworks are exhibited locally and internationally. He has participated in many group exhibitions and has had many successful solo exhibitions. His work is highly regarded and enjoyed by art-educated and non-art-educated audiences alike. Harvey aims to make artworks that engage people in a playful way, making them reflect on the relationships between humans and domestic creatures.

WWW www.blueterrace.com/hinchinbrook/artists/harvey.php
http://robingibson.net/exhibitions/geoff-harvey

TEACHER NOTE

As a class, discuss the ways in which Geoff Harvey's sculptures seem playful.

Student worksheet

Creatures of the street

Our streets are a public domain. We use them as a way to get from one place to another. They are also used as playgrounds and meeting places. The streets are owned by no-one, and everyone; that is what makes them the perfect place for artists to create artworks. Postmodern street artists display their artworks in public places for a general audience, often treading the fine line between artmaking and vandalism.

Artmaking sequence	Form	Artists

Let's make an artwork I
Inflated creatures
	Sculpture	• *Joshua Allen Harris*
		• Jason Hackenwerth,
		  Dan Steinhilber,
		  Tone Holmen

Let's make an artwork 2 *Sticky creatures*	Sculpture, installation	• *Mark Jenkins, Banksy* • Juan Muñoz, Antony Gormley

Let's make an artwork 1
Inflated creatures

Coming up with ideas   ARTMAKING PRACTICE

Create a creature made from plastic bags or recycled plastic materials.

Discussion, research and planning in your visual arts diary

CONCEPTUAL FRAMEWORK	PRACTICE	FRAMES
Artist Artwork World Audience	Ideas and actions	Postmodern—experimenting with new materials and methods in artmaking Structural—exploring materials and methods in artmaking

Student worksheet

Jason Hackenwerth (1970–), USA, *Traverse City Film Festival Megamite*, 2009. Balloon sculpture. © Jason Hackenwerth.

Tone Holmen, contemporary artist, Norway, *Baby Polar Bear*. Polystyrene, sheet, chicken mesh and plastic bags, 76 × 38 × 36 cm. © Tone Holmen.

Dan Steinhilber (1972–), USA, *Untitled*, 2002. Plastic rubbish bags and wet/dry vacuum bags 304.8 × 365.8 × 365.8 cm. © Dan Steinhilber. Image: G Fine Art Gallery.

Look at the artworks by the artists on page 97, as well as that of **Joshua Allen Harris** further ahead in the chapter.

In your visual arts diary:

- discuss the ideas of each artist
- investigate 'street art' and explain how it is different to the art seen in galleries
- explain how the personal and wider world of these artists may have influenced their ideas, using the Conceptual Framework table in the Introduction to help you
- list two important artmaking actions each artist takes
- decide which Frame each artist is working in (using the Frames table in the Introduction to help you) and list the qualities of each Frame that you can see in the artworks
- describe the ways that each artist engages their audience
- sketch your ideas for creating a sculptural street creature, using your knowledge of these artists' ideas and actions.

Research and experiment with the methods and materials that you could use to create a sculptural creature.

WWW www.jasonhackenwerth.com/
http://admin2.clikpic.com/toneholmen/

TEACHER NOTE

Collect a range of plastic bags, plastic lids and plastic containers that students can use to make artworks.

Taking action   ARTMAKING PRACTICE
Option 1   Sculpture

- Collect photographs or other images of creatures to use as visual reference for a 3-D plastic bag sculpture.
- Look at the works of Joshua Allen Harris on page 100, and Dan Steinhilber on page 97.
- Draw up plans for your creature artwork, breaking the creature down into simplified shapes.
- Use the simplified shapes to create a paper pattern for your 3-D plastic bag sculpture.

- Cut pieces from plastic bags to match your pattern and join them together using clear sticky tape. Make sure you leave an opening at the base of your sculpture for air to enter and inflate it.
- Use ties made from pieces of plastic bag to attach your creature to a fan or other wind source, and slowly inflate it.
- Alternatively, you could breathe air into your sculpture and seal it with tape so that it is permanently inflated like a balloon.

Option 2 Sculpture

- Look back at the artworks of Tone Holeman and Jason Hackenwerth on page 97.
- Refer to the sketches of a sculptural street creature you made in your visual arts diary and collect photographs and other images of creatures to use as visual reference. Observe the patterns, textures and visual qualities of your chosen creature as you plan your work.
- Create a wire frame or use an inflated balloon as the base for your sculpture and build around it using a range of plastic materials. You may even like to include some found plastic objects.
- Use the Structural Frame to make choices about the colours, textures and shapes that you will use in making your sculpture.
- Use a variety of methods to construct your sculpture, such as gluing with a hot glue gun, weaving, sewing, tying, layering and threading your materials together.

In-depth study

Joshua Allen Harris

CRITICAL AND HISTORICAL INTERPRETATIONS

CONCEPTUAL FRAMEWORK: WORLD

Joshua Allen Harris is a Postmodern street artist. His world is that of bustling and busy New York City.

ARTIST FRAMES: POSTMODERN/STRUCTURAL

Harris is a street artist who works in the Postmodern Frame, using unconventional materials and methods to create large-scale inflatable artworks in the urban environment. He positions his plastic bag creatures so that they become inflated and animated when trains pass through the train tunnels and expel air though grates in the footpath.

ARTWORK FRAMES: POSTMODERN/STRUCTURAL

In Harris's *Polar Bear Plastic Bag Installation* on page 100, two white plastic bag polar bears are tied to a train tunnel grate and come to life, rising up and dancing on the pavement as they are filled with blasts of warm air from trains passing under the street. Harris's incidental audiences must ask themselves whether these plastic creatures emerging from a pile of plastic rubbish on the footpath could possibly be art.

incidental: occurring by chance

PRACTICE: IDEAS

As polar bears are often a symbol associated with global warming, Harris's artwork could be interpreted in terms of concerns about global warming and the destruction of our environment. However, this artwork is just one of numerous animal, creature and monster plastic-bag installations Harris has created.

TEACHER NOTE

Discuss with the class the way in which Harris's material artmaking choices also reflect his concern for the environment.

Joshua Allen Harris, *Polar Bear Plastic Bag Installation*, 2008. © Joshua Allen Harris. Contemporary artist, USA

PRACTICE: ACTIONS

Harris uses sticky tape and discarded plastic shopping bags to create giant inflatable animals, such as these polar bears, which are fastened to footpath grates and air vents. The exhaust air that is expelled by trains passing under the street fills the plastic bags, causing the creatures to slowly come to life, moving and swaying with the rhythmic blasts of warm air. When the train has passed and the air runs out again, the creatures slowly deflate, becoming piles of plastic rubbish once again. His artworks are documented through videos and photographs that are then posted on the internet.

AUDIENCE

Harris creates his artworks primarily for his own pleasure but also wants to create installations that come to life, surprising and intriguing people as they pass by them in the street.

He claims that he had no idea that his artworks would get so much attention. However, once someone posted an image of his polar bear sculptures on the Wooster Collective street-art website, his images began appearing all over the internet. He has since been interviewed by *New York Magazine* and now has a global audience.

WWW   www.woostercollective.com
www.inhabitat.com
http://nymag.com

 Student worksheet

Let's make an artwork 2
Sticky creatures

Coming up with ideas ARTMAKING PRACTICE

Create a tape sculpture of a creature and install it in a public place.

Discussion, research and planning in your visual arts diary

CONCEPTUAL FRAMEWORK	PRACTICE	FRAMES
Artist Artwork World Audience	Ideas and actions	Postmodern—experimenting with new materials and methods in artmaking Structural—exploring materials and methods in artmaking Cultural—exploring ideas, beliefs and values through artworks

Student worksheet
eText

Juan Muñoz (1953–2001), Spain, *Two Seated on the Wall*, 2000. Cast sculpture. © Juan Muñoz, image courtesy of the Estate of Juan Muñoz, photo by Attilio Maranzano.

Mark Jenkins (1970–), USA, *Untitled (9/09, Seoul, Korea)*, 2009. Newspaper and packing tape. © Mark Jenkins.

Antony Gormley (1950–), UK, *Passage*, 2000. Cast iron sculpture (×2), installation view, Caumont, Picardie, France, 197 × 48 × 26 cm (each). © the artist.

Look the work of the three artists above, as well as the additional artwork by **Mark Jenkins** further ahead in the chapter. Choose one of the artists who has installed their artwork in the streets. In your visual arts diary:

- describe your chosen artist's ideas and actions
- describe how audiences react to and interact with this artist's work
- explain how the personal and wider world of this artist may have influenced their artmaking ideas and actions, using the Conceptual Framework table in the Introduction to help you
- describe how the artist communicates meaning to their audience through their artwork

- describe which Frames the artist is working in (using the Frames table in the Introduction to help you) and list the qualities of each Frame
- list and sketch your own artmaking ideas, using your knowledge of this artist's artmaking ideas and actions.

WWW www.juanmunoz.org

Taking action   ARTMAKING PRACTICE
Option 1   Sculpture

- Use an image of a creature as the inspiration for a sculpture made of tape.
- Look at the tape sculptures created by Mark Jenkins on pages 101 and 103. You may find it helpful to view one of his online tape sculpture tutorials.

WWW www.tapesculpture.org

- Use newspaper and masking tape to create the form of your creature sculpture.
- Once you have sculpted the basic form, wrap it in a layer of clear plastic.
- Cover your sculpture with multiple layers of clear packing tape. Add layers of tape so that the shell of plastic wrap is quite rigid.
- Ask your teacher to supervise as you use a craft knife to carefully cut your creature's packing tape shell in half to release the paper mould inside.
- Remove the newspaper and carefully tape your creature back together again so that all that remains is the transparent form of your creature.

Option 2   Installation

- Work in a group with some of your classmates to create an installation of large packing tape sculptures.
- Follow the steps for Option 1 to create large tape sculptures.
- Install your tape creatures in a public place. You could hang them in an indoor space, place them somewhere in the school playground or install them so that they are walking up a staircase.
- Document your installation using photographs or video and record the way that your audience responds to and interacts with your sculptures.

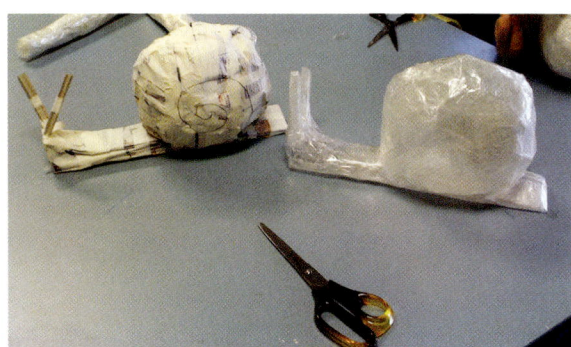

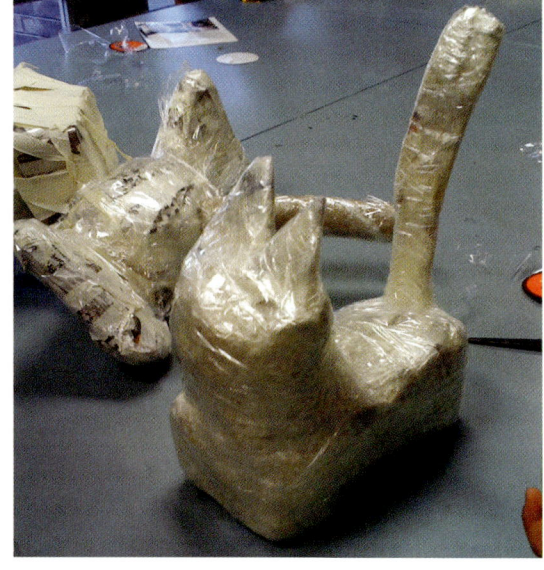

In-depth study
Mark Jenkins

CRITICAL AND HISTORICAL INTERPRETATIONS

CONCEPTUAL FRAMEWORK: WORLD

Mark Jenkins is a contemporary American artist whose world is that of the urban city. He has become well known for his street sculpture installations created using packing tape.

ARTIST FRAMES: CULTURAL/POSTMODERN

Jenkins is interested in the world around him, particularly his social environment, and considers himself to be as much of a social experimenter as an artist. He is always interested to see how people will react to and interact with his artworks. Jenkins is known to be a bit of a prankster and often places his artworks in unlikely locations that make people stop and smile.

ARTWORK FRAMES: STRUCTURAL/POSTMODERN

The artwork shown here is an almost life-sized sculpture of a giraffe made from clear packing tape. Jenkins installed the giraffe on a patch of grass on the corner of a Washington street. It appears as if the giraffe is eating a yellow plastic bag out of a nearby tree. The giraffe is recontextualised, taken from its home in the wild and placed in the urban landscape. While Jenkins's artwork would have been installed on the street for only a short amount of time, he documents his tape sculpture installation photographically.

Mark Jenkins, *Untitled (2/06 Washington, DC)*, 2006. Packing tape. © Mark Jenkins. (1970–), USA

PRACTICE: IDEAS

Jenkins's artmaking ideas grow out of his desire to play and create. An early influence on his artmaking practice was the Spanish sculptor Juan Muñoz who placed sculptures of human figures in architectural environments and unexpected settings, see page 101 for an example. It was seeing the work of Muñoz that gave Jenkins a deeper understanding of what it meant to create an art installation. Jenkins is challenged by the impersonal nature of the city and strives to bring life back to the city by creating artworks that make ordinary things look strange and intriguing. While he does not intend for his sculptures to become like traditional sculptures or monuments, his artworks reference the traditions of public sculpture and act as Postmodern monuments that challenge the audience to interact with the urban environment in new ways.

PRACTICE: ACTIONS

Jenkins claims that he discovered his packing tape sculpture technique when, as a child at school, he used to make tape casts of his pencil case during class. He begins a sculpture by selecting a creature or object and carefully wrapping it in clear plastic wrap. He then takes a roll of transparent packing tape and covers the plastic wrapped object in layers of packing tape. Jenkins then cuts the packing tape shell from the original object and tapes it back together to form a replica of the object made entirely from packing tape. Next, without official permission and often with the help of friends, he installs (or as he says 'drops') his tape sculptures in public places. Jenkins's artworks are a form of street art. They are playful, transparent and impermanent. Unlike some forms of street art, they do not deface the city in any way; if anything, they make ordinary things appear more extraordinary.

replica: copy or imitation

AUDIENCE

Jenkins's artworks are accessible to a wide audience, from people who view his tape sculptures in the street, to those who come in contact with his works in art galleries, books, newspapers, magazines, via the internet or through his artmaking workshops. While Jenkins seeks to engage his audiences, he never really sets out with an intentional message. He would prefer that those who view his works are intrigued by what they see, so that they begin to ask questions of their own like 'Is this art?' It is his hope that his playful installations, and the element of surprise they create as people pass by them in the street, will inspire audiences to see their everyday world in new ways.

WWW www.xmarkjenkinsx.com
www.myartspace.com
www.themorningnews.org/archives/galleries/let_no_man_scare_you.php

Extension

Banksy (1974–), UK, *Parachuting Rats* (Melbourne, Australia), 2001. Black spray-paint stencilled graffiti. Photo: Astred Hicks, Design Cherry.

Banksy, *Street Cleaner*, date unknown. Spray-paint stencilled graffiti. Image: Corbis.

ARTIST FRAMES: CULTURAL/STRUCTURAL

Banksy's artworks often include creatures and make witty comments about political, cultural, and ethical issues. His distinctive style of street art, which combines free-hand graffiti and stencilling, has appeared in numerous cities all around the world.

WWW www.banksy.co.uk
www.banksyunmasked.co.uk

Look at the works of Banksy on page 104.

- Use your own photographs of creatures or images that you have collected to create an artwork using stencils.
- Create a stencil of a creature cut from thick paper or cardboard.
- Use acrylic paints mixed with mediums such as impasto to create rich textures, and paint through your stencil onto thick paper or **MDF board**. (Do not paint on walls unless you have permission). Repeat the design to create a dynamic composition.
- You may like to also include shapes cut from patterned and textured papers to add another dimension to your artwork.

ONLINE RESOURCES
Banksy

MDF board: multi-density fibreboard, a manufactured wood product made by breaking down wood into fibres, combining it with glues and compressing it to form dense, strong wooden panels

Chapter 10

Creatures of the air

Humans have always had a fascination with creatures of the air. We are envious of their freedom, their ability to spread their wings and fly high above the earth. Creatures of the air are beautiful, majestic and powerful and artists have often depicted them in their artworks.

Artmaking sequence	Form	Artists
Let's make an artwork 1 *Henpecked chooks*	Painting	• *Lucy Culliton* • William Robinson, Joanna Braithwaite, Lauren Potts
Let's make an artwork 2 *Constructed creatures of flight*	Sculpture	• *Abby Glassenberg* • Tamar Mogendorff, Brett Whiteley, Leo Sewell

Let's make an artwork 1
Henpecked chooks

Coming up with ideas   ARTMAKING PRACTICE

Paint a captivating creature of the air.

Discussion, research and planning in your visual arts diary

CONCEPTUAL FRAMEWORK	PRACTICE	FRAMES
Artist Artwork World Audience	Ideas and actions	Structural—exploring materials and methods in artmaking Cultural—exploring ideas, beliefs and values through artworks

Student worksheet

William Robinson (1936–), Australia, *Chookyard*, 1982. Oil on canvas, 110.6 × 135.8 cm. Image: Phillip Bacon Gallery.

Joanna Braithwaite (1962–), New Zealand/Australia, *Egg n Spoon*, 2007. Oil on canvas, 112 × 137 cm. Image: Darren Knight Gallery.

Lauren Potts (1985–), contemporary artist, Australia, *Boo Who*. Acrylic on canvas, 70.2 × 95.5 cm. Image: Harrison Galleries.

Looking at the artworks on page 107, as well as that of **Lucy Culliton** further ahead in the chapter, examine the ways in which these artists have been inspired by creatures of flight.

In your visual arts diary:

- describe which Frame each artist is working in, using the Frames table in the Introduction to help you
- research and make notes on the different methods and materials used by each artist
- explain how each artist has captured the interest of their audience
- research and make notes on the symbolism associated with birds and creatures of flight
- collect some images from different cultures in which creatures of flight have been depicted.

Plan your own painting based on your knowledge of these artworks and the works of other artists who have been inspired by creatures of flight.

Taking action   ARTMAKING PRACTICE
Option 1   Painting

- Look at the painting created by Lucy Culliton on page 109.
- Use your own photographs or images you have collected of creatures of flight as visual reference to paint a large close-up image of a bird.
- Use the Structural Frame to plan and compose your close-up image and refer to the composition of Lucy Culliton's *Game Bird* as a guide.
- Use acrylic paint and impasto to build up layers of interesting texture.
- Create visual interest by including collage elements such as string, PVA glue, tissue paper and sand with your paint.

Option 2   Painting

- Look back at the artwork by William Robinson on page 107.
- Collect images of chooks in a chookyard. Use your own images or images from books or the internet as inspiration for your artmaking ideas.
- Use the Structural Frame to design a composition based on a detailed area of a chookyard that has strong tonal contrasts, patterns, textures, a variety of colours and contains creatures of flight.
- Use a variety of drawing materials such as pencils, chalks and charcoals, as well as washes of acrylic paint, to build up layers of interesting detail in your artwork.

In-depth study
Lucy Culliton

CRITICAL AND HISTORICAL INTERPRETATIONS

CONCEPTUAL FRAMEWORK: WORLD

Lucy Culliton began her career as a graphic designer before completing her studies at the National Art School in Sydney. Her world is that of contemporary Australian visual arts.

ARTIST FRAMES: CULTURAL/STRUCTURAL

Culliton is interested in the visual qualities of her subjects. She is renowned for her paintings of everyday things such as roosters, shells, crockery, cakes, cups and saucers, knitted toys, cacti, animals and prize displays at local country shows. She is an accomplished painter who aims to paint ordinary things, making them appear extraordinary.

ARTWORK FRAMES: STRUCTURAL

In the artwork shown here, Culliton has painted a close-up image of a game bird, or rooster. She approaches her subject matter in an unconventional way by cropping the image of the bird closely and painting it so that it dominates the composition.

PRACTICE: IDEAS

Culliton's ideas come from the world around her. She draws inspiration from the things that she encounters while living in country New South Wales. She likes to paint familiar but often-overlooked objects and works with mundane subject matter in order to capture and amplify its beauty. She doesn't make the objects any more beautiful than they are; she just paints her subjects in a way that makes audiences more aware of their true beauty.

Lucy Culliton, *Australian Game Bird*, 2003. Oil on board, 63 × 48 cm. Image: Ray Hughes Gallery. 1966–, Australia

mundane: ordinary

PRACTICE: ACTIONS

Culliton paints with oil paints on board. She uses thick creamy textured impasto paint and bright rich pastel colours in her paintings. These techniques and material choices give her artworks an expressive quality.

AUDIENCE

Culliton presents familiar objects in new ways; therefore, her artworks have universal appeal. She has won a number of prestigious art prizes and her artworks are increasingly being shown in art galleries and on gallery websites in Australia and around the world.

WWW www.rayhughesgallery.com
http://jrmedia.blogspot.com/2007/03/lucy-culliton.html

Let's make an artwork 2
Constructed creatures of flight

Coming up with ideas   ARTMAKING PRACTICE

Make a sculpture of a creature of flight using scraps of fabric and other found materials.

Discussion, research and planning in your visual arts diary

Student worksheet

CONCEPTUAL FRAMEWORK	PRACTICE	FRAMES
Artist	Ideas and actions	Structural—exploring materials and methods in artmaking
Artwork		
World		Cultural—exploring ideas, beliefs and values through artworks
Audience		

Tamar Mogendorff, contemporary artist, Israel/USA, *Peacocks*, 2008. Soft sculptures. Images: Ngoc Minh Ngo.

Brett Whiteley (1939–1992), Australia, *Blue Wren*. Mixed-media sculpture. Collection: Brett Whiteley Studio. © Wendy Whiteley.

Leo Sewell, contemporary artist, USA, *Duck*. Found plastic object sculpture 40.6 × 20.3 × 40.6 cm. © Leo Sewell.

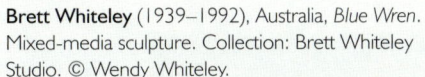 www.leosewell.net
www.tmogy.com

Look at the works of the artists above and on page 110, as well as that of **Abby Glassenberg** further ahead in the chapter.

In your visual arts diary:

- list the type of creature of flight that each artist creates
- explain each artist's ideas and artmaking actions
- describe the qualities of at least two of the Frames used in creating each of the artworks, using the Frames table in the Introduction to help you.

Use books and the internet to research one type of creature of flight in detail. Begin planning and sketching ideas for a soft sculpture of your own, listing in your visual arts diary the Structural Frame qualities and materials and methods that you intend to use in your artmaking.

Taking action   ARTMAKING PRACTICE

Option 1   Sculpture

- Choose an image of the creature of flight that you have researched and sketch your creature, breaking it down into simple shapes and forms. Look at the artwork of Abby Glassenberg on page 113 for inspiration.
- Use your drawings to create a pattern for a three-dimensional sculpture. Cut out your paper pattern.
- Use your pattern to cut shapes out of fabric or sheets of bubble wrap.
- Sew, staple or glue the shapes of your creature together, leaving a small gap in a seam so that you can fill the completed figure with stuffing.
- If you are using bubble wrap, you may like to stuff your creature with paper; otherwise, use the cotton or polyester stuffing that is used to fill soft toys.
- Add extra decorative detail to your creature by painting, gluing or sewing on beads, feathers or other decorative details and objects.

- Use wire or other found materials to create your creature's eyes and feet and attach them by gluing them with a hot glue gun and sewing them in place so that they are secure.

Option 2 Sculpture

- Choose an image of the creature of flight that you have researched and sketch your creature, breaking it down into simple shapes and forms. Look back at the artwork of Leo Sewell on page 111 for inspiration.
- Create the basic shape of your creature using a chicken wire frame or a frame made out of plastic bottles and milk cartons.
- Use a hot glue gun or pieces of wire to attach small found plastic objects and trinkets to your wire frame, covering your creature of the air with found objects.

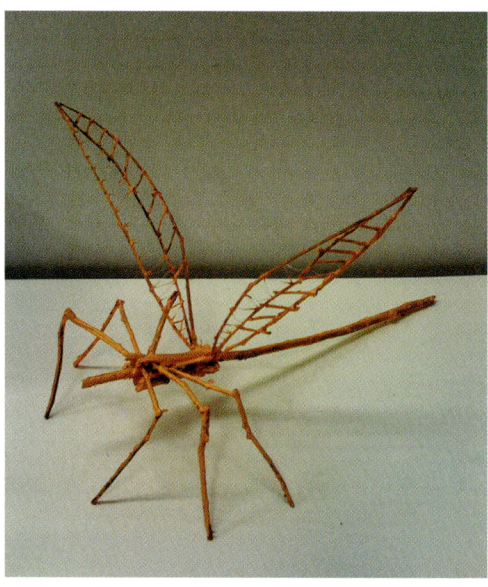

In-depth study
Abby Glassenberg

CRITICAL AND HISTORICAL INTERPRETATIONS

CONCEPTUAL FRAMEWORK: WORLD

Abby Glassenberg's world is that of contemporary American art, craft and design. She was once a primary school teacher but now spends the majority of her time caring for her two young daughters. For two hours a day while her children sleep, Glassenberg makes art.

ARTIST FRAMES: STRUCTURAL/CULTURAL

From an early age Glassenberg loved to make things and always kept a craft box in her bedroom filled with supplies. At 13 years of age she purchased her first sewing machine, which she still uses to make her soft sculptures today. Glassenberg is a contemporary sculptor and mixed-media artist. She is interested in creating complex sculptural artworks that can be admired by both adults and children.

ARTWORK FRAMES: STRUCTURAL

Glassenberg's artwork *Owl* is a soft sculpture made from fabrics, wool stuffing, wire and found materials. It is life-like in proportion and detail. Glassenberg works with a palate of neutral coloured fabrics, which she arranges carefully in order to make the most of the variety of patterns in each piece of fabric. The tones and textures of the folded fabric create visual interest and make the owl appear more life-like. The soft fabric body of the sculpture is firmly packed with stuffing so that it holds its shape. Details such as the owl's bound wire feet, and layered beige and gold fabric feathers give the owl a personality of its own.

PRACTICE: IDEAS

Glassenberg explores ideas about the relationships between art and craft, and between art, nature and her everyday world. She is interested in making artworks out of scrap materials that would otherwise be thrown away. Her inspiration comes directly from nature, as she observes birds and creatures at play. Once she has a bird or creature in mind, to further refine her concept, Glassenberg researches the species online and in books, examining the shapes, physical dimensions and features of the creature that she intends to make. She also examines the material practice of other toymakers, sculptors and artists to see how they have constructed their artworks.

Abby Glassenberg, *Owl*, 2009. Fabric and found materials. © Abby Glassenberg.
Photo: Elena Clayman.
1975–, USA

PRACTICE: ACTIONS

From her initial research, Glassenberg creates sketches of a bird, breaking it down into simple shapes. She then creates a paper pattern as the starting point for the construction of her sculpture. Glassenberg traces her pattern onto carefully selected pieces of fabric, and cuts out the fabric shapes ready for sewing. For the main body of her creatures she likes to work with Kona Cotton, a strong fabric that allows her to stuff her creatures very firmly with wool stuffing so that they become rigid. Other scraps of fabric that she uses include remnants of flour sacks, clothing tags and vintage fabrics. She sews her creatures on a sewing machine and finishes the finer details by hand. Other artmaking tools that she uses include scissors, sewing needles, thread and surgical forceps, which enable her to turn very small pieces of fabric inside out, and stuff, poke and clamp her creatures as they take shape. She creates the feet and other features of the birds using wire, scraps and found objects that she collects from around her house and from the local rubbish dump.

AUDIENCE

Glassenberg reaches her audience in a variety of ways but mainly through her online blog and website. She also exhibits her artworks in galleries. Articles and interviews with Glassenberg and critical writings about her work can be found online, often in blogs written by others who are interested in soft sculpture and craft. She has an online store with Etsy, which enables her to sell her artworks to the general public. She is currently writing a book about her artmaking practice, which will include patterns for her bird sculptures. Glassenberg's audiences are not always art-educated; they are made up of a range of people who simply share her passion for making things.

 Student worksheet

WWW www.abbyglassenberg.com
www.whileshenaps.typepad.com

Part three

THE WORLD OF OBJECTS

Chapter 11

Ordinary objects/ extraordinary objects

The things we surround ourselves with are often the ordinary objects of everyday life. But they can have an importance beyond their everyday use. We use objects to tell other people who we are and what we value in life. Artists can take ordinary objects and portray them in such a way that they become extraordinary.

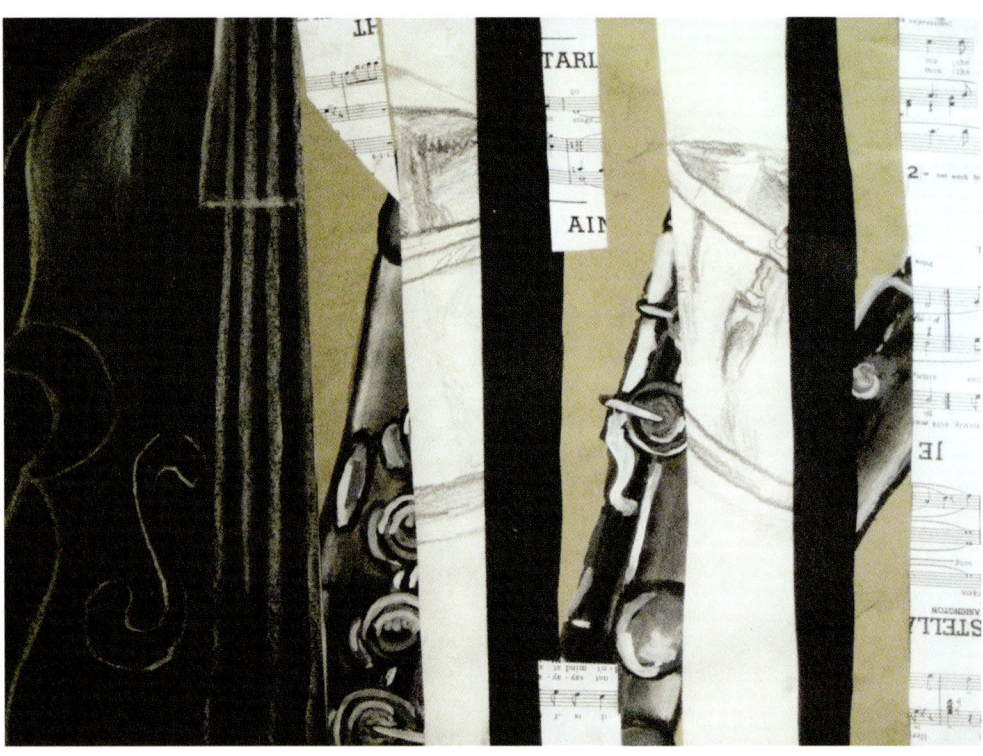

Artmaking sequence	Form	Artists
Let's make an artwork 1 *Transforming objects*	Photography	• *Kevin Best* • Jo Gregory, Michal Fanta, Christo
Let's make an artwork 2 *Eating objects*	Painting	• *Vika Prokopaviciute* • Nanda Palmieri, Pablo Picasso, Cornelis de Heem
Let's make an artwork 3 *Playing with objects*	Drawing	• *Juan Gris* • Tom Wesselmann, Brett Whiteley, Kevin Lincoln

Let's make an artwork   1
Transforming objects

Coming up with ideas   ARTMAKING PRACTICE

Take a series of still-life photographs of everyday objects.

Discussion, research and planning in your visual arts diary

CONCEPTUAL FRAMEWORK	PRACTICE	FRAMES
Artist Artwork World Audience	Ideas and actions	Structural—using symbolism to give meaning, visual qualities, planned composition Postmodern—borrowing ideas and actions from other artists

Student worksheet

Jo Gregory (1969–), Australia, *Still Life*, 2006. Black and white digital photograph, 300 dpi. © Jo Gregory.

Michal Fanta (1987–), Czech Republic, *Gummy Bears*, 2009. Digital photograph, 3888 × 2592 pixels. © Michal Fanta.

Look at the works of the two photographers above, as well as the work by **Kevin Best** further ahead in the chapter.

ONLINE RESOURCES

Jo Gregory
Michal Fanta

In your visual arts diary:

- note the types of objects each artist photographs
- discuss each artist's ideas in relation to the choice of these objects
- list two important actions each artist takes
- describe which Frame you think each artist is working in (use the Frames table in the Introduction to help you) and describe the qualities of that Frame you can see in the photographs
- choose one of the photographs that uses objects as symbols, and list the symbols, explaining what you think they tell us about the meaning of the photograph
- explain one way each artist sets out to interest the audience.

Borrowing ideas from these photographs, discuss with your friends the types of objects you can use in still-life photographs that are relevant to your life and culture. Explore some ideas for your symbolic still-life photographs, and sketch these in your visual arts diary.

TEACHER NOTE

Set up a digital photo shoot over several lessons so that the class can take a series of portrait shots of each other, as well as self portraits.

ONLINE RESOURCES

How to set up a photo shoot

Taking action   ARTMAKING PRACTICE

Option 1   Photography

- Share school cameras, or use your own camera or mobile phone camera.
- Working in small groups, and using the Structural Frame, take a series of photographs of objects that are symbolic of your world. Look at the photographs by Jo Gregory and Michal Fanta on page 117 and Kevin Best on page 120 for inspiration.
- Use a variety of different lighting conditions, such as available light from a window, light from a reading lamp or coloured spotlight, or even candlelight.
- Experiment with different viewpoints; for example, from above, from the side, from the front, extreme close-up, a dark background and so on.
- Download the images onto a school or home computer. Use photographic editing software to enhance, adjust or add effects to capture what you want to communicate to an audience.

Option 2   Photography

TEACHER NOTE

Organise for students to bring in party food and drink during an extended or double period.

- Arrange a selection of party food and drink out on a table to create small still-life compositions. Look at the photographs of Michal Fanta on page 117 and Kevin Best on page 120 for inspiration.
- Take a series of photographs of the food (you can eat it when you've finished!).
- Use a variety of different lighting conditions, such as available light from a window, or light from a reading lamp or coloured spotlight.
- Experiment with different viewpoints; for example, from above, from the side, from the front or an extreme close-up.
- Download the images onto a school or home computer. Use photographic editing software to enhance, adjust or add effects.

Extension

Look at the photograph by Jo Gregory on page 117, and the Christo installation here.

- Using the Postmodern Frame, borrow the idea of wrapping a series of objects to be photographed in white paper so they are still clearly recognisable.
- Like Jo Gregory, choose a humorous theme, such as breakfast with toast and jam!
- Take photographs using the same lighting conditions—the objects placed in a darkened place and lit from slightly above and to one side.
- Emphasise the tonal contrasts between the brightly lit objects and the dark background. Try to create strong shadows.
- Download the images onto a school or home computer. Use photographic editing software to enhance, adjust or add effects.

Christo (1935–), Bulgaria, *Wrapped Bottles and Cans*, 1958–1960. Cans, bottles, lacquered canvas and twine, 28 × 74 × 28 cm. Copyright Christo 1958–1960. Photo: Eeva Inkeri.

In-depth study
Kevin Best

CRITICAL AND HISTORICAL INTERPRETATIONS

CONCEPTUAL FRAMEWORK: WORLD

Although Kevin Best lives in 21st-century Australia, his world is really in an **atelier** in 17th-century Holland.

atelier: artist's studio

ARTIST FRAMES: POSTMODERN/STRUCTURAL

Best is a Postmodern photographer who borrows the style and methods of Dutch 17th-century still-life **vanitas** painters such as Pieter Claesz, Willem Kalf and David Bailly. However, he reproduces what they did using modern photographic technologies.

ARTWORK FRAMES: POSTMODERN/STRUCTURAL

In *Disposable Still Life with Fruit and Ham* on page 120, transparent plastic containers of shaved ham, diced fruit and muffins are arranged on white plastic picnic plates strewn with plastic cutlery, a pepper grinder and some olives. An empty plastic drinking flute lies on its side and a plastic cup is filled with water from a plastic bottle. To draw our eyes into this contemporary version of a feast, a white table napkin is draped over the edge of the table.

vanitas: a still-life painting with objects symbolising the fleeting nature of life and its vain, pointless ambitions ('vanitas' is Latin for vanity), such as skulls, unlit candles, dying flowers and hourglasses

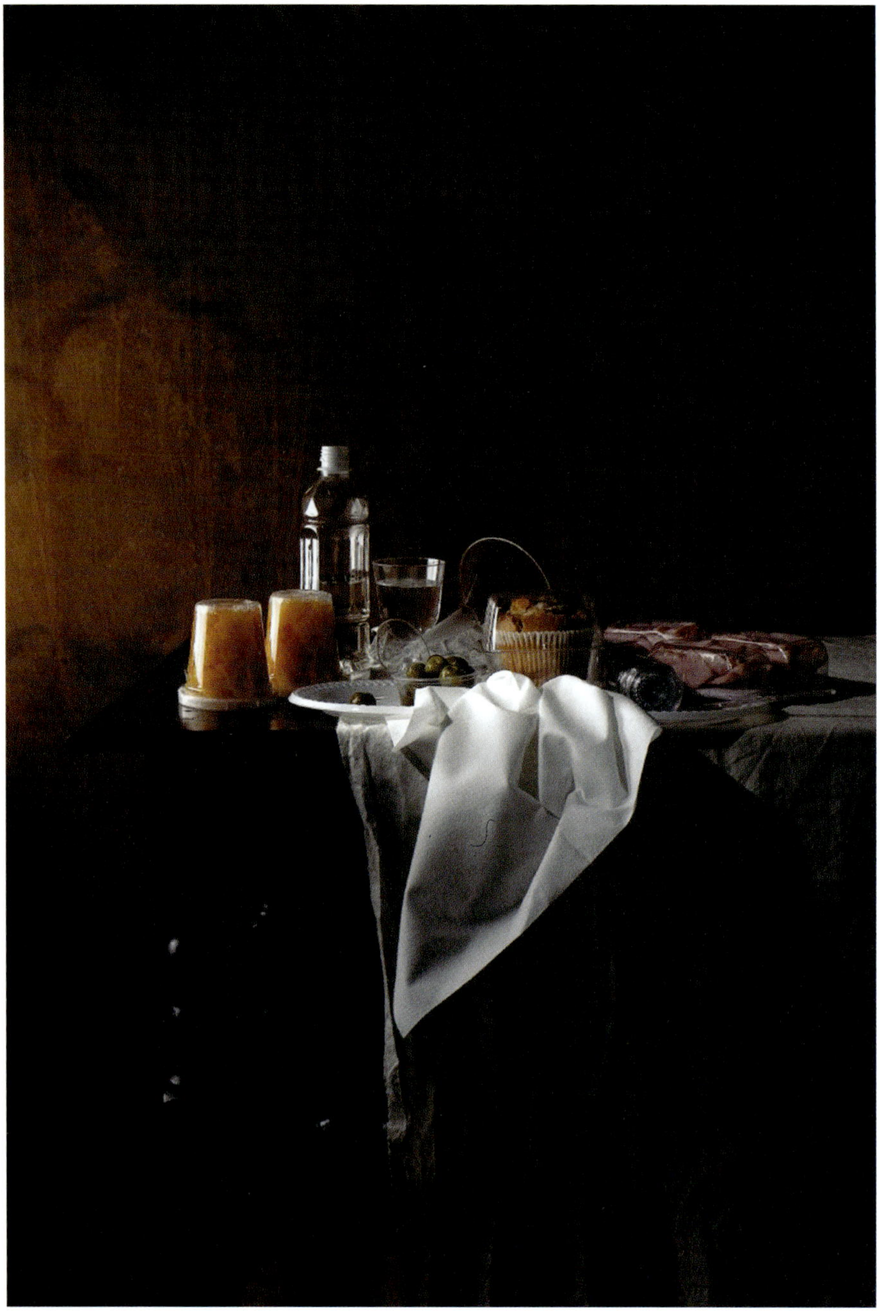

Kevin Best, *Disposable Still Life with Fruit and Ham*, 2006. Digital photograph, 300 dpi.
Courtesy of Kevin Best.
1960–, Australia

PRACTICE: IDEAS

Best has explored the idea that he can take a photograph of modern objects but use the technology so cleverly that it looks like a 17th-century Dutch painting. He also plays with the idea that the objects of luxury in the original artworks had symbolic meaning. This was usually related to the wealth and status of the people the Dutch artists painted for, and the shortness of the life they had in which to enjoy the luxuries. With this in mind, Best seems to ask what mass-produced food in mass-produced packaging could symbolise for today's audience.

PRACTICE: ACTIONS

Best has chosen a setting and objects that have the same neutral colours and range of tones that an artist in the 17th century would have used. He arranges some ordinary, everyday contemporary objects as if they are the same type of luxury objects used in still-life paintings in the 17th century. He uses the same qualities of light from the side to create reflections and shadows. The light makes the forms look so solid and real that we could almost lift the plastic bottle and drink the water.

AUDIENCE

Kevin Best sets out to visually engage an audience with his skills but he then asks them to think about the meaning of his photographs.

www www.flickr.com/photos/
kevsyd/3708707339

Let's make an artwork 2
Eating objects

Coming up with ideas ARTMAKING PRACTICE

Paint food and everyday objects from the kitchen that are interesting to you and have some symbolic meaning.

Discussion, research and planning in your visual arts diary

CONCEPTUAL FRAMEWORK	PRACTICE	FRAMES
Artist Artwork World Audience	Ideas and actions	Structural—using symbolism to give meaning, visual qualities, planned composition Subjective—expressive and imaginative qualities Cultural—ideas and beliefs of society Postmodern—borrowing ideas and actions from other artists

Student worksheet

ONLINE RESOURCES

Nanda Palmieri

Nanda Palmieri, contemporary artist, USA, *Cupcakes*, 2006. Oil on canvas, 122 × 122 cm. © Nanda Palmieri.

Pablo Picasso (1881–1973), Spain/France, *Guitar and Violin*, c. 1912. Oil paint on canvas, 65.5 × 54.3 cm. Image: DACS/Viscopy/Bridgeman Art.

Cornelis de Heem (1631–1695), Netherlands, *Still Life with Oysters, Lemons and Grapes*, c. 1660. Oil paint on oak panel, 35.5 × 45.0 cm. © Residenz Gallery, Salzburg, Austria.

Look at the works of the three artists on page 121 as well as the paintings of **Vika Prokopaviciute** further ahead in the chapter.

In your visual arts diary:

- note the types of objects each artist paints
- discuss each artist's ideas in relation to the choice of these objects
- list two important actions each artist takes to create each artwork
- describe which Frame you think each artist is working in (use the Frames table in the Introduction to help you) and describe the qualities of this Frame that you can see in the paintings
- choose one artwork that uses objects as symbols, and list these symbols, explaining what you think they tell us about the meaning of the painting
- choose the artist whose work most appeals to you and explore some aspects of their world that have affected their artmaking (use the Conceptual Framework table in the Introduction to help you)
- describe one way each artist sets out to catch and hold the interest of the audience.
- discuss the types of objects you can use in still-life paintings that are relevant to your life and culture
- list some ideas for symbolic still-life paintings (for example 'The good things in life' or 'Objects from the kitchen')
- sketch some ideas for compositions, borrowed from these artworks.

Taking action   ARTMAKING PRACTICE
Option 1   Painting

- Arrange a selection of party food and drink out on a table to create small still-life compositions. Look at the work of Nanda Palmieri on page 121 and Vika Prokopaviciute on page 123 for inspiration.
- Take photographs of the table—before and after you eat the food!

- Discuss with your teacher how to use suitable media (such as large brushes and acrylic paint mixed with impasto medium) for spontaneous, expressive painting.
- Use the Subjective Frame to paint before and after images of the party-food setting, using the photographs as visual reference. Keep looking at the food in the photographs and paint quickly. Experiment with expressive brushstrokes and thick paint. Use some simple shapes, bright colours and distortion to express the liveliness of a party.

Option 2 Painting

- Look at the Cubist still life by Picasso on page 121 and borrow, using the Postmodern Frame, some aspects of the Cubist style to produce still-life paintings of objects from the kitchen.
- Use the Structural Frame to produce a planned still life of objects from the kitchen. Use a variety of painting techniques and materials and focus on formal elements (such as outline, repeated patterns and subdued colour) and other visual qualities (such as hard edges, fragmented and geometric shapes and flatness rather than perspective).

In-depth study
Vika Prokopaviciute
CRITICAL AND HISTORICAL INTERPRETATIONS

ONLINE RESOURCES
Vika Prokopaviciute

Vika Prokopaviciute, *McDonald's Before*, 2009, *McDonald's After*, 2009. Both acrylic on canvas, 60 × 80 cm each. © Vika Prokopaviciute.
1983–, Russia

CONCEPTUAL FRAMEWORK: WORLD

Vika Prokopaviciute is a young Russian artist whose world is that of contemporary painting. Her work is influenced by artists such as Van Gogh, Simon Birch and Jenny Saville. These artists share an expressive approach to the way they use paint as well as the use of cool shadows, warm highlights and pure colours.

ARTIST FRAMES: SUBJECTIVE

Prokopaviciute is an artist who wants to paint her subjects quickly and spontaneously so that her audience can experience the moment with her. The artist says:

> *I love to make a work in one breath; it seems more fresh and eye-catching. I use bright colours, active brushstrokes, the paint flows, and of course, I was so hungry!*
>
> Vika Prokopaviciute

ARTWORK FRAMES: SUBJECTIVE

diptych: a pair of paintings that together make one artwork

The artworks on page 123 are a diptych. In the first painting a typical takeaway meal from McDonald's is arranged in a casual composition and we see it as if we're just about to sit down and eat. The second painting shows the after-effects of eating a takeaway meal with the remains of the food and drink strewn across the painting.

PRACTICE: IDEAS

The idea for this artwork was to capture a simple moment of everyday living, eating a takeaway, and at the same time conduct a fun experiment with food and art.

PRACTICE: ACTIONS

The artist paints using direct observation of the McDonald's takeaway meal spread out on a sheet. Using thin acrylic paint the image is drawn quickly and then the shadows, patterns and colours are added with thicker paint. Because the paint is used so quickly, drips and smudges become part of the work and add to the feeling of the actual experience. The artist then ate the food and documented the resulting mess using the same approach.

AUDIENCE

As a young contemporary artist who does not yet have a history of showing her work to an audience in an art gallery, Vika Prokopaviciute uses the contemporary technology of her own website to make her artwork accessible to an international audience. She invites her audience to experience her world and feel what she is feeling through her expressive and spontaneous artmaking practice.

 Student worksheet

WWW http://artportions.blogspot.com
www.prokopaviciute.com

Let's make an artwork 3
Playing with objects

Coming up with ideas   ARTMAKING PRACTICE

Make a series of still-life drawings using the objects that interest you.

Discussion, research and planning in your visual arts diary

CONCEPTUAL FRAMEWORK	PRACTICE	FRAMES
Artist	Ideas and actions	Structural—using symbolism to give meaning, visual qualities, planned composition
Artwork		
World		Subjective—expressive and imaginative qualities
Audience		

Student worksheet

Tom Wesselmann (1931–2004), USA, *Drawing for Still Life #12*, 1962. Charcoal on paper, 120 × 120 cm. Art Institute of Chicago. Photo licensed by Viscopy.

Elisabeth Cummings (1934–), Australia, *Still Life*, 2009. Charcoal on paper. © Elisabeth Cummings. Image: King Street Gallery.

Kevin Lincoln (1941–), Australia, *Spotted Guitar*, 1991. Charcoal drawing on paper, 70 × 49 cm. Photo by Emma Phillips.

Look at the drawings of the three artists above, as well the artwork of **Juan Gris** further ahead in the chapter.

In your visual arts diary:

- note the types of objects each artist draws
- briefly list each artist's ideas in relation to the choice of these objects
- list two important actions by each artist, using the Artmaking Practice table in the Introduction to help you

- list the Structural Frame or Subjective Frame visual qualities in the drawings, using the Frames table in the Introduction to help you
- choose one of the artworks and list the symbols used, explaining what you think they tell us about the meaning of the drawing
- indicate one way each artist sets out to interest the audience, using the Conceptual Framework table in the Introduction to help you.

Taking action   ARTMAKING PRACTICE

Option 1   Drawing

- Look back at Tom Wesselmann's drawing on page 125.
- Set up a still life of everyday objects and light them from one side.
- Discuss with your teacher suitable media for monochrome drawings using the Structural Frame (such as brush with pen and ink, conté crayons, white chalk and charcoal on either black or white paper) and how to use these.
- Explore visual qualities (such as forms, textures, patterns and tones of the objects) through direct observation of the objects, and structured drawing.

Option 2   Drawing

- Look back at Brett Whiteley's drawing on page 125.
- Set up a still life of everyday objects.
- Discuss with your teacher suitable media for monochrome drawings using the Subjective Frame (such as brush with pen and ink, conté and pastel crayons, white chalk and charcoal on either black or white paper) and how to use these.
- Draw spontaneously to explore expressive visual qualities, such as broken lines, colours used to show emotion, imaginative use of textures, patterns created by torn strips of white, black and brown paper and distortion of forms.

Extension

- Look at the drawings of Kevin Lincoln and Juan Gris on pages 125 and 128 respectively.
- Set up a still life of musical instruments.
- Discuss with your teacher suitable media for monochrome drawings using the Structural Frame (such as brush with pen and ink, conté crayons, white chalk and charcoal on either black or white paper) and how to use these.
- As you draw your still life, explore similar visual qualities to those used by the Cubists: fragmented or flattened shapes, textures and patterns, Cubist perspective, and use of collage and text.

 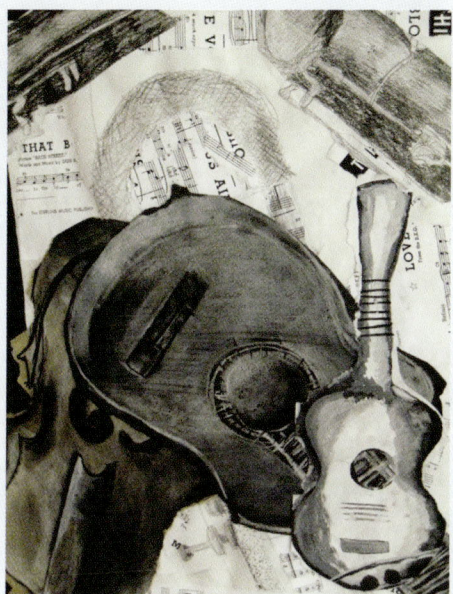

In-depth study
Juan Gris

CRITICAL AND HISTORICAL INTERPRETATIONS

CONCEPTUAL FRAMEWORK: WORLD

Juan Gris lived his life in Paris and was part of the group of artists who were inventing new ways to make art at the beginning of the 20th century: the Cubists. This was a time of rapid social and industrial change; a world of machines, of the growth of cities and of speed. The Cubists set out to make art suitable for this new, modern world.

ARTIST FRAMES: STRUCTURAL

Gris painted with Picasso and Braque, who invented the Cubist style. He then developed his own personal Cubist style, called synthetic Cubism. The visual qualities he used included the use of collage, repetition and compositions based on a grid.

Juan Gris, *Still Life with Guitar*, 1912–1913. Drawing, pencil and gouache on paper.
1887–1927, Spain

ARTWORK FRAMES: CULTURAL/ STRUCTURAL

Juan Gris's subjects were almost all taken from his immediate surroundings. As bars and cafés were popular meeting places for the Cubist artists in Paris, the people and objects in these places often featured in their artworks. These included glasses, bottles, pipes, tables and chairs, newspapers and musical instruments used to entertain in the bars. This drawing of a guitar is a fragment of his everyday world that has been simplified into a series of geometric lines and split, flattened shapes placed in an unreal space with some decorative splatter patterns and wood textures.

PRACTICE: IDEAS

The artist used this simple still-life drawing as a way of experimenting with the Cubist style. His idea is to ask what is true and what is false in this simplified and flattened Cubist representation of a real guitar when it is combined with unreal space.

PRACTICE: ACTIONS

Gris used structured methods of drawing the guitar based on direct observation. He draws a grid of lines as his composition and within the grid he places the flat, fragmented parts of the guitar. These pencil lines are strong and dark contrasting with the more delicate wood patterns and areas of spattered gouache. He strengthens other areas with flat black gouache. To add tonal contrasts, he silhouettes light against dark.

AUDIENCE

Gris has included enough visual information (the strings, frets, tuning pegs, the sound hole and the wooden body) to enable an audience to recognise the object he draws easily.

www www.juangris.org/
www.artchive.com/artchive/G/gris.html

Shells, fossils and bones

Shells, fossils and bones are the traces and structures of lives once lived. They are memories and imprints of what's left when life has been stripped away. Because of this, we can find them fascinating, fearful or funny.

Artmaking sequence	Form	Artists
Let's make an artwork 1 *Memories*	Sculpture/installation	• *Subodh Kerkar, Christopher Locke* • Robyn Gordon, Rosalie Gascoigne, Robert Smithson, Jitish Kallat
Let's make an artwork 2 *Dem bones*	Drawing	• *Locust Jones* • Leonardo da Vinci, Jordan Massengale, Kamila Szczesna

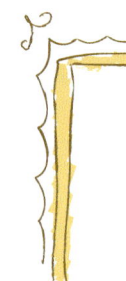

Let's make an artwork 1
Memories

Coming up with ideas   ARTMAKING PRACTICE

Make sculptures and installations based on shells, fossils and bones.

Discussion, research and planning in your visual arts diary

Student worksheet

CONCEPTUAL FRAMEWORK	PRACTICE	FRAMES
Artist Artwork World Audience	Ideas and actions	Structural—using symbolism to give meaning, visual qualities, planned composition Subjective—expressive and imaginative qualities Postmodern—using non-traditional materials and methods

Robyn Gordon (1943–), Australia, *Delicacy, Beauty, Extreme Vulnerability*, 2008. Metal blades, with assorted materials, 46 × 46 × 7 cm. © Robyn Gordon. Image licensed by Viscopy.

Rosalie Gascoigne (1917–1999), New Zealand/ Australia, *Untitled (25 scallop shells)*, 1984. Sculpture, scallop shells on wood, 55 × 56.5 × 7 cm. © Rosalie Gascoigne. Image licensed by Viscopy.

Robert Smithson (1938–1973), USA, *Spiral Jetty*, 1970. Earthwork installation (Great Salt Lake, Utah), black rock, salt crystals, earth, red water (algae). Image: Corbis.

Looking at the works of the three artists on page 130, as well as works by **Subodh Kerkar** and **Christopher Locke** further ahead in the chapter, explore the main idea in each artwork. Research the symbolism of shells, fossils and bones in different times and cultures using the library or the internet.

In your visual arts diary:

- record your research findings
- discuss how the idea of each artwork relates to shells, fossils or bones
- describe each artist's use of the Structural Frame (the use of shells, fossils or bones as symbols of other things), using the Frames table in the Introduction to help you
- list two important actions each artist takes in each artwork
- make notes on assemblage and installation as types of sculpture
- indicate one way each artist sets out to interest the audience
- choose the artist whose work appeals to you most and explore some aspects of their world that have affected their artmaking, using the Conceptual Framework table in the Introduction to help you
- plan your own sculptures and installations based on your knowledge of shells, fossils and bones and the work of these other artists
- collect images, sketches and lists of ideas for your own shell, fossil or bone artmaking.

Start to collect objects such as shells, bones, sticks and stones to give you more ideas or to use in a sculpture or installation of your own. Keep your collection in a shoebox. Search the internet for free images of shells, fossils and bones to inspire you or to use in your artmaking.

Taking action   ARTMAKING PRACTICE
Option 1   Sculpture/installation

- Plan a mini installation in a box based on the theme of shells, fossils and bones. Look at the artworks of Robyn Gordon and Rosalie Gascoigne on page 130 for inspiration. Plan the composition carefully in your visual arts diary using visual qualities and symbols that will give your artwork particular personal meaning.
- Find a box, preferably a wooden crate, of about 40 cm × 50 cm in size. Or, make a box with some scrap pieces of wood.
- Make a series of small, detailed pastel, pen and ink sketches of some of the images or objects you have collected.
- Use assemblage methods to construct the installation in the box.
- Photograph your completed work.
- Work with your classmates to design and assemble a larger group installation and photograph this.
- Exhibit both the artworks and the photographs.

assemblage: in sculpture, the joining of individual pieces or objects into an arrangement using any suitable equipment, such as PVA glue to join wood, or a soldering iron to join metal

TEACHER NOTE

Organise an excursion to a beach, lake or river so students can make an installation and document it photographically. Alternatively, there may be suitable areas within school grounds.

site-specific installation: a work of art designed for a specific place and relating in some way to that place

Option 2 Sculpture/installation

- Look at the installations of Robert Smithson on page 130 and Subodh Kerkar on pages 133 and 134.
- Brainstorm the types of simple, symbolic shapes that are suggestive of shells, fossils and bones—for example, the spiral relates to both shells and fossils.
- Choose your own shape and make a collection of everyday materials and found objects that you can use to make your shell or fossil shape in the natural environment.
- Plan a site-specific installation (either during an excursion organised by your teacher or in a suitable part of the school grounds, chosen by your teacher) based on shells and fossils as symbols. Use the Structural and Postmodern Frames. Respond to the particular site so that you communicate your idea in an interesting and thought-provoking way to an audience, and use some symbolic objects from the site itself, such as shells, sand, pebbles and driftwood.
- Construct your installation. Because you will later need to dismantle it, document your installation with photographs throughout the artmaking process.
- Act as an audience for each other's work and discuss the visual impact of each work.
- Present a series of at least six photographs of the completed installations in your visual arts diary, or exhibit the photographs.

Option 3 Sculpture

- Make your own modern fossil based on an object that reflects today's world, to be unearthed by an archaeologist in 10 000 years' time.
- Use materials and methods that are not traditional in artmaking.
- Refer to Christopher Locke's artwork on page 135 and borrow his idea of a modern fossil.
- Brainstorm and list contemporary objects that reflect our modern world.
- Collect a found object that reflects modern culture, such as a discarded mobile phone, a soft-drink bottle, an old watch or a broken skateboard.

- Sketch how your object will look after 10 000 years—very old, embedded in stone, becoming stone itself.
- Experiment with a variety of sculptural materials and techniques to suit the reproduction of your object as a modern fossil. For example, try dipping your found object into a PVA glue and water solution and then sprinkling with earth and sand to 'fossilise' the object; or make moulds of found objects using new products like poly clay.
- When all sculptures are completed, photograph them singly and together as if just unearthed.

WWW www.jaedworks.com/clayspot
www.polymerclayworld.com/polymerclayfossil.shtml
www.elvenwork.com/tips.html#five

> *poly clay:* a bendable sculpting clay made from plastic polymers that does not dry out and can be fired to hardness at temperatures low enough to use a normal kitchen oven

In-depth study
Subodh Kerkar
CRITICAL AND HISTORICAL INTERPRETATIONS

Subodh Kerkar, *Sea Anemone II*, 2007. Installation, sand, lights, shells. © Subodh Kerkar.
1959–, India

Subodh Kerkar, *The moon and the tides I, 2008*. Installation, sand, lights, shells. © Subodh Kerkar.
1959–, India

CONCEPTUAL FRAMEWORK: WORLD

Subodh Kerkar was once a member of the medical profession. His world is now that of experimental contemporary artmaking in India and internationally. He specialises in land art and site-specific installations. Growing up in Goa, India, by the sea, he has developed a deep and abiding love of light, the sea and the beach.

ARTIST FRAMES: STRUCTURAL/ SUBJECTIVE

Kerkar is an artist who wants to communicate his feelings and thoughts about the natural environment of the seaside. He does this, as an artist who works in the Subjective Frame, in a poetic, expressive and imaginative way. He also works in the Structural Frame using planned and ordered compositions as well as symbols of the environment and sea creatures to give meaning to his artworks.

ARTWORK FRAMES: STRUCTURAL/SUBJECTIVE

In *Sea Anemone II* on page 133, Kerkar works at night, using a hollow in the sand, ringed with white shells to suggest the edges of an anemone. He places lights in the hollow to give the work an eerie, orange glow. This is a poetic, imaginative approach, rather than a realistic one. However, the work is also planned and uses the symbols of light, natural shape and colour to suggest the mystical qualities of nature and life. In *The moon and the tides I*, above, a large circle composed of carefully placed shells sits as a shining moon-disk on the sand as a symbol of one of the important cycles of nature's rhythms: the rise and fall of the tides, influenced by the gravitational pull of the moon.

PRACTICE: IDEAS

Kerkar explores ideas about the magic and mystery of nature and natural cycles using his love of the beach, the sea and light as his way of expressing his ideas.

PRACTICE: ACTIONS

Kerkar uses a contemporary form of artmaking, the site-specific installation. His method is to use what is in the environment so that his materials are around him: in this case, sand, shells and the sea. He brings electric lights in from outside the natural environment as a way of emphasising the beauty and mystery of nature and to also symbolise humankind in nature.

AUDIENCE

Kerkar wants his audience to feel the same passions about nature and its rhythms as he does. But his installations are **ephemeral** and cannot be seen by a large audience. They are documented photographically and the photos can be seen by audiences in art galleries or on the artist's website.

ephemeral: existing for only a short period of time

WWW www.subodhkerkar.com

In-depth study
Christopher Locke
CRITICAL AND HISTORICAL INTERPRETATIONS

Christopher Locke, *Playstation Controller*, 2009, from the series *Modern Fossils*. Moulded concrete, with the words 'Ludustatarium temperosony' inscribed on the reverse, life-size. © Christopher Locke.
1978–, USA

CONCEPTUAL FRAMEWORK: WORLD

Christopher Locke's world is that of contemporary sculpture, and communication and entertainment technologies. He sees his world as one of over-consumption and waste, because the technological gadgets we produce are almost instantly outdated.

ARTIST FRAMES: POSTMODERN

Locke is a Postmodern artist who uses **parody**. He makes fake fossils by copying items of popular technology, like iPods, hard drives, mobile phones and older Nintendo products. He does this in a humorous way. Just like real fossils in a museum, Locke's 'fossils' have a scientific name in nonsense Latin.

parody: imitation of something else in a humorous way

ARTWORK FRAMES: POSTMODERN

In *Playstation Controller*, the artist uses non-traditional materials imitating the plastic and metal of a Playstation controller. The 21st-century device is shown as if embedded in excavated stone and, as a form of **irony**, the artist calls it a modern fossil.

irony: when a meaning is given that is opposite to the real meaning

PRACTICE: IDEAS

Locke is worried about the environmental effects of our culture's consumerism and wastefulness. He imagines what 21st-century artefacts archaeologists will unearth in

10 000 years' time. His idea is to make modern fossils based on technology that was recently cutting-edge, but has become outdated almost immediately.

PRACTICE: ACTIONS

Locke's fossils are made using a mould taken from the items of technology he wants to copy. He then uses mixed media such as concrete, plaster, clay, resins, sand, earth and foam. The works are made to look ancient, with the look and feel of real stone fossils.

AUDIENCE

Locke makes full use of contemporary technology to present his artworks to an audience. He exhibits and advertises his work for sale on his own website rather than using a traditional fine art gallery.

WWW http://heartlessmachine.com/section/79989_Modern_Fossils.html

Extension

Look at the artwork by Jitish Kallat.

WWW http://jitishkallat.in

Explore the artist's world. In your visual arts diary:

* describe the artist's ideas and how they relate to his world
* discuss the actions the artist takes, including methods and materials
* place this artist's work within a particular Frame
* discuss the effect this artwork could have on an audience.

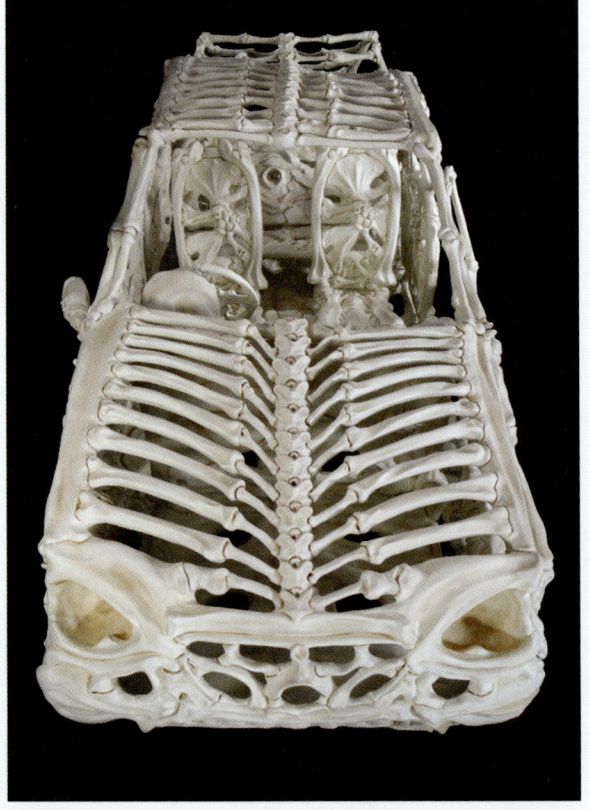

Jitish Kallat (1974–), India, *Collidonthus*, 2007. Resin, paint, brass, life-size. © Jitish Kallat. Photo: Iris Dreams, Mumbai/Jitish Kallat.

Let's make an artwork 2
Dem bones

Coming up with ideas   ARTMAKING PRACTICE

Draw detailed images of skeletons, skulls and other bones and use these in your artmaking.

Discussion, research and planning in your visual arts diary

CONCEPTUAL FRAMEWORK	PRACTICE	FRAMES
Artist Artwork World Audience	Ideas and actions	Structural—using symbolism to give meaning, visual qualities, planned composition Subjective—expressive and imaginative qualities Postmodern—using non-traditional materials and methods

Student worksheet

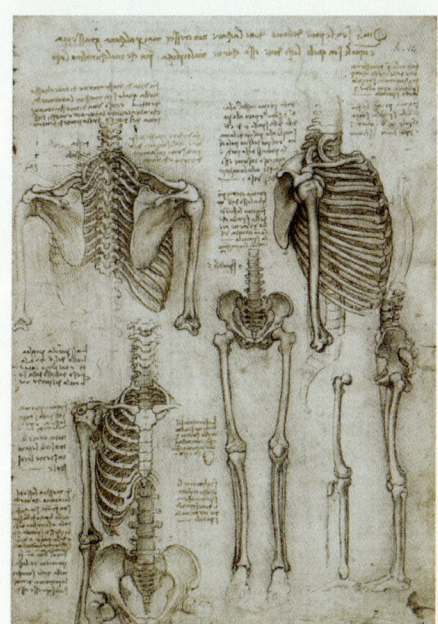

Leonardo da Vinci (1452–1519), Italy, *The Skeleton*, c. 1510. Pen and ink with wash over black chalk, 28.8 × 20.0 cm. The Royal Collection © 2009 Her Majesty Queen Elizabeth II.

Kamila Szczesna (1974–), Poland/USA, *Gesture Drawing of a Specimen no.15*, 2008. Ink on mylar, 30.0 × 22.5 cm. © Kamila Szczesna.

Look at the works of the two artists above, as well as that of **Locust Jones** further ahead in the chapter, and explore the different ideas each artist has about drawing the human skeleton.

In your visual arts diary:
- write some possible reasons for humans' fascination with skeletons and skulls
- make a list of expressive words that could describe images of skeletons and skulls, such as 'macabre', 'spooky' and 'funny'

- list the ways each artist communicates with the audience
- identify and explain each artist's use of a particular Frame, using the Frames table in the Introduction to help you
- explore the actions of each artist, referring to materials, methods and styles in their drawings
- collect images (such as photographs, free images from the internet or your own sketches) of skeletons and skulls, showing patterns of lines and contrasts between dark and light.

WWW www.leonardo.net/north.html
www.gfmer.ch/International_activities_En/Leonardo_anatomical_drawings.htm

Taking action   ARTMAKING PRACTICE
Option 1 Drawing

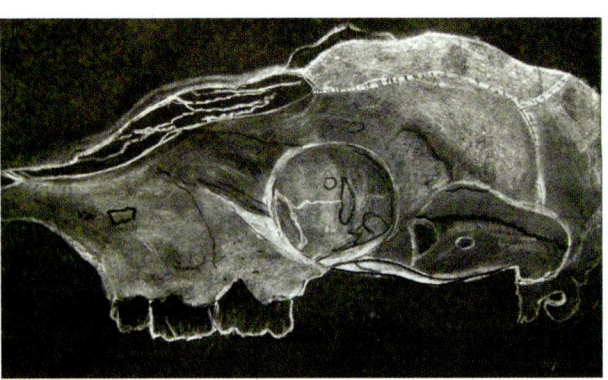

- Using the images of skeletons, skulls and bones you have collected for reference, draw some detailed bone images. Use a variety of drawing media on a variety of different types and colours of paper.
- Look at the artworks you have studied in class to guide you, but develop your own idea to communicate to your audience. Your idea might be something like 'We've all got skeletons!' or 'Bones are interesting/scary/funny'.
- Choose a particular Frame to guide your artmaking actions. For example: Structural—use visual qualities, composition and symbolism to give meaning; Cultural—depict skeleton, skull or animal bones as though you are a forensic scientist; Postmodern—borrow an idea or style from another artist; Subjective—emphasise gruesome and frightening aspects.
- Using your classmates as models, do a series of full-body drawings.
- Cut out your full-body drawings and assemble these with your skeleton and bone drawings to form a composite image symbolising what we are now and what we will become.

Option 2 Drawing

- Make a large detailed drawing of a human or animal skull by closely observing its shape, volume, textures and details. You may have access to a real animal skull to observe, but you can look at photographs if necessary.
- Use a variety of drawing media, such as pastels, charcoal and chalk, on white, brown or black paper.
- Make use of rendering light and dark, using hatching, cross-hatching and shading, to create volume and contrast.

Option 3 Drawing

- Using the images of skeletons, skulls and bones you have collected for reference, draw some detailed bone images. Use a variety of drawing media, such as pastels, charcoal and chalk, on black, brown and white paper. Look at the artworks you have studied in class to guide you.

- Make one larger, detailed drawing of a skull to be the centrepiece, and collage the other images around the skull to create a study of bones. Make use of rendering light and dark, using hatching, cross-hatching and shading, to create volume and contrast. Use the Structural Frame (planned visual qualities and composition) to guide your artmaking actions.

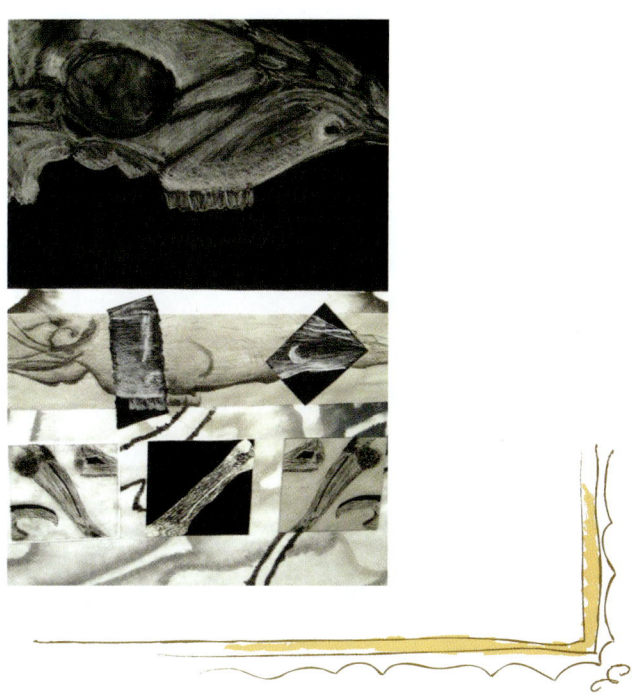

In-depth study
Locust Jones

CRITICAL AND HISTORICAL INTERPRETATIONS

CONCEPTUAL FRAMEWORK: WORLD

Locust Jones's world is that of contemporary art and politics. He is interested in commenting on the big picture in his artworks, and especially what's wrong with the world.

ARTIST FRAMES: SUBJECTIVE

Jones is an artist who comments on what he sees as the ills of the world in a personal way. He expresses his feelings of anguish and isolation with images and a drawing style that are dark, pessimistic and striking.

ARTWORK FRAMES: SUBJECTIVE

Self Portrait of Sorts, as shown on page 140, is a large-scale pencil drawing of a series of fragmented skulls and skeletons with a tall city building in the background. The work is full of emotional energy, with expressive lines and patches of scribbled dark tones scrawled over the surface of the paper.

PRACTICE: IDEAS

Although he calls it a self portrait, this almost X-ray style of drawing gives us no idea of what Locust Jones looks like. Instead his idea is to express his feelings of being pulled apart, stripped bare and made defenceless.

PRACTICE: ACTIONS

Jones is influenced by graffiti art. His drawing style is rough and raw because he draws rapidly and on a large scale just like street artists. Jones uses a deliberately child-like way

Locust Jones, *Self Portrait of Sorts*, 2005. Graphite on paper, 105 × 150 cm. Image courtesy of the artist and Karen Woodbury Gallery, Melbourne.
1963–, New Zealand/Australia

of drawing the skeletons. He distorts their shapes, simplifies and breaks them up and keeps changing their size. He uses large graphite pencils to give a dark background to many of the skulls and to highlight the patterns of ribs and other bones. He uses a black and white grid to show the windows of the building and this, as well as the lighter grey areas of pencil shading, adds to the lively patterns. He doesn't use the traditional style of shading to make his skeletons look three-dimensional; he is more interested in tonal contrast and pattern.

AUDIENCE

Locust Jones wants his audience to react as strongly to his artworks as he felt when making them. To do this he makes his works large, and full of movement and energy, and he often chooses subject matter that is controversial or intriguing.

www   www.locustjones.com

Stop the machines!

Chapter 13

The machines are taking over!

Every day machines play an increasingly important role in our lives. They make our lives easier by doing some of the difficult or unpleasant work for us, leaving us more time to do the things we want to do, like making art. For this reason, we love machines; but we worry about them as well. They can be big, dangerous, noisy and threatening. They control many aspects of our lives, sometimes leaving us with the feeling that they are taking over.

Even in art it's not so easy to avoid using machines, from cameras and computers, to tools and even robots! Looks like it won't be easy to stop the machines.

Artmaking sequence	Form	Artists
Let's make an artwork 1 *Build a robot*	Sculpture	• *Jeremy Mayer* • Raoul Hausmann, *Star Wars* puppet, Robert Klippel
Let's make an artwork 2 *Moving art*	Collage, sculpture	• *Theo Jansen* • Richard 'Doc' Nagy (Datamancer), Leonardo da Vinci, Jean Tinguely
Let's make an artwork 3 *Animate!*	Flip book animation, stop-motion animation	• *Anthony Lucas* • Frederick Rowland Emett, *Modern Times, I,Robot*

Let's make an artwork 1
Build a robot

Coming up with ideas   ARTMAKING PRACTICE

Build a robot sculpture using found materials, scraps and odds and ends. Make the robot poseable.

Discussion, research and planning in your visual arts diary

Student worksheet

CONCEPTUAL FRAMEWORK	PRACTICE	FRAMES
Artist	Ideas and actions	Structural—symbolism, visual qualities and composition
Artwork		Postmodern—use of non-traditional materials
World		Subjective—spontaneous, imaginative and expressive qualities
Audience		

ONLINE RESOURCES

Raoul Hausmann

Robert Klippel

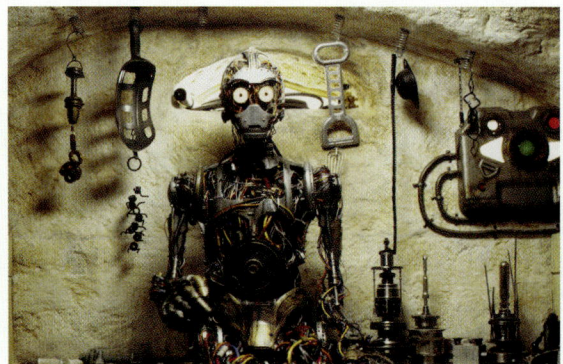

Raoul Hausmann (1886–1971), Austria, *Mechanical Head (The Spirit of Our Age)*, c. 1920. Assemblage with objects such as a ruler, measuring tape and tin cup. Photo: RMN.

C3PO robot from the film *Star Wars: Episode I*, directed by George Lucas, Lucasfilm, 1999. © Lucasfilm/The Kobal Collection/Picdesk.

Robert Klippel (1920–2001), Australia, *No. 247, Metal construction*, 1965–1968. Welded and brazed steel, found objects, wood, 269 × 145 × 126 cm. Queensland Art Gallery, Queensland.

TEACHER NOTE

Discuss the conventions of movie robots: Do they look human? Do they speak or use beeps? Are they good or bad? *WALL·E*, (PIXAR Disney Studios, 2008) is one of many excellent films about robots.

Using found objects and discarded rubbish in art is not new. Artists such as Raoul Hausmann and Robert Klippel have recognised the sculptural qualities of ordinary objects such as rulers, shop dummies and typewriter parts. As time goes on and old machines and their pieces change and become unrecognisable, the sculptures take on even more meaning and interest. One day audiences may look at the work we make in wonder at the technology they no longer use or recognise.

Look at the three artworks on page 142 and at the work of **Jeremy Mayer** further ahead in the chapter. Discuss with your friends how artists use different materials to make their works.

In your visual arts diary:

- describe how the choice of materials each artist has made affects the look and meaning of the artwork
- identify some pieces of technology you use commonly today, and suggest how they might change in the future
- list some current technology that might seem strange and wondrous to a future audience, giving reasons for your answers
- present some sketches and ideas about future technology we don't have yet.

Begin to plan an artwork of a robot that you will make, taking the following into consideration:

- What characteristics of real robots will you apply to your robot sculpture? Research the roles and functions of real robots.
- What will your robot look like? Will it look human? Or will it have the design style of the different functional machines that surround you in your daily life, such as white goods like fridges and stoves, or the distinctive style of a game console, MP3 player or mobile phone?
- How will you make your robot poseable? Look at some diagrams of the human skeleton, and observe the way the bones connect and the joints bend. If you decide to make your robot look human, it will need to move in all the right places.
- Will your robot have visible wires, lights and technology that you can see? Because robots are functional objects, the technology to make them work is often visible and part of the look and design.

WWW http://en.wikipedia.org/wiki/Raoul_Hausmann
www.lucasfilm.com
www.starwars.com
www.qag.qld.gov.au

Other websites about robots in art:
http://robotart.homestead.com/lawrencenorthey.html
www.bennettrobotworks.com
www.senster.com/
http://libarynth.org/art_robots
www2.ntj.jac.go.jp/unesco/bunraku/en/

Taking action   ARTMAKING PRACTICE
Option 1   Sculpture

- Collect objects and materials to use to build a robot sculpture. You could use discarded computer parts, old clocks and rubbish such as milk cartons, soft drink containers and scrap plastic.
- Build a frame or skeleton out of soft, bendable wire so that the robot can be posed. Your robot should reflect the kind of work it does: Does it collect garbage? Does it explore space or work as a servant?

- Use your found materials and paint to make a convincing, poseable robot.
- You may like to combine efforts and work as a group to make one large, full-size robot, with each person in the group responsible for constructing a particular part of the robot.

Option 2 Sculpture

- Make a robot puppet, similar to the puppets and marionettes that are often used in films. Sometimes these puppets are small models made for miniature sets, which are filmed to look much larger than they are; or they can be large puppets the same size as a human, and operated by a human on set, using the Japanese technique of Bunraku, where the human is dressed to blend in with the background and operates the robot from behind it.
- You can use the same materials as in the previous option; however, you may decide to use string and flexible wire to make your robot easy to manoeuvre.

In-depth study

Jeremy Mayer

CRITICAL AND HISTORICAL INTERPRETATIONS

CONCEPTUAL FRAMEWORK: WORLD

Jeremy Mayer's art responds to the fast-paced and constantly changing world of technology. Machines become obsolete almost as soon as they are produced and today's trendy gadget is tomorrow's rubbish. Mayer's sculptures use the parts of machines we no longer use or value—typewriters. Now replaced by computers, typewriters were once highly valued machines. Well-made and beautiful, they were largely discarded when they were replaced. Mayer's sculptures remind us of the beauty and quality of these lost machines. He gives them new life through his figure sculptures.

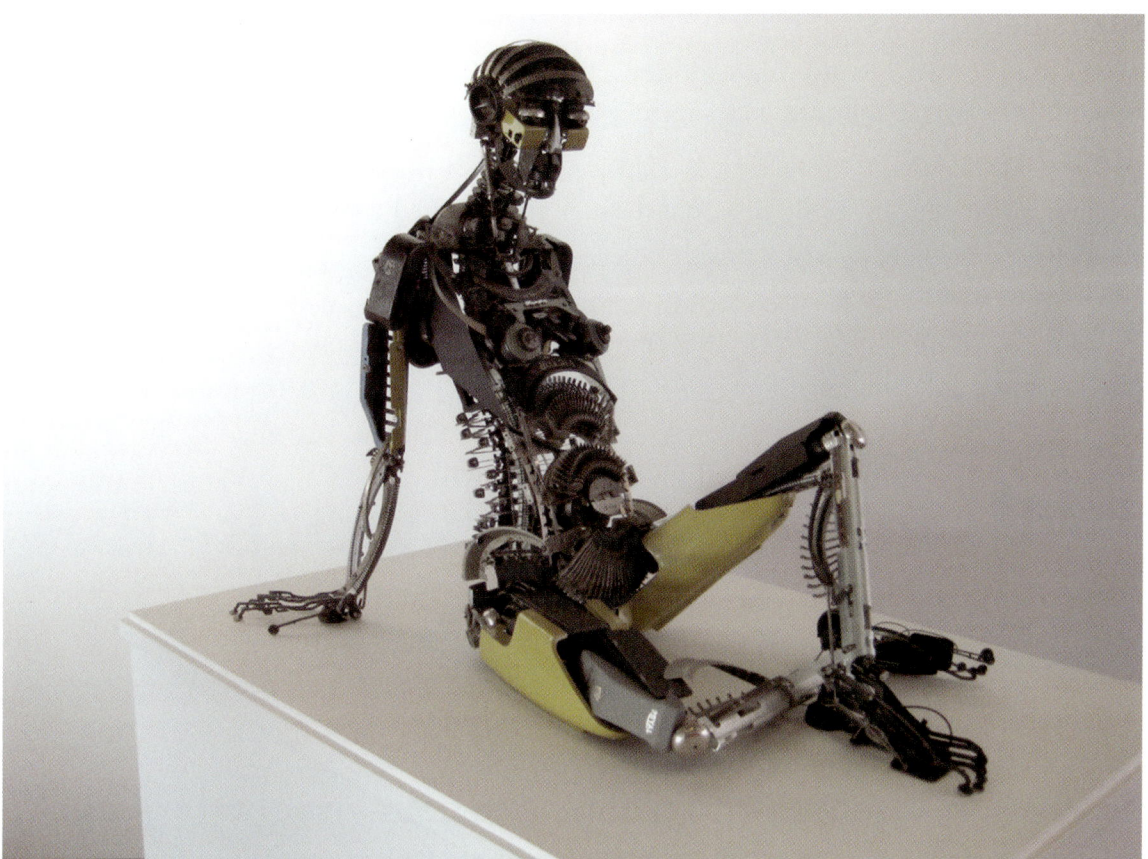

Jeremy Mayer, *Nude III (Olympia)*, 2007. Typewriter parts, 94 × 121 × 121 cm. © Jeremy Mayer.
1972–, USA

ARTIST FRAMES: STRUCTURAL/SUBJECTIVE

Ever since he was a boy, Jeremy Mayer has been fascinated by typewriters. He started by taking apart his mother's typewriter. Later, his interest blossomed into a full-time career as an artist making sculptures from collected typewriter parts.

ARTWORK FRAMES: STRUCTURAL/POSTMODERN

Nude III (Olympia) is a figure sculpture that presents a reclining woman made out of non-traditional materials—old typewriter parts. The face, arms, legs and body use all existing parts of a typewriter, from keys for the teeth, to the ribbon wheels for eyes. The sculpture looks relaxed and human despite the material it is made from.

PRACTICE: IDEAS

Mayer is a sculptor who uses found objects and discarded rubbish to make wild and interesting art. His work recycles things we think of as useless and worthless and turns them into interesting things that people want. He creates all sorts of characters and figures using typewriter parts. Mayer sees typewriters as another natural material, like wood or stone. His sculptures make us think about how we value machines and the role they play in our world. When machines fail or are complicated to use, we tend to attribute personalities to them. Perhaps because we spend so much time with machines, there can be a tendency to form emotional connections with them. Mayer is also a Postmodern artist in that he has made a classically traditional figure sculpture in very non-traditional materials. He is challenging what we consider to be art.

PRACTICE: ACTIONS

Mayer does not weld or glue his sculptures. He carefully puts together the typewriter pieces by finding ways that they can lock together like a giant jigsaw puzzle.

AUDIENCE

Student worksheet

Jeremy exhibits mainly in the USA, but through his website he is able to reach a wide international audience.

WWW http://jeremymayer.com/

Let's make an artwork 2
Moving art

Coming up with ideas   ARTMAKING PRACTICE

'Refit' some machines or machine images to create new artworks.

Discussion, research and planning in your visual arts diary

Student worksheet

ONLINE RESOURCES

Steampunk

Leonardo da Vinci

Jean Tinguely

CONCEPTUAL FRAMEWORK	PRACTICE	FRAMES
Artist	Ideas and actions	Structural—use of symbolism, methods and materials to give meaning
Artwork		
World		Cultural—representing a group or culture
Audience		Postmodern—use of non-traditional materials

Richard 'Doc' Nagy (Datamancer), contemporary artist, *Steampunk Laptop*, 2007. Refitted Hewlett-Packard ZT1000 laptop, mixed media. Image: Datamancer.

Leonardo da Vinci (1452–1519), Italy, design for a tank, late-15th to early-16th century. Illustration from journals. Image: Getty Images.

'Steampunk' is a style movement in which people imagine what might have happened if they had kept using steam power as the main form of energy. It's an imaginary world with all the technology we have today, but run by complex and bulky steam engines, with all the focus on decoration and craftsmanship that such engines had in the past. This is in contrast to the functional and minimal nature of the mass-produced machinery we live with in today's world. An example of steampunk style might be an MP3 player or laptop computer that is powered by steam and decorated with fancy Victorian brass patterns.

Look at the works of the three artists on page 146 and here as well as the artwork by **Theo Jansen** further ahead in the chapter. All these artworks involve movement and engineering. Discuss with your friends the role engineering plays in art.

Explore the visual style of each artwork. In your visual arts diary:

- identify which Frame each artwork fits into, using the Frames table in the Introduction to help you, and describe the qualities of this Frame that you can see in the artwork
- list the symbols used in one of the artworks and explain what you think they tell us about the meaning of the artwork
- collect images of kinetic sculpture from books, magazines and the internet to use as visual reference
- collect images of consumer goods such as refrigerators microwaves and washing machines from sales catalogues to use as visual reference
- research and collect images of contemporary design as visual reference
- research and collect images of the Victorian style of design, including styles of architecture and furniture
- borrow and sketch some ideas for compositions based on these artworks and your own collection of images and come up with some ideas of your own for collages and sculptures
- indicate one way each artist sets out to interest the audience, using the Conceptual Framework table in the Introduction to help you.

WWW www.datamancer.net/steampunklaptop/steampunklaptop.htm
www.sonypictures.com/movies/steamboy
www.tinguely.ch
www.dailysteampunk.com/steampunk_laptop.jpg

Jean Tinguely (1925–1991), Switzerland, *Meta-Maxi*, 1986. Mixed media. Potsdamer Platz, Berlin, Germany. Image: Bridgeman Art.

TEACHER NOTE

Show students some steampunk movies for inspiration, such as the 2004 anime movie *Steamboy* (directed and co-written by Katsuhiro Otomo).

kinetic: describing art in which moving parts are a key element, either involving audience participation (for example, with buttons to push), or using motors or natural forces like wind for power

Victorian: describing a style of design from the early 1800s to the beginning of the 20th century, with a focus on elaborate decoration

TEACHER NOTE

Have a class discussion about ways in which the artists in this section engage the interest of the audience. Have students take notes in their visual arts diaries.

Taking action   ARTMAKING PRACTICE

Option 1   Collage

- Collect some photos and sales catalogue images of contemporary objects, such as televisions, MP3 players and other electronic goods.
- Using pens and paint, 'refit' a series of objects in a Victorian design style. You might decide to make decorative patterns on the objects or to show some of the details of their function, such as steam stacks and boilers. Look back at the *Steampunk Laptop* artwork on page 146 for inspiration.
- Collect your images together and create a Steampunk sales catalogue, using the Victorian style and language.
- You could also collage decorative designs found in old Victorian illustrations over contemporary designs. For example, you could create a mechanical, steam-powered game station with thick hose pipes connecting the player consoles, or a chunky metal MP3 player with bolts and wires and light bulb-valves.

Option 2   Sculpture

- Collect some discarded consumer goods, such as an old mobile phone or a broken appliance.
- Alternatively, use strong cardboard and paint to make models of these objects.
- Decorate the goods in the steampunk style. For example, you could paint or refit an old mobile phone to look like it is made of wood and brass.

TEACHER NOTE

Students should take care with old discarded goods, ensuring they are not plugged into a live electrical supply. You may wish to have power cabling removed before the project starts.

*Batteries for mobile phones should be recycled.

In-depth study
Theo Jansen
CRITICAL AND HISTORICAL INTERPRETATIONS

Theo Jansen, *Strandbeest*. Kinetic sculpture, PVC electrical conduit, dimensions variable (3–4 m tall). Image: Theo Jansen/Loek van der Klis/Viscopy. 1948–, Netherlands

CONCEPTUAL FRAMEWORK: WORLD

Theo Jansen is, like Leonardo da Vinci, an artist, a scientist and an engineer. He has designed special sculpture machines that move under their own power, generated by the wind. He makes them out of electrical tubing and they wander about on a beach in the Netherlands, like grazing animals.

ARTIST FRAMES: POSTMODERN/STRUCTURAL

The materials Jansen uses to make his sculptures are not traditional art materials. His use of industrial materials like electrical tubing is very Postmodern. Jansen sees his sculptures as almost living things—see *Strandbeest* above. When he talks about them he speaks as if he is describing animals:

> *Since 1990 I have been occupied creating new forms of life. Not pollen or seeds but plastic yellow tubes are used as the basic material of this new nature. I make skeletons that are able to walk on the wind, so they don't have to eat.*

Over time, these skeletons have become increasingly better at surviving the elements such as storms and water and eventually I want to put these animals out in herds on the beaches, so they will live their own lives.
www.strandbeest.com

ARTWORK FRAMES: CULTURAL

Jansen's sculptures are a great example of how art and engineering can combine to produce amazing artworks. His sculptures are wind-powered and require no electricity to move.

PRACTICE: IDEAS

Jansen is trying to draw attention to our human potential to come up with new and amazing ways to make art. Jansen's work draws attention to the beauty of great machines in their design and the way they work.

PRACTICE: ACTIONS

Jansen uses electrical conduit piping which he cuts and binds to form the skeletal structures of his 'beests'. The piping is combined with fabric that catches the wind to propel the beasts forward.

AUDIENCE

Initially only people in the Netherlands knew of Jansen's work. However, videos of the works screened on the website YouTube have proved very popular, with viewers marvelling over the moving sculptures. Jansen is now famous and has appeared on television and in magazines all over the world. His artworks are in high demand as are the engineering ideas behind how they work.

WWW www.strandbeest.com
www.youtube.com

Let's make an artwork 3
Animate!

Coming up with ideas   ARTMAKING PRACTICE

Make an animation featuring machines.

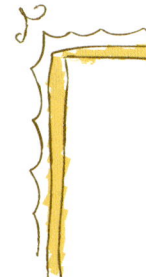

Student worksheet

Discussion, research and planning in your visual arts diary

CONCEPTUAL FRAMEWORK	PRACTICE	FRAMES
Artist	Ideas and actions	Structural—visual qualities, formal elements, symbols, planning
Artwork		
World		Subjective—spiritualism
Audience		Postmodern—use of non-traditional materials

Creating a traditional animation involves taking a series of photographs or still video frames of an object that is slowly moved and altered. When the images are played in

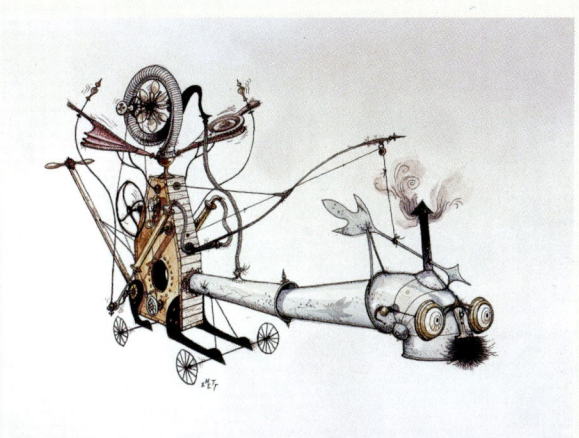

Frederick Rowland Emett (1906–1990), UK. Concept illustration from the film *Chitty Chitty Bang Bang*. Image: Warfield/United Artists/The Kobal Collection/Picdesk.

A still from the film *Modern Times*, directed by Charlie Chaplin, Charles Chaplin Productions, 1936. Image: Chaplin/United Artists/The Kobal Collection/Picdesk.

quick succession, the object will appear to be moving. The minimum rate at which that these images can pass the eye is about 14 frames per second; any less than this, and the movement will appear jumpy or static. Some animations use around 30 frames a second—this means you would need 90 still pictures to create a three-second shot!

Complete the following activities, making notes in your visual arts diary, as background research.

A still from the film *I, Robot*, directed by Alex Proyas, 20th Century Fox, 2004. CGI by Digital Domain. Image: 20th Century Fox/The Kobal Collection/Picdesk.

- Watch some different animated films, such as the 2004 anime film *Steamboy* or the 2008 animated film *WALL·E*. Pause each film and move frame by frame through the shots, observing the change in position of the subject. How far does an arm or leg move in each frame to give the appearance of walking?

- Look at some comic books or graphic novels and take note of how they plan and present movement and action. Comic book artists are very good at focussing on key moments to depict in order to get the story across and convey a sense of movement in just a few pictures. Focussing on key moments will be useful when planning your own animation.

- Create a motion comic. A motion comic is partway between a full moving animation and an original-style comic book. Make a series of sequential drawings and put them into a program like PowerPoint or Movie Maker. By zooming and panning across the still pictures, you get a sense of movement and action.

Look at the images of artworks above. In your visual arts diary:

- discuss the attitude towards technology presented in each work
- describe the materials each artist or creator has used to make their work
- compare each work with the animation of **Anthony Lucas** further ahead in the chapter and list the common elements that can be found in all the artworks.

www http://www.imdb.com/title/tt0027977/
www.digitaldomain.com
www.foxmovies.com

Taking action   ARTMAKING PRACTICE
Option 1   Flip book animation

- Look at the bottom-right corner of this book, and you will see that a section of the book comprises a flip book animation.
- Using a tripod or resting your camera on a stable surface, take some digital photographs of the robot you made in 'Let's make an artwork 1'.
- Between taking each shot, move your robot a little in one direction. Make sure the camera does not move at all during the entire process. You will need to take at least 30 photographs.
- You might prefer to change your background, instead of the robot. If so, draw or paint a background on a long piece of paper, set it up behind your robot and move it slowly in each photograph to create a sense of movement.
- Print your photographs in a small format and glue them to some thin but stiff pieces of cardboard. (Alternatively, you could use a thick sketchbook instead of pieces of cardboard.)
- Attach all the pieces of card together like a book by stapling one end of the cards together. By flipping the other end, you will create a short animated movie.

Low-tech alternative

- Instead of using a camera, draw pictures of your robot onto cardboard or the pages of a thick sketchbook.
- Trace each following drawing from the original, changing one aspect of the robot, such as the position of its arms.

Option 2 Stop-motion animation

- Create a stop-motion animation of your robot from 'Let's make an artwork 1'.
- Start by carefully storyboarding your movie. A storyboard is a series of pictures drawn in the planning stage that tell the story of your movie. Your storyboard should focus on the key points of your movie so that you know exactly what is supposed to be happening. Animation is hard work and can be very time-consuming—you may need to take between 15 and 30 still shots for every second of the movie. It is important you don't waste time photographing things pointlessly.
- Mount a video camera or a digital camera on a tripod or a stable surface so that it does not move during the process.
- Take single photos (or shoot single moments if using a video camera), moving your robot slightly between each shot.
- Use photographic editing software to edit your footage together into an animation.

In-depth study
Anthony Lucas
CRITICAL AND HISTORICAL INTERPRETATIONS

Anthony Lucas, contemporary director, *The Mysterious Geographic Explorations of Jasper Morello*, 2005, 3D Films. Image: 3D Films/AFC/Film Victoria/ SBS Indpendent.
Australia

CONCEPTUAL FRAMEWORK: WORLD

Anthony Lucas is an Australian animator who currently makes short films. His 2005 short film *The Mysterious Geographic Explorations of Jasper Morello* was nominated for an Academy Award.

ARTIST FRAMES: POSTMODERN/STRUCTURAL

The artist says this about his way of working:

> *I've always collected things since I was a kid. It's a family trait . . . If Julia has a broken peg from the clothesline, I will save it. There's a lot you can do with that—you've got the spring and then you've got the two pieces and you could connect that to something else quite easily. To throw something away is just an evil day . . . you just never know when it's going to be of use.*
>
> Anthony Lucas, quoted by Lindy Percival, 'My Space—Anthony Lucas', www.theage.com.au, 19 September 2009

ARTWORK FRAMES: CULTURAL/SUBJECTIVE

The Mysterious Geographic Explorations of Jasper Morello is a steampunk adventure which substitutes sea ships for airships in a drama about a mysterious plague that needs a cure. The style and imagery in *The Mysterious Geographic Explorations of Jasper Morello* is drawn heavily from the work of Frederick Rowland Emett and even references Leonardo da Vinci. The technique of animation used is a combination of stop-motion, which is relatively low-tech, and CGI images.

PRACTICE: IDEAS

Anthony says this about his ideas:

> *I just love the ugliness of industry. There's a beauty in the ugly, in the oil and the grease and the rust, the repetition of shape—it's a real graphic appreciation of it . . . it's really form being more important than function.*
>
> Anthony Lucas, quoted by Lindy Percival, 'My Space—Anthony Lucas', www.theage.com.au, 19 September 2009

Student worksheet

PRACTICE: ACTIONS

Lucas uses an interesting technique in animating his films. The images are all mounted on a **light box** so that the shapes to be animated are all silhouetted. It's a technique similar to shadow puppetry.

light box: a glass-topped table or box lit from underneath the glass by fluorescent lights, usually used to view slides or transparencies such as X-rays

AUDIENCE

Lucas's works range from children's films to films with content aimed at a mature audience. His nomination for an Academy Award has significantly raised his profile.

WWW www.jaspermorello.com

Personal objects

All of us have objects that we keep with us or handle every day. Mobile phones, MP3 players and memory sticks are as much a part of our wardrobe as jewellery and clothing. Some objects we don't even notice and are constantly thrown away as rubbish and replaced. Artists have always taken inspiration from objects close at hand. They have used personal objects as the subjects of paintings, sculptures—in fact, all forms of art. The personal objects we keep say a lot about the people we are and the world we live in.

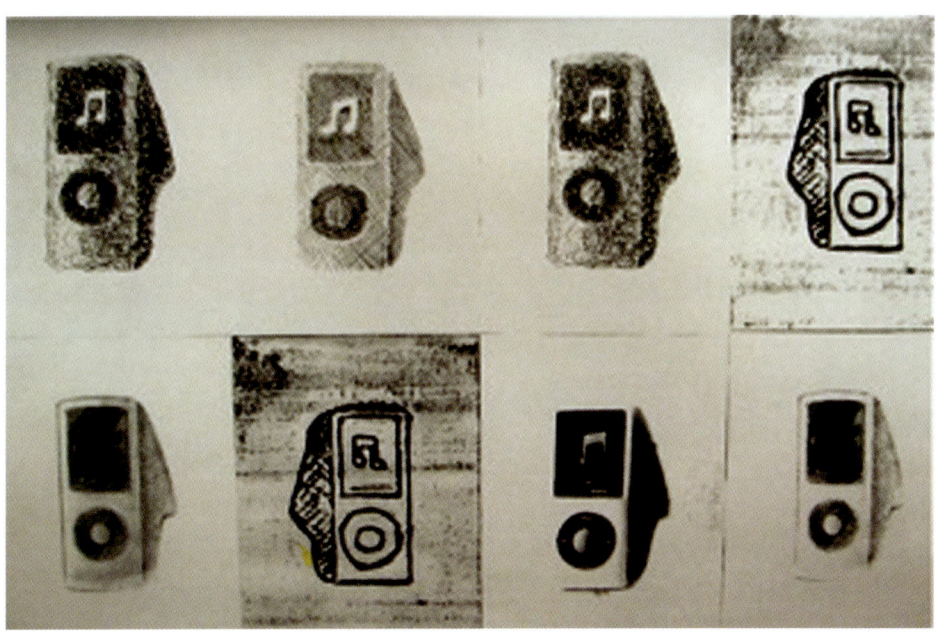

Artmaking sequence	Form	Artists
Let's make an artwork 1 *My stuff is me*	Drawing, scratchboard, painting	• *René Wirths, Samuel van Hoogstraten* • Giorgio Morandi, Jason Salavon, Gwyn Hanssen Pigott
Let's make an artwork 2 *All about me and my stuff*	Textiles, assemblage	• *Barbara Schulman, Adrienne Doig* • Tony Cragg, Joseph Cornell
Let's make an artwork 3 *Stuffed with stuff*	Assemblage	• *James Powditch* • Chris Jordan, Clare Healy and Sean Cordeiro

Let's make an artwork 1
My stuff is me
Coming up with ideas   ARTMAKING PRACTICE

Make artworks representing personal objects that have significance to you.

Discussion, research and planning in your visual arts diary

Student worksheet

CONCEPTUAL FRAMEWORK	PRACTICE	FRAMES
Artist Artwork World Audience	Ideas and actions	Structural—visual qualities, formal elements, symbols, planning Postmodern—questioning art rules, use of non-traditional technologies and materials Subjective—referencing the artist's own world and experiences

TEACHER NOTE

Discuss with the class what defines an object as 'personal': is it daily use, emotional attachment, status or physical proximity? Analyse the role of personal objects in the still-life genre.

Giorgio Morandi (1890–1964), Italy, *Still life*, 1957. Oil on canvas, 60.8 × 60.8 × 4.4 cm. Image: DACS/Viscopy/Bridgeman Art.

Jason Salavon (1970–), USA, *Still Life II (Glassware)*, 2007. Custom software and industrial LCD panel, played on a continuous loop. Photo: courtesy of the artist.

ONLINE RESOURCES

Giorgio Morandi

Jason Salavon

Gwyn Hanssen Pigott

Gwyn Hanssen Pigott (1935–), Australia, *Dark Still Life with Bowl*. Two bottles, two beakers, one bowl, 33 × 27 × 14 cm. Photo: courtesy of Gwyn Hanssen Pigott.

Looking at the three still-life artworks on page 156, as well as the works by **René Wirths** and **Samuel van Hoogstraten** further ahead in the chapter, think about how each artist has dealt differently with the same subject matter.

In your visual arts diary:

- list the Structural Frame qualities in each artwork, using the Frames table in the Introduction to help you
- list and sketch some ideas about how you might replace the objects in the images with those more common to your own everyday life
- describe how each artist has approached the idea of personal objects in a new way
- list the qualities of one of the Frames (apart from the Structural Frame) used in any one of these artworks using the Frames table in the Introduction to help you
- indicate one way each still-life artist and each personal-objects artist sets out to interest the audience
- list and sketch some ideas for the personal objects you will arrange and draw.

www http://collection.artgallery.nsw.gov.au/collection

TEACHER NOTE

Have a class discussion about ways in which each artist in this section sets out to interest their audience. Have students take notes in their visual arts diaries.

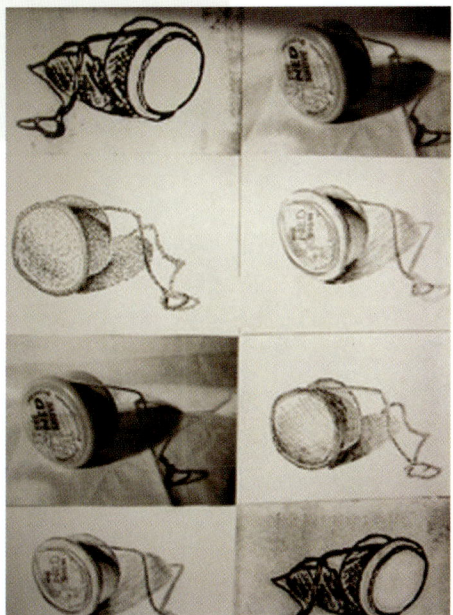

Taking action   ARTMAKING PRACTICE
Option 1   Drawing

- Choose some personal objects. Arrange them on a table in front of you. The arrangement can be in order of importance to you or it can be random. Take your time to observe these familiar objects and get the arrangement exactly how you want it.
- If you can, put the objects in front of a dark background.
- If possible, use a reading lamp or portable light to highlight one side of the objects to create contrast and volume. If you don't have a lamp, position yourself sideways to a window, so that your view of the objects is more brightly lit on one side.
- Do a series of drawings of the objects. Set a time limit for the drawings, starting out with a longer time and gradually getting faster until you have to make very quick sketches.
- Finally, take photographs of your objects to keep as a reference in your visual arts diary.

Option 2   Scratchboard

- Choose some personal objects. Arrange them on a table in front of you. The arrangement can be in order of importance to you or it can be random. Take your time to observe these familiar objects and get the arrangement exactly how you want it.
- Draw your personal objects in pencil on some scratchboard. Scratchboard can be bought, or you can make it by painting white melamine with a coat of flat black paint.

- Use a scalpel or the point of a compass on your scratchboard to lightly scratch away the drawn lines, revealing the white underneath. There is no shading possible with a scratchboard, and you will have to use lines in different ways to give your objects volume. Crosshatching is one technique you can use.

Option 3 Painting

- First complete the steps in Option 1.
- Use your sketches or photographs to make a painting of your personal objects as a vanitas still life. Vanitas paintings use dark backgrounds and dramatic lighting to make the objects look important and valuable.
- Sketch the painting in light pencil or watery light paint first, and then gradually add more detail using light layers of paint.
- Finish up with thicker paint and a dark background.

In-depth study
René Wirths

CRITICAL AND HISTORICAL INTERPRETATIONS

René Wirths, *Audio-Kassette*, 2007. Oil on canvas, 70 × 110 cm. Courtesy of Galerie Daniel Templon Paris and the artist.
Copyright: B. HUET/TUTTI.
1967–, Germany

CONCEPTUAL FRAMEWORK: WORLD

René Wirths lives and works in Germany. His world is that of contemporary painting.

ARTIST FRAMES: STRUCTURAL/POSTMODERN/SUBJECTIVE

Wirths is an artist who paints large, highly **photorealistic** paintings of his personal objects. The objects he paints are not glamorous or unique, they are the ordinary, everyday things he has accumulated around him. We are told nothing about these objects in the paintings. There is no background painted to explain where the objects were sitting. The objects are not precious-looking, and many are worn and used. They look much like the sorts of things you would find lying around in your own home. Wirths has avoided choosing items that are too specifically about him. There are no photos or pets in his images and he has carefully avoided painting backgrounds that might give us too much information about him. The objects are very personal, but the stories about them are a mystery.

Photorealistic: belonging to a style of painting and drawing in which the artist tries to produce images as clear as photographs, even reproducing photographic flaws such as lens flares, distortions and reduced depths of field

ARTWORK FRAMES: STRUCTURAL/SUBJECTIVE

The type of painting Wirths does is highly detailed and very time-consuming. It takes a tremendous amount of effort to paint these humble objects. In the painting *Audio-Kassette*, Wirths has carefully included a secret surprise. The painting is so detailed that although there is no background, you can see the artist's studio in the reflection of the plastic. Look more closely and you will see Wirths staring intently at the object as he paints it. What he has in fact done is paint a self portrait of the artist at work.

PRACTICE: IDEAS

Wirths paints the sorts of objects we often give little thought to, despite the fact that they play a significant role in our everyday lives. A well-worn soccer ball, a pair of glasses, a bicycle wheel and even an old audio cassette are all part of the clutter that inhabits our world. By painting these objects on a large scale using high-art materials such as canvas and oil paint, Wirths makes us look at these objects in a fresh way and gets us to think about the importance of objects like these in our own lives.

PRACTICE: ACTIONS

Wirths paints in oil paint that, because of its slow drying time, allows plenty of time to work on the fine detail in his pictures. His paintings are like photographs as they have a flatness to them that is further emphasised by the plain white background.

AUDIENCE

When we look at the objects Wirths paints, we start to notice all the worn scrapes and details. As an audience, we begin to become aware of the history of the objects. We can't possibly know their story, but we can see that each object *has* a story. Wirths is sending a very significant message in this mysterious work. He is saying that when we paint something that is a personal object and part of our lives, we are in fact painting about ourselves. We are painting a self portrait in another way.

WWW www.renewirths.de

In-depth study
Samuel van Hoogstraten
CRITICAL AND HISTORICAL INTERPRETATIONS

Samuel van Hoogstraten, *Still-life*, 1666–1668. Oil on canvas, 63 × 79 cm. State Art Gallery (*Staatliche Kunsthalle*), Germany. 1627–1678, Netherlands

CONCEPTUAL FRAMEWORK: WORLD

Samuel van Hoogstraten's world was that of the 17th-century **Renaissance** artist.

ARTIST FRAMES: STRUCTURAL

Van Hoogstraten was a Dutch painter who, like René Wirths, painted ordinary personal objects. Unlike Wirths, van Hoogstraten painted a collection of objects that combine to tell a coded story. At the time that van Hoogstraten was painting, it was common for artists to paint collections of objects, called still lifes. These paintings were careful compositions of objects that could show off the skill of a painter. At the time, artists felt that it was important to be able to paint as realistically as possible. The more realistic the objects looked, the more skilled the painter and the higher they were paid.

ARTWORK FRAMES: STRUCTURAL/SUBJECTIVE

In *Still-life*, van Hoogstraten has presented a number of different objects that appear to be hung on some red leather straps. The objects are all very personal: a pen, some letters and a small diary, lots of personal grooming items like soap and lice combs as well as a locket and coins. It's as if the painter has emptied the contents of a purse or bag on a table. The objects

> *Renaissance:* a historical period in which artists became fascinated with the Classic Age of Rome and Greece, and adopted the styles and subjects of many Classical artworks

are all very detailed and realistic, demonstrating a highly skilled understanding of painting. The work shows off the artist's skill.

PRACTICE: IDEAS

The types of objects 17th-century artists such as van Hoogstraten would paint were usually grand and stylish—fine glassware and silver with exotic fruits and foods, for example. These objects were difficult to paint because of their shiny surfaces and reflections. They were also objects of desire, wealth and prestige. They were painted to be bought as statements of style and success.

PRACTICE: ACTIONS

The objects that a 17th-century painter chose, and the way they were arranged, demonstrated the level of difficulty of painting them, and hence the skill of the painter. In van Hoogstraten's painting on page 160, the objects are all different and have lots of detail, which is hard to paint. He has also piled objects up on top of each other, making the painting even more complicated. His painting demonstrates a mastery of tone and colour. Van Hoogstraten was a very confident painter and he even went so far as to try and play tricks on his audience. He has painted all the objects as if they have been strapped down with nailed strips of leather stuck to two pieces of wood. When the painting was hung it was meant to look as if the objects were not painted at all but were actually hanging on the wall! Today many of the meanings may seem lost to us but looking closely at a painting can reveal some symbolic ideas the artist was trying to represent.

AUDIENCE

In van Hoogstraten's still life, we are actually given a detailed portrait of a person. The clues and symbols in the objects pictured can reveal much to us, and would have revealed even more to a 17th-century audience.

Let's make an artwork 2
All about me and my stuff

Coming up with ideas   ARTMAKING PRACTICE

Create an artwork using personal objects that have significance to you.

Student worksheet

Discussion, research and planning in your visual arts diary

CONCEPTUAL FRAMEWORK	PRACTICE	FRAMES
Artwork Artist World Audience	Ideas and actions	Structural—visual qualities, formal elements, symbols, planning Postmodern—questioning art rules, use of non-traditional technologies and materials Subjective—referencing the artist's own world and experiences

TEACHER NOTE

Have students do a 'stocktake' of personal objects they carry with them daily. Discuss common objects, such as mobile phones. Brainstorm ways that personal objects can be featured in artworks.

Tony Cragg (1949–), UK, *Red Indian*, 1982. Plastic. Image: Bridgeman Art.

Joseph Cornell (1903–1972), USA, *Untitled (for Stephanie)*, c. 1945. Box construction 48.9 × 36.2 × 12.7 cm. Image: NGA/VAGA/Viscopy.

TEACHER NOTE

Have a class discussion about what the artists in this section chose to include in, or reject from, their artwork. Discuss the common elements included.

Discuss with your friends some ways an artist might go about collecting material for an assemblage artwork. Think about some routine tasks that an artist might adopt to generate material for an artwork. For example, they might decide to save the paper coffee cup from their daily coffee for a year, or to keep all their train tickets or shopping dockets.

Look at the work of the two artists above, as well as the work of **Barbara Schulman** and **Adrienne Doig** further ahead in the chapter.

In your visual arts diary:

- identify some of the many elements that make up each of the works
- list the Structural Frame qualities in the artworks, using the Frames table in the Introduction to help you
- choosing one of the examples of assemblage, write which Frame the artist was working in and use the Frames table in the Introduction to help you list the qualities of this Frame.
- using this knowledge, list and sketch some ideas in your visual arts diary for an assemblage artwork of your own.

Taking action   ARTMAKING PRACTICE

Option 1   Textiles

- Draw a still-life arrangement of some of your own personal objects onto a piece of fabric.
- Carefully use a needle and thread to stitch the image onto the fabric, using your drawn lines as a guide.

- You might also like to add some text to your work that tells something personal about you.
- Display your finished work as a wall-hanging.

Option 2 Assemblage

- Collect material that can be used to make a wearable artwork. You might collect bus or train tickets, ATM receipts or shopping dockets. Look at the work of Barbara Schulman on page 164 for ideas.
- Join the objects by stitching, stapling or gluing them together to make a wearable cloak.

In-depth study

Barbara Schulman

CRITICAL AND HISTORICAL INTERPRETATIONS

CONCEPTUAL FRAMEWORK: WORLD

Barbara Schulman is an American textile artist who makes work that comments on society's obsession with consumerism and materialism.

ARTIST FRAMES: POSTMODERN/SUBJECTIVE

Schulman uses traditional weaving and textiles techniques in new and unconventional ways, often by combining found or collected objects. Some of the objects Barbara has collected in her work are personal refuse—the sorts of objects we might handle and dispose of every day without thinking. Bus and train tickets are sewn and woven into the two- and three-dimensional objects she creates. Schulman also uses other objects with strong

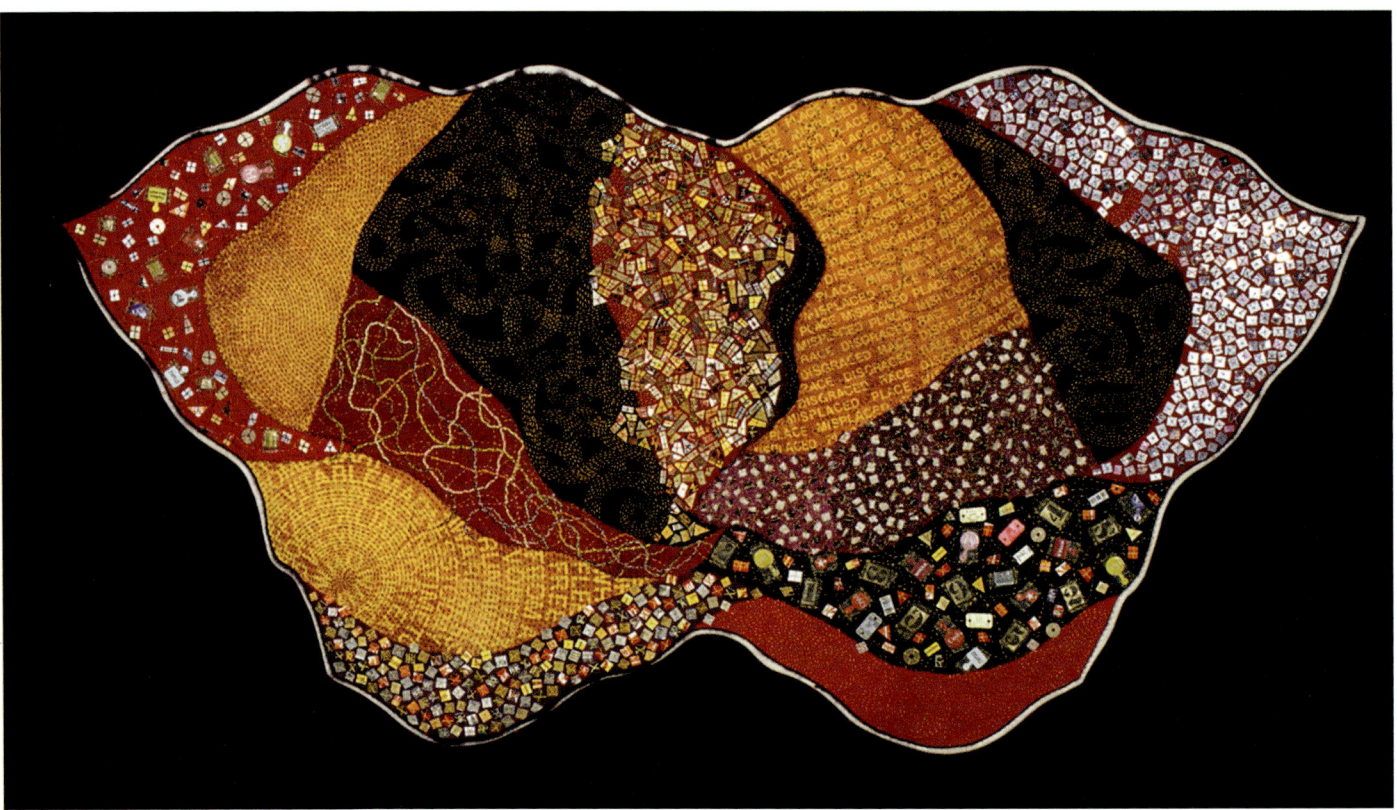

Barbara Schulman, *Cape for a Protectress*. Credit card fragments, museum badges, brass stencil letters, subway tokens and other found objects; stitched on dyed industrial wool felt, with spray paint stencils, 94 × 178 cm. © Barbara Schulman.
Contemporary artist, USA

symbolic meaning and value, such as credit cards. These objects are often made of the same materials as the rubbish, and yet because of their power to buy material goods, credit cards have a strong aura of power. Barbara subverts this power by cutting up the cards, making them powerless: a cut credit card has no more value than a piece of plastic rubbish. To give credit cards a greater aura of power, they are often decorated with grand and alluring designs, gilt edges and gold and silver colours. Barbara reconfigures these elements to create beautiful textile objects that are beautiful and attractive, but at the same time seek to undermine our obsession with material things.

ARTWORK FRAMES: STRUCTURAL/SUBJECTIVE

Cape for a Protectress is a wearable cape made from a large collection of embroidered found objects, including New York City subway tokens. It has a magical quality about it, suggesting that it might protect the wearer from all the pitfalls of living in a large city like New York. The pitfalls are suggested through the choice of materials and also by the embroidered words (such as 'flee', 'escape' and 'run away'), which suggest a mantra or spell the wearer might use to cast aside potential threats. The processes and controls of moving around a city on a daily basis are represented by the subway tokens and bus tickets. The need for money in an expensive city is represented by the credit card fragments, which both acknowledge the magical power of waving a credit card at a problem and also attack it, because the cards are cut up. Schulman perhaps hopes that by wearing the cape she can be a sort of superhero who is impervious to these everyday challenges.

PRACTICE: IDEAS

Schulman's practice makes us aware of the worthlessness of material objects. She suggests expensive objects are essentially worthless, and that beauty and worth can be found in disposed-of objects.

PRACTICE: ACTIONS

Schulman has used the traditional art form of needlework to craft *Cape for a Protectress*, combining an assortment of everyday items.

AUDIENCE

Schulman's work appeals to audiences through its use of attractive materials and seductive designs. Barbara's audience is the urban art gallery goer who appreciates the perils and stresses of living in a busy city, but who also can appreciate the traditional craft forms she uses.

WWW www.barbaraschulman.com

In-depth study
Adrienne Doig
CRITICAL AND HISTORICAL INTERPRETATIONS

Adrienne Doig, *Dies in Horto*, 2008. Embroidery on linen, 53 × 255 cm. Collection O'Hallorans Corporate Lawyers. Photo by Jenni Carter. Contemporary artist, Australia

CONCEPTUAL FRAMEWORK: WORLD

Adrienne Doig's world is that of the postmodern sculptor, painter and performance artist. Adrienne has exhibited widely in Australia and overseas. Her work is specific in its Australian references, but the ideas she explores are universal.

ARTIST FRAMES: POSTMODERN/SUBJECTIVE

Doig is an artist who uses herself and her own experience as a basis for her work. Much of her work features Doig engaged in different activities. Her works often feature symbolic personal objects. These objects may appear to be ordinary, meaningless parts of everyday life, but actually have significant meaning to the artist. Doig's work is intensely personal, sometimes requiring the audience to decode the meanings. She often uses jokes and humour to communicate her ideas. Her artworks sometimes tell stories about her life and sometimes these stories comment on the wider roles of women in today's world.

ARTWORK FRAMES: POSTMODERN/SUBJECTIVE

In the wall-hanging *Dies in Horto*, Doig contrasts the everyday activities in her work by representing them in the style of a famous artwork: the *Bayeux Tapestry*. She uses the style and language of the ancient artwork but represents herself doing ordinary things like gardening. The use of Latin and the historic style of the *Bayeux Tapestry* makes the ordinary things that she is doing seem important and historical. This also adds humour to the work.

PRACTICE: IDEAS

As well as being an artwork, the *Bayeux Tapestry* is a significant historical document. The tapestry tells the story of the Norman conquest of England in 1066 and is more than 500 years old. By borrowing its design and material practice in her work, the artist is making a comment about how we value our personal histories and objects.

PRACTICE: ACTIONS

Doig has carefully hand-stitched the wall-hanging using needle and thread. The work is a drawing in thread. Adrienne has used mangle cloth as a surface for the work. This is a fine linen usually reserved for formal tablecloths. Perhaps Adrienne has recycled this cloth from her personal collection.

AUDIENCE

Doig exhibits her work in solo and group shows. Often a curator has commissioned her to produce a work for a particular theme or idea; more often she is approached to supply a work for an exhibition. Her work has been included in exhibitions about the type of materials she uses (such as the textiles) and also because of the ideas she represents (such as women artists and their lives).

Student worksheet

Let's make an artwork 3
Stuffed with stuff

Coming up with ideas   ARTMAKING PRACTICE

Make an artwork using discarded personal objects that have significance to you.

Discussion, research and planning in your visual arts diary

Student worksheet

CONCEPTUAL FRAMEWORK	PRACTICE	FRAMES
Artist	Ideas and actions	Structural—visual qualities, formal elements, symbols, planning
Artwork		Subjective—spiritualism
World		Postmodern—questioning art rules, using non-traditional technologies and materials
Audience		

Chris Jordan (1963–), USA, *Intolerable Beauty*, 2004. Depicts 426 000 cell phones, equal to the number of cell phones retired in the US every day. Archival inkjet print 152 × 254 cm. Copyright Chris Jordon, courtesy of Kopeikin Gallery, Los Angeles, USA.

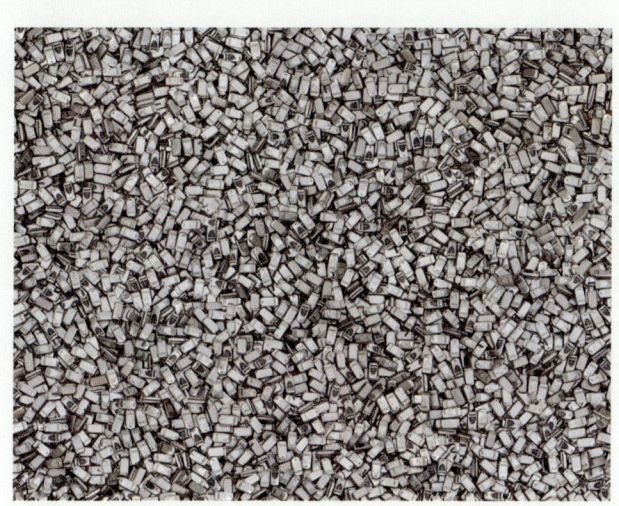

Detail of Chris Jordan's *Intolerable Beauty*. Copyright Chris Jordon, courtesy of Kopeikin Gallery, Los Angeles.

Claire Healy (1971–) and Sean Cordeiro (1974–), Australia, *Deceased Estate*, 2004. Installation, found detritus from artists' warehouse. Photographer: Christian Schnur. Photo: courtesy of the artists and Gallery Barry Keldoulis.

Looking at the works of the artists above, as well as that of **James Powditch** further ahead in the chapter, discuss with your friends the ideas of each artist.

In your visual arts diary:

* list the different ways each artist has used discarded materials to make an artwork
* list the Structural Frame qualities in each artwork, using the Frames table in the Introduction to help you
* choose one example of sculpture, decide which Frame the artist is working in (using the Frames table in the Introduction to help you) and list the qualities of this Frame

- make a list of things that you buy, consume or dispose of everyday (for example, milk containers, chip packets and soft-drink cans), keep a record of how much you use and work out how much you would use in one month, one year or even in a lifetime
- make a 'desert island list' of 10 things you would take with you on a desert island.

WWW www.chrisjordan.com
www.claireandsean.com

Other artists who have made work about consumerism:
Rob Pettit: www.robpettit.com
Alex Martin, a woman who made and wore a dress for a year: www.littlebrowndress.com
John Freyer, who sold all his possessions: www.allmylifeforsale.com
Peter Menzel, photographer: www.menzelphoto.com

Taking action   ARTMAKING PRACTICE
Option 1   Assemblage

- Collect disposable personal objects that you use over the course of a few weeks. For example, you may drink a container of fruit juice every day, or a bottle of milk or eat an apple with a sticker on it, or a meat pie in a tin foil container.
- Using the collected objects create an assemblage work to represent your consumption. You might choose to assemble it in a frame or box. Include some photocopied personal images (don't use precious originals!).
- Give your assemblage an appropriate name. Will it be *Chip Packet Girl*? Or *Soft Drink Can Man*?
- Take photographs to document the creation of your assemblage.

In-depth study
James Powditch

CRITICAL AND HISTORICAL INTERPRETATIONS

CONCEPTUAL FRAMEWORK: WORLD

James Powditch is an assemblage artist. His world is that of Australian contemporary art.

ARTIST FRAMES: STRUCTURAL

Powditch collects a range of materials that have interesting or personally significant qualities and arranges them like a jigsaw puzzle. This is time-consuming, because it requires a large collection of all sorts of different objects and materials. In some cases, the artist has an idea for a work and collects pieces to fit. Other times, he may be inspired by things he finds in his collection, which make connections with each other. Powditch carefully considers the shapes, colours and forms of his objects. His artworks explore ideas about line and tone in the way he arranges his pieces in his box. James has been influenced by a number of artists, including James Cornell who made small collection boxes that told stories about some of the interests and experiences in his life.

ARTWORK FRAMES: STRUCTURAL/ POSTMODERN

Made in Canada is an assemblage work featuring a number of objects and materials that have a reference to Canada. The artwork carries what appears be lots of images of and instruments of calibration and measurement, such as map grids and rulers. The map shows part of Canada and it frames objects such as an old paper Coke cup with a Montreal Olympics logo, ticket stubs and map keys all referencing or measuring some sort of 'Canadianess'. All of the materials are old, suggesting that the artwork might be recording an event from the past. The materials have been glued and assembled in a sort of geography lesson display, with careful consideration given to colour (the red cup complements the small red cow icon and the section of red card).

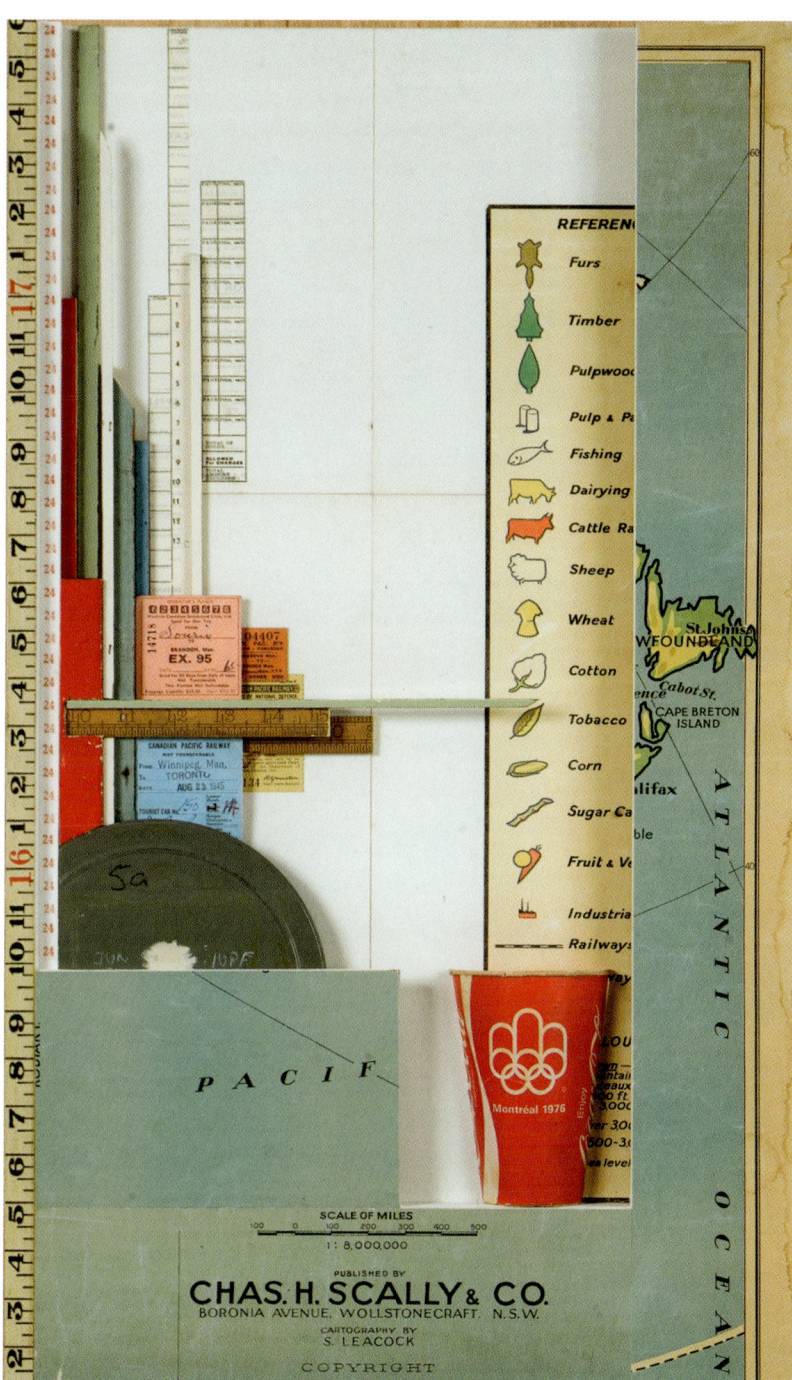

James Powditch, *Made in Canada*, 2009. Mixed media, 61 × 91 cm. © James Powditch. 1966–, Australia

PRACTICE: IDEAS

The title suggests that the artist, the artwork or the materials might be 'made in Canada', but actually this is not true. Powditch has chosen to feature the map-maker's logo, which clearly shows the map was made in Australia. Perhaps this is an artwork about an Australian understanding of, or experience with, Canada. Perhaps the artist once visited Canada and collected some keepsakes.

PRACTICE: ACTIONS

Powditch is an avid collector of material. His process of assemblage is very considered. He carefully finds connections between different pieces of material, whether it is colour or age or common references, such as the Olympics or Canada. He assembles the material so that the works can also be appreciated purely for the formal way the shapes and colours relate to each other.

AUDIENCE

Made in Canada was part of an exhibition that featured works whose titles began *Made in . . .* Each work was about a different country, but featured materials collected in Australia. The audience for this series of works is wide, due to careful design considerations that make the artworks colourful and attractive. The series would also appeal to people with an interest in the wider world beyond Australia, or perhaps those who have settled here from somewhere else.

 Student worksheet

WWW www.jamespowditch.com.au/

Part four

THE WORLD OF PLACES AND SPACES

Looking down on the land

Ever since human beings first looked up into the sky they have dreamt about flying and about the view from the sky down to the land below. Until the advent of flight, the closest people could get to an aerial view was to climb a high mountain. Artists have always been fascinated with high views and there are many artworks about looking down on the land.

Artmaking sequence	Form	Artists
Let's make an artwork 1 *Bird's-eye view*	Photography	• *Narelle Autio* • John Olsen, Kathleen Petyarre, Richard Woldendorp
Let's make an artwork 2 *The view from here*	Drawing, painting	• *John Wolseley* • William Robinson, Eugène von Guérard, Elizabeth Mpetyane

Let's make an artwork 1
Bird's-eye view

Coming up with ideas   ARTMAKING PRACTICE

Take a series of photographs based on the idea of 'a bird's-eye view'. The images can refer specifically to the life of a bird (for example, a day in the life of a school pigeon), or they can be more about the angle and perspective of a bird's-eye view.

Discussion, research and planning in your visual arts diary

CONCEPTUAL FRAMEWORK	PRACTICE	FRAMES
Artist Artwork World Audience	Ideas and actions	Structural—symbolism, visual qualities and composition Postmodern—borrowing ideas and actions from other artists Cultural—representing a group or culture

Student worksheet

John Olsen (1928–), Australia, *Spring at Rydal*, 1992. Oil, mixed media on board, 80 × 400 cm. Image courtesy of Tim Olsen Gallery, Sydney/licensed by Viscopy.

Kathleen Petyarre (born c. 1930s), Australia, *Mountain Devil Lizard Dreaming*, 2009. Synthetic polymer on Belgian Linen, 167.4 × 214.0 cm. © Kathleen Petyarre. Image: Gallerie Australis, Adelaide, South Australia.

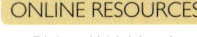

ONLINE RESOURCES

Richard Woldendorp

Richard Woldendorp (1927–), Netherlands/Australia, aerial photograph of Forrest River, WA, 2002. Inkjet print, 116 × 208 cm. Photo courtesy of Boutwell Draper Gallery.

Look at the work of the three artists on page 173, as well as the work of **Narelle Autio** further ahead in the chapter.

In your visual arts diary:

- list the important actions each artist takes (using the Artmaking Practice table in the Introduction), referring to the forms used, the materials and the methods
- write which Frame each artist is working in (using the Frames table in the Introduction to help you) and describe the qualities of that Frame you can see in the artworks
- choose one of the works and discuss the artist's world and how this has affected their representation of the land, referring to the Conceptual Framework table in the Introduction
- make notes and sketch some ideas for your own representations of the land from an aerial perspective, borrowing ideas from these artworks to help you.

TEACHER NOTE

Have a class discussion about the ideas of each artist in this section in relation to representing the land from an aerial view. Refer to the Artmaking Practice table in the Introduction.

aerial: a perspective of the landscape as seen from high in the air, such as the view from an aircraft, crane or high building

Taking action ARTMAKING PRACTICE
Option 1 Photography

- During an outdoor walk with your class, take a series of photographs and do some quick sketches to map each stage of your journey through the land.
- Take photos along the way looking up at higher parts of the land. Take photos looking across at the land.
- Take a series of photographs and do a series of sketches from the highest point of your walk, looking down on the land.
- Use some aspects of the Structural Frame in your photos and sketches—emphasise the visual qualities of the land, patterns, colours and tones, and the different perspectives.
- Download the images onto a school or home computer. Choose three images taken from an aerial perspective, giving a bird's-eye view of the land.
- Use photographic editing software to adjust, enhance and add effects to these three photos to create images with abstract qualities like those in the artworks of John Olsen, Richard Woldendorp and Kathleen Petyarre on page 173.

TEACHER NOTE

Take students on a walk to a high place in the local area with a good view, (e.g. a tall building, hill or lookout). Alternatively, your school grounds may have suitable high areas.

ONLINE RESOURCES

Organising a journey through the land excursion

Low-tech alternative

- Collect aerial images of the landscape from magazines and the internet.
- Make a photo collage using the images.
- Borrow the simplified, abstract patterns, lines and tones of the artworks of John Olsen, Richard Woldendorp and Kathleen Petyarre on page 173 by cutting, rearranging and pasting your images by hand.

Option 2 Photography

- Take a series of photographs of an artificial bird's-eye view using models and toys.
- Arrange small-scale objects to create the illusion of height and depth.
- Look back at the artworks of John Olsen, Richard Woldendorp and Kathleen Petyarre on page 173, and at the artwork of Narelle Autio on page 176, for inspiration.
- Use some aspects of the Structural Frame, for example, such visual qualities as patterns, placement of figures, shadows, colours and tones to emphasise the bird's-eye view.
- Use your camera to make a short stop-frame animated movie of your bird's-eye view by taking a series of photographs of the scene, moving the figures slightly between each shot.
- Download your photos onto a school or home computer. Use photographic editing software to enhance or adjust your photographs, and then play them back in sequence to view your stop-frame animation movie.

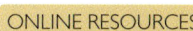

Extension

- Make a series of prints using paper etching plates. Look back at the artworks of John Olsen and Kathleen Petyarre on page 173 for inspiration.
- Base the initial design for the print on a fragment of one of your bird's-eye view photos.
- Use the Structural Frame, for example, lines, tones and colours, planned composition and printing method used, to give meaning to your artwork.
- Use a variety of methods to prepare the paper or acetate plate and in the printing technique.
- Use a planned composition, simplification of shapes, and dark tones to contrast with lighter tones. Emphasise pattern and texture rather than lines.

ONLINE RESOURCES

Etching using paper and acetate plates

In-depth study
Narelle Autio
CRITICAL AND HISTORICAL INTERPRETATIONS

Narelle Autio, *Untitled (cat#16)*, 2001, from *Not of this Earth*. Photograph, archival inkjet prints on canvas, 66 × 100 cm. © Narelle Autio. Image: Stills Gallery.
1969–, Australia

CONCEPTUAL FRAMEWORK: WORLD

Narelle Autio's world is that of contemporary photography. She responds to people in the everyday world around her and attempts to present them in a way that is fresh and unexpected. By doing this she makes us think differently about the world we live in.

ARTIST FRAMES: STRUCTURAL

Autio is a structural artist who uses photography to explore new and unusual ways of discovering the landscape and the people who live in it.

ARTWORK FRAMES: STRUCTURAL

In the artwork above, Autio uses a high bird's-eye perspective to create a surprising and unusual image of some people relaxing on a grass lawn. The high angle and the absence of any other details except for some birds flying overhead create a very simple and minimal image.

PRACTICE: IDEAS

Autio explores ideas about human beings in the landscape. Her subjects are ordinary people engaged in everyday activities. When we first look at the image we are confused. The people appear to be standing up or floating. There is very little information in the image to explain the angle we are looking from.

PRACTICE: ACTIONS

Autio uses the traditional practice of photography in an unconventional way. A recognisable signature of her work is the use of unusual perspectives of everyday scenes. She has used high bird's-eye views to show landscapes and low underwater angles to show people swimming.

AUDIENCE

The artworks of Narelle Autio have a very wide appeal. She chooses subjects that many people identify with, such as people relaxing in parks or swimming in the sea. Her unusual perspectives produce images that are exciting and visually engaging for the audience.

www www.stillsgallery.com.au/artists/autio

Student worksheet

Let's make an artwork 2
The view from here

Coming up with ideas   ARTMAKING PRACTICE

Make an artwork depicting your local landscape from a high view—it could be a view from the top of a hill, a tall building or another high place that has meaning for you.

Discussion, research and planning in your visual arts diary

CONCEPTUAL FRAMEWORK	PRACTICE	FRAMES
Artist Artwork World Audience	Ideas and actions	Structural—symbolism, visual qualities and composition Subjective—expressive and imaginative qualities, expressive colour, changes in size and proportion Postmodern—borrowing ideas and actions from other artists

Student worksheet

TEACHER NOTE

Take students on a walk to a high place in the local area with a good view, (e.g. a tall building, hill or lookout). Alternatively, your school grounds may have suitable high areas.

ONLINE RESOURCES

William Robinson

Eugène von Guérard

William Robinson (1936–), *Ridge and gully in the afternoon light*, 1992. Oil on canvas, 138 × 198 cm. Image: Phillip Bacon Galleries.

Eugène von Guérard (1811–1901), Austria/Australia, *Govett's Leap and Grose River Valley, Blue Mountains, New South Wales*, 1873. Oil on canvas, 68.5 × 106.4 cm. National Gallery of Australia, Canberra.

Look at the artworks of the artists on page 177, as well as the work by **John Wolseley** further ahead in the chapter.

In your visual arts diary:

- list the important actions each artist takes (using the Artmaking Practice table in the Introduction), referring to the forms used, the materials and the methods
- write which Frame each artist is working in (using the Frames table in the Introduction to help you) and describe the qualities of that Frame you can see in the artworks
- choose one of the works and discuss the artist's world and how this has affected this representation of the land, referring to the Conceptual Framework table in the Introduction
- indicate one way each artist sets out to interest the audience
- make notes and sketch some ideas for your own representations of the land from a variety of perspectives, borrowing ideas from these artworks to help you.

Taking action ARTMAKING PRACTICE

Option 1 Drawing

- Use your photographs and drawings taken during the class walk you went on in 'Let's make an artwork 1' as the starting point for a drawing.
- Isolate one of the details of your photos and drawings that gives an aerial perspective, looking down on the land, and has a strong composition.
- Work in the Structural Frame—use of methods and materials to give meaning, visual qualities that emphasise the aerial perspective, simplification of lines, tone and textures, stylisation, and a planned composition. Look further ahead to the work of John Wolseley for inspiration.

Option 2 Painting

- Use your photographs and drawings taken during the class walk you went on in 'Let's make an artwork 1' as the starting point for a painting in the form of a map. Your map will show a view looking down on the land, similar to John Wolseley's work, but it will also serve as a record of your journey *through* the land. It will also include other perspectives, such as views across the land and looking up.
- Use the Structural Frame—use of symbolism, methods and materials to give meaning, visual qualities that emphasise the aerial perspective, simplification of lines, tone and textures, stylisation and a planned composition.
- Also use the Subjective Frame—expressive and imaginative qualities, expressive colour, and changes in size and proportion.
- Make a further connection with the audience by including text in the painting, such as a description of your walking journey.
- Complete your painting by including some collaged sketches from your journey.

In-depth study

John Wolseley

CRITICAL AND HISTORICAL INTERPRETATIONS

John Wolseley, *Camel Gate Border Track SA/VIC*, 2006–2007. Watercolour and carbonised wood on paper, 209.0 × 195.5 cm. Image: Australian Galleries/licensed by Viscopy. Photo: Terence Bogue.
1938–, UK

CONCEPTUAL FRAMEWORK: WORLD

John Wolseley came to Australia in 1976 and has made countless journeys into the Australian desert that intrigues him, attempting to understand the spirit of the place. His world has become a series of journeys mapping the different histories of the land.

ARTIST FRAMES: STRUCTURAL/SUBJECTIVE

Wolseley is an artist who makes work about the Australian landscape, usually in remote areas. He does this by spending time in a place and by making work that does more than just represent what the landscape looks like but expresses what he experiences in it. He uses skilful and expressive drawing and painting methods and a range of both conventional and unconventional materials to communicate these experiences to an audience so they can share them.

Detail of John Wolseley's *Camel Gate Border Track SA/VIC*. Image: Australian Galleries/licensed by Viscopy. Photo: Terence Bogue.

ARTWORK FRAMES: STRUCTURAL/SUBJECTIVE

Camel Gate Border Track SA/VIC is a series of small views and notations that together give us a rich experience of Wolseley's journey in the desert. He uses a combination of looking down on the land and looking across at it. He shows us landforms such as waterholes, hillocks and particular trees, as well as man-made structures such as fences, gates and dams. Unlike a conventional map, however, Wolseley alters size and distance and treats some things in a sketchy, linear way while others are rich with detail and painterly effects. He also records such events as birds and insects going about their normal activities, their tracks or their flight paths.

PRACTICE: IDEAS

Wolseley's idea is to have his audience experience what it's like to be in a particular place. His work is a record of his experiences in the Australian desert landscape and not just a copy of the view. Wolseley wants us to feel and understand a wider range of sensory experiences—the heat, the dust, the sounds, the textures—rather than a merely visual representation of the landscape. He also wants us to understand some of his personal relationships with the landscape, including a record of his artmaking with tears and smudges on the surface. He includes details and evidence other artists usually don't include, subjecting his paper to the same kinds of physical things as the land experiences: drought, rain, fire and dust storms.

PRACTICE: ACTIONS

Wolseley's practice involves documenting his trips into the landscape using drawings, painting, map-making and collections of found materials. These make up a record of his experience in a particular place, in this case on the border between South Australia and Victoria, in the desert. *Camel Gate Border Track SA/VIC* also examines the landscape in much more detail than a simple picture would do. He worked on site in this landscape, not in his studio. The process of making the work in this place becomes part of the work. Rips, tears and smudges that come from working on rough, dusty ground have become part of the story of this artwork and help tell us about his experience in the landscape. He uses pigments gathered on site to make paint, charcoal from his campfire or from burnt trees and makes rubbings of the textures and surfaces of the place he is in.

AUDIENCE

Wolseley has a wide audience. It ranges from people who may never have been in the bush, who view his work in a spotless art gallery far removed from the place where the work was made, to artists and people familiar with the bush who can recognise the signs of his experiences in the landscape in the work.

Student worksheet

WWW www.johnwolseley.net
www.australiangalleries.com.au/ag/artist/john_wolseley

Extension

Elizabeth Mpetyane, contemporary Utopia artist, Australia, *Bush Plum Dreaming*. Acrylic on canvas, 51 × 66 cm. Image: Ironwood Arts.

There are many different types of Aboriginal art, including bark painting, rock art carvings and paintings, weaving and wooden sculptures. Traditionally, Aboriginal people also decorated their bodies for ceremonies.

The contemporary Aboriginal art movement rose to prominence in the early 1970s at Pupunya, a community in the Western Desert of Western Australia. Today, Aboriginal art is known the world over and is highly valued. The use of dots in paintings is perhaps the most widely recognised feature of contemporary Aboriginal art. Dots can have many different meanings in a work. They can also sometimes be used to hide the meanings of symbols that are meant to be kept secret.

Aboriginal art refers to the stories and histories of its people. Aboriginal people have a deep connection with the land and this is reflected in their art whether it is traditional or contemporary. Aboriginal paintings are as much pictures *about* the land as they are pictures *of* the land. Their work represents a different way of 'seeing' the landscape.

Elizabeth Mpetyane is an Aboriginal artist from Utopia in the Northern Territory. Although a contemporary artist who makes work using conventional art materials such as acrylic paint and canvas, Mpetyane's work involves stories and traditions that are thousands of years old.

In *Bush Plum Dreaming*, Mpetyane has used different coloured dots to make a complex and beautiful painting. The way she has painted the dots gives the painting rhythm and texture. Some dots are larger and closer together than others and some dots are different colours. The dark background contrasts with the white and coloured dots, which adds to the painting's texture. Dots are applied one by one by dipping a small stick in paint and applying it to the canvas.

In your visual arts diary:

- list two important actions Elizabeth Mpetyane has taken to make this landscape painting, using the Artmaking Practice table in the Introduction to help you
- list the Structural Frame qualities in *Bush Plum Dreaming*, using the Frames table in the Introduction to help you
- list the symbols used and explain what you think they tell us about the landscape.

Discuss with your friends the different ways that artists respond to and interpret the landscape. Consider the work of Elizabeth Mpetyane as well as the work of all the other artists you have studied in this chapter. Discuss how a landscape painting can be both a visual and symbolic representation of the land. Refer to the Conceptual Framework chapter in the Introduction. Use this knowledge to list and sketch some ideas for more paintings and prints in your visual arts diary.

Responding to the landscape

Apart from the human body, the landscape is perhaps the most common subject for artists to depict in their work. In the past, artists have made work that responded to the landscape by copying it. Artists also made work to be placed in the landscape.

Land artists respond to the landscape by making it a vital part of the artwork itself. The work can be made from the land or interact with it in a direct way.

Artmaking sequence	Form	Artists
Let's make an artwork 1 *Bring it, weave it/find it, leave it*	Installation, textiles/ installation	• *Rani Brown* • Denise Litchfield, Andy Goldsworthy
Let's make an artwork 2 *Big things, little things*	Sculpture, collage	• *Anna-Maria O'Keeffe, Margarita Sampson* • Bronwyn Oliver; Sean O'Keeffe, Francis Scognamiglio and Robert Dyson, Richard Long

Let's make an artwork 1
Bring it, weave it/find it, leave it

Coming up with ideas   ARTMAKING PRACTICE

Make a site-specific installation in a natural or urban environment.

Discussion, research and planning in your visual arts diary

Student worksheet

CONCEPTUAL FRAMEWORK	PRACTICE	FRAMES
Artist	Ideas and actions	Structural—visual qualities, formal elements, symbols, planning
Artwork		Subjective—imagination, expression, spontaneity
World		Postmodern—questioning art rules, use of non-traditional technologies and materials
Audience		

Denise Litchfield, contemporary artist, *The Knitted Tree*, Australia, 2009. Knitted yarn, dimensions variable. © Denise Litchfield.

Andy Goldsworthy (1956–), UK, *Rowan leaves with hole*. © Andy Goldsworthy.

Look at the works of the two artists above, as well the artwork by **Rani Brown** further ahead in the chapter.

In your visual arts diary:

- discuss the ideas of each artist in relation to the rural or the urban landscape
- list two important actions each artist takes to make their artwork
- write which Frame each artist is working in (using the Frames table in the Introduction to help you) and describe the qualities of this Frame
- indicate one way each artist sets out to interest the audience.

Artists like Andy Goldsworthy, who make site-specific art in urban and natural landscapes, speak about understanding the language of the land. They do this by spending time in the landscape trying to understand how different elements relate to each other.

The works are always different because the land is always different and changing constantly. In the past, land artists often used materials such as steel and concrete to make work that intervened with the landscape, sometimes in permanent or destructive ways. Today we have a greater understanding about our impact on the world we live in. Artists have become increasingly sensitive to this in their creation of land art, and the trend is towards more impermanent work that often uses the natural materials of a chosen space in a non-destructive way. In order to make artwork that works with the landscape, it is important to spend time getting to know your particular place, as well as thinking about the materials and methods you will use to create your artwork.

- Decide whether you will make land art in a natural setting or an urban setting.
- Go for a walk in your chosen landscape. Identify likely places for your work. Don't forget to take into consideration the way you will photograph the work later.
- Take a good look at the materials available in your chosen landscape. What will you use to make your artwork?
- Will you choose to introduce or add materials to the landscape in order to make your work? Or will you make an impermanent work that has minimal impact on the natural landscape?
- Sketch some ideas and make notes in your visual arts diary for the works you will be making.

Taking action   ARTMAKING PRACTICE
Option 1   Installation

- Once you have identified a site for your work, and have checked a weather report to make sure you will have suitable weather, collect materials from the site to create your work. Discuss this with the rest of the class in order to guarantee a good distribution of what's available. Be mindful of the natural environment—you might decide to use only dead or inorganic materials, such as rocks and sticks, rather than living plants. Be careful when moving rocks and wood in bushland areas. Snakes, spiders and other fauna use rocks and logs as a habitat and present a potential danger.

- Once you have gathered your objects, arrange them together to make your work. Consider the elements of art such as texture, shape and colour when arranging your objects. You might wish to arrange rocks in order of shape or tone.
- Share school cameras, or use your own camera or mobile phone camera, to photograph your work. Consider when might be the best time of day to photograph your work in order to convey your idea.

Option 2   Textiles/installation

- Form a group of people to make a textile site-specific installation, inspired by the work of Denise Litchfield on page 184 and Rani Brown on page 187. You will need enough people to be able to physically install your installation. Identify the site where you wish to install your work. If it is an urban or public space, get permission first and take care that the work does not cause any permanent damage.
- Be aware of the right of public access to public space. Do not obstruct walkways or fire escapes and consider the audience of your work.
- Discuss the materials you will use and how you will install the work with your group. Consider existing features that might add to or inspire how your work will be installed.
- Decide whether you will make the artwork on the spot, responding specifically to the space, or whether you will make pieces of the work in advance in the classroom and bring them already made to the site.
- Make sure someone is designated to take photographs of the work when it is finished. Consider how you will photograph the work. What time suites the artwork best to convey your idea?

In-depth study
Rani Brown

CRITICAL AND HISTORICAL INTERPRETATIONS

CONCEPTUAL FRAMEWORK: WORLD

Rani Brown's world is that of the contemporary artist, teacher and social activist. She trained in painting and sculpture in Sydney at the College of Fine Arts. There she began to incorporate natural materials and woven elements into her two-dimensional painting. She is also a weaver who constructs woven objects using vines and weeds found in natural environments. Brown lived for some years on the North Coast of New South Wales, where she made sculptural work using local materials and created paintings as a way of highlighting local issues about the environment. Brown has travelled extensively and lived in a number of countries. Her work is often a personal response to landscapes she is living in.

Rani Brown, images from the installation *From Away*, 2002. Mixed woven objects and natural pigment installed at Lake Cawndilla, New South Wales. Images courtesy of the artist.
1971–, Australia

ARTIST FRAMES: STRUCTURAL/POSTMODERN

Brown's woven works reference the human impact on the natural environment, such as the overabundance of weeds and vines in some forests that results from the imbalance created by human settlement. By making and documenting work in one place, and then exhibiting it in another place (a gallery), Brown is setting up a connection between the two places: one wild and natural and the other artificial and controlled. Her Postmodern approach uses non-traditional materials, such as weeds.

ARTWORK FRAMES: STRUCTURAL/POSTMODERN

In her desert work *From Away,* Brown is referencing the human impact on the environment by recent European settlement and its early farming practices.

PRACTICE: IDEAS

The materials Brown uses and the sites she installs at are all informed by her ideas about the environment. Her installation work shows how humans impact on the world through their activities. Even the far desert of Australia has been changed by human contact. Introduced weeds and plants have spread to places that may never have been visited by humans, extending the reach of human impact. Brown's work is also about time, because the objects she places in the environment break down and fall apart. Unlike the much slower pace of natural change, the handmade objects she has woven last only briefly, perhaps making a reference to the relatively short time span of human existence.

PRACTICE: ACTIONS

In her land art project *From Away*, Brown explored her personal relationship with the outback landscape of Kinchega National Park, and in particular Lake Cawndilla, a large lake in the inland of this arid region of far western New South Wales. Her approach was to weave and construct a number of sculptural objects using locally sourced materials and introduced species. The works were then installed in an impermanent way on the shore of the lake. She documented this process with photography and video that were later shown in an art gallery alongside the objects she created on location. Some works were left to deteriorate on site, and these were later photographed over a period of months as they changed and broke down. Small balls of red sand that had been put along the edge of the lake dried up during drought, and as the water receded, the balls served as markers of where the water line had once been. As the sand dried out, the balls collapsed and eventually blew away.

AUDIENCE

Like many examples of land art, Brown's artwork is able to be viewed in two ways. The first requires the audience to visit the artwork while it is installed at the site, often travelling great distances to get there. The second, more common way is to view the exhibition of images of the installation in an art gallery. This way, the audience can get a sense of the installation experience heightened by the photographic skills of the artist. Land art photographs are sometimes made into books, which present the work to an even wider audience who may never have visited the actual site. Rani Brown has exhibited widely in galleries both in Australia and overseas, as well as site-specific sculpture exhibitions, such as 'Sculpture by the Sea'.

Student worksheet

Let's make an artwork 2

Big things, little things

Coming up with ideas   ARTMAKING PRACTICE

Make an artwork that imitates elements of a rural or urban landscape.

Discussion, research and planning in your visual arts diary

Student worksheet

CONCEPTUAL FRAMEWORK	PRACTICE	FRAMES
Artist	Ideas and actions	Structural—symbolism, visual qualities and composition
Artwork		
World		Subjective—imagination, expression, spontaneity
Audience		Postmodern—questioning art rules, use of non-traditional technologies and materials

Bronwyn Oliver (1959–), Australia, *Palm*, 1999. Copper structure, 190 × 180 × 180 cm. Sydney sculpture walk, Royal Botanic Gardens, Sydney. Image: Eiko Bron.

Sean O'Keeffe (1969–), Canada/Australia, **Francis Scognamiglio** (contemporary artist), Australia, **Robert Dyson** (1975–), Australia, *Big Bench*, 2003. Reinforced concrete, recycled timber. Image courtesy of the artists. Photographer: Robert Dyson.

Look at the works of the artists above, as well as the works by **Margarita Sampson** and **Anna-Maria O'Keeffe** further ahead in the chapter. Discuss with your friends how each artist has imitated an element of the landscape.

In your visual arts diary:

- explore the main idea in each artwork, identifying the different material choices the artists have made
- describe how some of the artists have manipulated the scale of their sculptures, and explain the role that scale plays in the impact of the images
- list two important actions each artist takes to make their sculpture
- write which Frame each artist uses (using the Frames Table in the Introduction to help you) and describe the qualities of that Frame you can see in the artworks
- indicate one way each artist sets out to interest the audience
- identify any elements in the sculptures that encourage audience interaction with the work
- collect images of outdoor sculpture from books, magazines and the internet to use as visual reference
- borrow and sketch some ideas for compositions of your own, based on these artworks and your own collection of images
- research and make notes on the methods and materials you will use.

Go for a walk in your local area to choose a site for a sculpture of your own. List and sketch some interesting objects or features of the space in your visual arts diary. You might like to take some photographs of the site as well.

Taking action   ARTMAKING PRACTICE

Option 1   Sculpture

- Using your notes and sketches of your chosen space, pick an element you will base your sculpture on. It might be a natural feature, such as a tree or a large rock, or an artificial feature, such as a picnic table, fire hydrant, post box or piece of rubbish.
- Consider the materials you will use to make your sculpture. How will these materials help communicate your idea? Will your sculpture be an exact copy of an object with every detail reproduced or will it explore the object in a totally new way?
- Using your sketches and photographs as visual reference, make your sculpture. Consider the scale of the object you have chosen. How will you distort or manipulate scale to make an impact with your work? Think about the colour of the object: how might this be used to create an impact?
- Once you have completed the construction of your object, take it back to the site (or a similar environment) and install the work. Watch for reactions to your installation by passersby and take photographs to document your work in the landscape.

Option 2   Collage

- Using some photographs and drawings you have made of your chosen site, make a collage of the site that shows what an imagined sculpture might look like in the space.
- You might choose to do these as collected photocopies or using photographic editing software.

In-depth study
Anna-Maria O'Keeffe
CRITICAL AND HISTORICAL INTERPRETATIONS

Anna-Maria O'Keeffe, *Small Mountain*, 2006. Mixed media, steel-welded support rods. Image courtesy of the artist.
1980–, Australia

CONCEPTUAL FRAMEWORK: WORLD

Anna-Maria O'Keeffe is an Australian artist from Melbourne currently living and working in Berlin. Her world is that of the international contemporary artist.

ARTIST FRAMES: POSTMODERN/STRUCTURAL

O'Keeffe is a Postmodern artist who makes work that challenges our understanding of what art can be. She uses the materials and techniques of hobby modellers to make new kinds of artwork.

ARTWORK FRAMES: POSTMODERN/STRUCTURAL

O'Keeffe makes land art, like *Small Mountain*, by literally reproducing sections of land as small suspended or raised objects, which she then exhibits as sculpture in art galleries.

PRACTICE: IDEAS

The pieces O'Keeffe makes show the effects of human habitation on the environment. Her land chunks suffer from erosion and degradation by humans. The pieces are often supported on miniature steel girders or hanging from small industrial crane supports. This makes reference to the devastating effect of human industry on the land.

PRACTICE: ACTIONS

O'Keeffe uses the same techniques that architecture and train set modellers use to create her sculptures. She carefully researches her land forms with visits, drawings and photographs. A skilled draughtsperson, Anna-Maria is able to pre-plan every detail of her work. The support cranes are all handmade from individually cut and welded steel rods. However, unlike train and architecture models, Anna-Maria's sculptures do not celebrate the achievements of industry. Her landscapes are carefully researched in order to convey a sense of accuracy. They are similar to the photographs made by other land artists, documenting the land that has been affected by the artist in order to maximise the impact of their idea.

AUDIENCE

Now living in Europe, O'Keeffe exhibits to an international audience through art galleries. Her works comment about the land by being away from it, because her sculptures are pieces of land that have been removed from their natural site and put on display.

WWW annamariaokeeffe.blogspot.com/
www.westspace.org.au/program/anna-maria-o-keeffe.html

In-depth study
Margarita Sampson

CRITICAL AND HISTORICAL INTERPRETATIONS

CONCEPTUAL FRAMEWORK: WORLD

Margarita Sampson's world is that of Norfolk Island, an island in the Pacific Ocean between Australia and New Zealand. Margarita studied art in Australia, and lived and worked in Australia and Europe before returning home to Norfolk Island.

ARTIST FRAMES: POSTMODERN/STRUCTURAL

Sampson is a Postmodern artist who makes work in response to the environment of Norfolk Island and the South Pacific. Her work references natural forms, such as sea anemones and plant life.

ARTWORK FRAMES: CULTURAL/SUBJECTIVE

Big Mumma and the Kittens is a large sculptural work that mimics the textures and form of sea anemones. The artwork is also Sampson's response to her personal relationship with Norfolk Island. She is responding to the physical as well as social geography of the island. All her works are metaphors about the natural and social history of Norfolk, which includes the Polynesian history as well as the colonial history. Margarita is an avid cat lover, and this work may in fact be a self portrait.

Margarita Sampson, *Big Mumma and the Kittens*, 2006. Variable-sized installation, PVC textiles, beading, polystyrene beads. Image courtesy of Adrian Tan.
1969–, Australia

PRACTICE: IDEAS

Margarita is interested in the beauty and complexity of natural forms. Her work is influenced by the crosscurrents between the traditional European and Pacific Islander cultures of Norfolk Island. She has a special interest in both cultures' use of handcraft skills such as needlework.

PRACTICE: ACTIONS

Big Mumma and the Kittens has been hand-stitched using nylon and PVC. The materials are not natural and serve to contrast with the natural subject matter. The process Sampson uses to make these objects is a traditional one. The hand-stitching makes a reference to the cultural traditions of women on Norfolk Island. It also highlights the amazing alien nature of undersea plant life. Margarita, like Denise Litchfield, has taken a traditional practice and made a contemporary statement about cultural traditions.

AUDIENCE

Sampson installs her work back into the environments that were its inspiration. Regularly exhibited at popular outdoor sculptural events such as 'Sculpture by the Sea', her work creates a link between the natural environment that draws human interest and the artificial reality of the urban human world. Sampson's attention to detail and startling choice of materials encourages a sense of wonder in the audience about the natural environment.

WWW www.margaritasampson.nlk.nf
www.sculpturebythesea.com

Student
worksheet

Extension

Crop circles, UK. Image: Steve Alexander.

Richard Long (1945–), UK, *Mahalakshmi Hill Line*, Warli Tribal Land, Maharashtra, India, 2003. Image: Haunch of Venison Gallery/licensed by Viscopy.

Uffington White Horse, UK. Image: Corbis.

- Look at the artworks above. What do you think is the purpose and meaning of each artwork? Answer in your visual arts diary.

- If you were going to make an artwork like the *Uffington White Horse*, what would you choose as an image? Why? Answer in your visual arts diary.
- Use the internet to view as many different crop circle designs as possible, and discuss them with your classmates.
- Using a digital camera or mobile phone camera, document a walk you do daily. Perhaps it is your walk to school, or a daily walk to the shops, or maybe you take your dog for a daily walk. Look for evidence of your walk on the way. Perhaps there is a worn patch of grass pathway, or other evidence of its regular use. Document this evidence.

www http://www.richardlong.org/sculptures/3

Chapter 17

It's my space

We all need a space to call our own. Sometimes it's a private space where we spend a lot of our time, keep things the way we want and where we feel safe; sometimes it's in public spaces where we feel comfortable and enjoy ourselves, like our neighbourhood, town or city; and sometimes our space exists entirely in our imagination as our ideal space.

Artmaking sequence	Form	Artists
Let's make an artwork 1 *Love my space*	Photography, photomontage	• *Les Slesnick* • Richard Hamilton, Isidro Blasco
Let's make an artwork 2 *Staying in/going out*	Drawing or painting, printmaking	• *Chico Monks* • Vincent Van Gogh, Martin Sharp, Matt Coyle, Brett Whiteley, Nikky Morgan-Smith

Let's make an artwork 1
Love my space

Coming up with ideas   ARTMAKING PRACTICE

Take a series of photographs or make a photomontage about private and public spaces.

CRITICAL AND HISTORICAL INTERPRETATIONS
Discussion, research and planning in your visual arts diary

CONCEPTUAL FRAMEWORK	PRACTICE	FRAMES
Artist Artwork World Audience	Ideas and actions	Structural—symbolism to give meaning, visual qualities, planned composition Subjective—expressive and imaginative qualities Cultural—your personal identity Postmodern—borrowing ideas and methods from other artists

Student worksheet

Richard Hamilton (1922–), UK, *Just What is it that Makes Today's Homes So Different, So Appealing?*, 1956. Collage, 26 × 25 cm. Image: DACS/Viscopy/Bridgeman Art.

Isidro Blasco (1962–), Spain, *Courtyard*, 2008. 3-D C print photographs, museum board, wood, hardware, 270 × 360 × 120 cm. Photo courtesy of the artist and Dominik Mersch Gallery.

Look at the works of the two artists above, as well as the work by **Les Slesnick** further ahead in the chapter.

In your visual arts diary:

- discuss each artist's ideas in relation to their concept of space
- list several important actions each artist takes, referring to the forms used, the materials and the methods

TEACHER NOTE

Have a class discussion about ways in which the artists in this section set out to interest the audience. Have students take notes in their visual arts diaries.

- write which Frame each artist is working in (using the Frames table in the Introduction to help you) and describe the qualities of that Frame you can see in the artworks
- list the symbols used in one of the works and explain what you think they tell us about the meaning of the artwork
- sketch and make notes on some ideas borrowed from these artworks to help you come up with your own representation of your space.

Taking action   ARTMAKING PRACTICE

Option 1   Photography

- Think about a private space of your own that you would like to photograph using the Structural Frame (symbolism to give meaning). Look at the work of Les Slesnick on page 200 for inspiration.
- Choose a part of your space that communicates something about you, and carefully arrange in this space the objects that are important in your life.

photomontage: an image made by combining photographs or parts of photographs, either by hand or using computer software

- Use a digital camera and experiment with using different lighting conditions from different angles to take a series of photographs.
- Download the images onto a school or home computer and use photographic editing software to manipulate the image until you feel it has the right mood and reflects what you want to communicate.

Option 2   Photomontage

- Plan a **photomontage** of your imagined ideal private space, using the Structural Frame (a planned composition), or the Subjective Frame (imaginative visual qualities) to express your feelings about your chosen space. Look back at the work of Richard Hamilton on page 197 for inspiration.
- Use a digital camera to take some photographs of a private space of your own, and collect more images from books, magazines and the internet.

- Download the photos onto a school or home computer and scan the book and magazine images into the computer. Use photographic editing software to assemble the images to create your ideal space.
- Manipulate your images to create different effects (such as bands of transparent and semi-transparent overlays) that express your emotional responses.
- Use the Cultural Frame and introduce aspects of your personal identity in the objects you choose.

Low-tech alternative

- Use either a digital or a non-digital camera to photograph your private space.
- Print out your photographs.
- Cut images from books and magazines, and print images from the internet.
- Cut and paste your photos and images to create a photomontage by hand.

Extension

- Take a series of digital photographs of a public space where you feel comfortable and enjoy yourself.
- Using the Postmodern Frame, borrow some ideas and methods from the work of Isidro Blasco on page 197.
- Print the photos, and then make multiple colour photocopies of them.
- Arrange the photos on stiff cardboard and/or foamcore.
- Manipulate the images by combining, repeating and overlapping them so that you begin to create 3-D spaces.
- When you are happy with the arrangement, use thin strips of wood or wooden dowel glued with PVA behind the images as a framework that will hold the work together and allows the work to stand up.

foamcore: lightweight board with a styrofoam centre often used to mount artworks or in architectural model construction

In-depth study
Les Slesnick

CRITICAL AND HISTORICAL INTERPRETATIONS

CONCEPTUAL FRAMEWORK: WORLD

Les Slesnick is a photographer who has always been interested in the movies and has taken photographs since he was nine or 10 years old. The black and white photography of Walker Evans, best known for his stark photographs of people in rural USA who were affected by the Great Depression, and Bruce Davidson's documentary photographs of the Civil Rights era in the USA are influences on his work.

ONLINE RESOURCES

Les Slesnick

Les Slesnick, *Dunedin Project #7*, 2007, from the series *Private Spaces*. Digital colour photograph. © Les Slesnick.
1942–, USA

ARTIST FRAME: STRUCTURAL/CULTURAL

Slesnick works within the Structural Frame using photographic technologies and techniques as well as strong compositions and striking visual qualities to give meaning to his photographs. But, because he is also interested in documenting the cultural values and identities of the people whose home he enters and photographs, he works within the Cultural Frame as well. He passes no judgment on these families, who he says tend to display in their homes what they value most in life. He asks no questions about their motives in what they display, seeing his role as being to record what is there and make beautiful photographs.

ARTWORK FRAME: STRUCTURAL/CULTURAL

The *Dunedin Project* is a glimpse into a little girl's bedroom. The wardrobe door is ajar and hanging in proud display are the costumes she wears in the talent and beauty pageants in which her mother enters her. On top is a still-life array of other things that are important to her, including a blonde wig, family photos, and a collection of small objects all in different shades of pink. The photograph was shot in a small town in Florida in 2007.

PRACTICE: IDEAS

The photographer's main idea in this image is to give his audience insights into the nature and identity of the little girl who owns this bedroom without actually including a portrait of her. His work has often been called 'people-less portraits'. Slesnick plays with the idea that we can know about the little girl by looking at her space and at the small ordinary things with which she surrounds herself. When he captures these in a photograph they take on new significance, revealing their meaning slowly over several viewings. He also explores the idea that out of this he is able to create an image that is beautiful and visually stimulating.

PRACTICE: ACTIONS

The photo shoot for the *Dunedin Project* took 17 days and needed extensive preparation ahead of time so that the photographer had access to many homes within the community of Dunedin at particular times. The people whose homes were being photographed had been asked not to change their homes but to allow them to be documented in their usual state. Like many contemporary photographers, Les Slesnick has moved to digital photography using a Nikon digital SLR camera and a wide-angle lens because he is usually working in very small rooms. He makes sure his shots are as faithful a representation of the scene as possible and then uses software such as Photoshop Elements to adjust tonal and light qualities.

AUDIENCE

Slesnick believes that his work appeals to any audience because it has a voyeuristic quality. The images are peeks behind the curtains into the bathrooms, living rooms, dining rooms, kitchens and bedrooms of the homes of strangers, and this feeds a natural curiosity about how others live. He uses the internet, making his work accessible to a wide audience.

WWW www.privatespaces.org/usa.htm
www.lesslesnick.com/uk.htm

Let's make an artwork 2
Staying in/going out

Coming up with ideas   ARTMAKING PRACTICE

Paint, draw or print images of your space.

Discussion, research and planning in your visual arts diary

CONCEPTUAL FRAMEWORK	PRACTICE	FRAMES
Artist	Ideas and actions	Structural—symbolism to give meaning, visual qualities, planned composition
Artwork		Subjective—expressive and imaginative qualities
World		Cultural—your personal identity
Audience		Postmodern—borrowing ideas and actions from other artists

Student worksheet

Vincent Van Gogh (1853–1890), Netherlands, *Bedroom at Arles*, 1888. Oil on canvas, 72 × 90 cm. The Art Archive/Musée d'Orsay Paris/Alfredo Dagli Orti/Picdesk.

Brett Whiteley (1939–1992), Australia, *Self Portrait in the Studio*, 1976. Painting, oil, collage, hair on canvas, 200 × 260 cm. Collection: Art Gallery of New South Wales, Sydney. © Wendy Whiteley.

Martin Sharp (1942–), Australia, *Fragments of a (f)unfair, lest we forget*, 1991. Screen-print on paper, 112 × 77 cm. Image: Historic Houses Trust of New South Wales/Viscopy.

Nikky Morgan-Smith (1979–), Vanuatu, *5 baths a day in shades of magenta*, 2008. Acrylic on ply, 90 × 123 cm. © Nikky Morgan-Smith.

Matt Coyle (1971–), Australia, *Self Portrait with Television*, 2007. Pen on paper, 40 × 36 cm. Image: Anna Pappas Gallery.

Look at the works of the five artists on page 202, as well as the artwork of **Chico Monks** further ahead in the chapter.

In your visual arts diary:

- list two important actions each artist takes, using the Artmaking Practice table in the Introduction to help you
- write which Frame each artist is working in (using the Frames table in the Introduction to help you) and describe the qualities of that Frame you can see in the artworks
- list the symbols used in one of the artworks and explain what you think they tell us about the meaning of the artwork
- explore some aspects of the world of the artist whose work most appeals to you, and describe how these have affected their artmaking, using the Conceptual Framework table in the Introduction to help you
- sketch and make notes on ideas borrowed from these artworks to help you come up with your own representation of your space.

TEACHER NOTE

Have a class discussion about each artist's chosen space. Refer to the Artmaking Practice table in the Introduction.

Taking action   ARTMAKING PRACTICE

Option 1   Drawing or painting

- Ask a friend or someone in your family to take a series of photographs of you in your own space, such as in your bedroom.
- Working from the photographs, make a drawing or painting of yourself in your space. Work in one of the following Frames:
  - **Structural Frame:** plan your composition and use methods and materials skilfully (look back at the drawing by Matt Coyle and the painting by Brett Whiteley on page 202)
  - **Cultural Frame:** communicate aspects of your identity to an audience (look back at the artworks by Van Gogh and Brett Whiteley on page 202 and look further ahead at the artworks by Chico Monks on page 205)
  - **Subjective Frame:** express yourself imaginatively in your space (look back at the artworks of Van Gogh, Nikky Morgan-Smith and Brett Whiteley on page 202, and look further ahead at the artworks of Chico Monks on page 205).
- Use the photographs as visual reference, but experiment with visual qualities, methods and materials that reflect the Frame you are using.
- You may want to draw a grid over any photographs you use to help get your composition and proportions looking natural.
- Include some of your personal images or symbols.
- Use some collage or found objects in your painting to add visual interest.

Option 2 Printmaking

- Think of a public space you've visited lately where your imagination was stimulated, where you felt comfortable and enjoyed yourself; for example, maybe you've recently been to a theme park such as Luna Park, or to a zoo or aquarium.
- Borrowing Martin Sharp's style of representation, see page 202 and make a lino print of this public space.
- Use the Structural Frame, such as visual qualities that communicate the unique lines, colours, shapes, textures and movement of the public space.
- Use one lino plate to print at least three colours by progressively cutting away more lino from the plate. Print each colour exactly over the top of the first colour. Print the lightest colour first.

In-depth study
Chico Monks

CRITICAL AND HISTORICAL INTERPRETATIONS

CONCEPTUAL FRAMEWORK: WORLD

Chico Monks has found himself in a clash of different worlds. He was born on the North Coast of New South Wales and he and his parents, who were artists, always lived in the bush in a house with no TV. Now he finds himself in the urban world of the city of Sydney where he has had to make the transition to becoming both a practising artist and a teacher of art at an inner-city college. His influences have been the Australian sculptor Robert Klippel, and both traditional and contemporary Aboriginal artists whose work he has come into contact with through his teaching.

ARTIST FRAMES: POSTMODERN/CULTURAL

Monks is an artist who makes sculptures and mixed-media paintings. He uses aspects of the Postmodern Frame and the Cultural Frame to make art. He often borrows images and ideas from the work of other artists when he is using collage. He also explores aspects of his own identity. He has Indigenous heritage but believes he does not know enough about this part of his heritage to think of himself as an Indigenous artist. He believes that just as his sense of self and identity is never quite resolved, and is always evolving, so is his artmaking practice.

ARTWORK FRAMES: SUBJECTIVE/STRUCTURAL

In *Stepsmall Long Bay*, Monks has divided the picture into four spaces. The whole work appears as if on a red, flat plane. Just above the red line in the centre are visual references to Long Bay Gaol with its row of gates and towers. From one of these is a plume of white smoke that is symbolic of the Indigenous smoking ceremony that purifies. The smoke travels across a collaged piece of an Aboriginal painting cut from an exhibition invitation and then exits at the top. Two mysterious words, 'step' and 'small', point to each other. Below the red line is the outside world. Here semi-abstract hills, mountains and the bush are beginning to turn into the buildings of the city in the lowest space. *House* makes use of a collection of found objects, some in relief and some fully three-dimensional, that together give the audience a glimpse into a more personal space.

PRACTICE: IDEAS

Stepsmall Long Bay was painted while the artist was teaching art in Long Bay Gaol and being confronted on a daily basis by the problems of his students, the prisoners. Some of his students seemed to have little sense of their own and other people's space or identity. The artist paints a space that he thinks might approximate what he and they were experiencing; although he is locked in with the prisoners during his teaching, unlike them, at the end of the day, he can leave. Monks's idea was to represent the different spaces of this Long Bay world using the same contained and fragmented spaces that make up the gaol itself and explore how it was affecting his own inner self and sense of space and identity. *House* is based on the artist's domestic space so he surrounds himself with things that reflect the idea of being at home and he presents them in a wooden framework that is divided into different rooms, like a house.

PRACTICE: ACTIONS

Monks is an artist who makes use of what's around him and uses painting and assemblage methods. He is influenced by the work of other artists to the point where he actually collages parts of the invitations to their exhibitions into his artworks. The surface of *Stepsmall Long Bay* resembles a relief sculpture but is still a flat painting, while *House* is more sculptural.

Chico Monks, *Stepsmall Long Bay*, 2008. Acrylic paint, mixed media, collage, felt-tip pens, textas in found frame, 32 × 40 cm. © Chico Monks. Image: Retrospect Galleries.
1978–, Australia

Chico Monks, *House*. Mixed media, 62 × 78 cm. © Chico Monks. Image: Retrospect Galleries.
1978–, Australia

Monks has used disassembled boxes, architectural and lettering stencils, felt-tip pens and MDF letters usually used in craft-making as stencils. For example: the smoke is formed by a series of 2s and a 9 joined together and painted white in *Stepsmall Long Bay*; in *House* he uses small plastic toy figures, and fragments of metal that he shapes into things such as an armchair, a cactus in a pot and a tiny yellow plastic house.

AUDIENCE

Monks has exhibited his work in art galleries in Sydney and Byron Bay and has his own website so that people who are interested in his work can access it easily. His audience consists of people who appreciate contemporary art.

WWW www.chicomonks.com/home.htm
www.robingibson.net/
www.retrospectgalleries.com

The built world

We build buildings for shelter, to live and work in and for sport and culture. We build on a small scale, but also on a towering scale. Sometimes our buildings look as though they are part of the natural world; at other times they are so big, and there are so many of them, that they make their own urban world: the city. The built world is an important part of our culture and we often refer to it in our art.

Artmaking sequence	Form	Artists
Let's make an artwork 1 *Urbana*	Photography, photomontage	• *Peter Hill, Dave Bowman* • Ezra Stoller, Justin Mackintosh, Sheila Smart
Let's make an artwork 2 *Suburbana*	Drawing, painting, printmaking	• *Paul Balmer* • Jonathan Farr, Peter O'Doherty, Anne Starling

Let's make an artwork 1
Urbana

Coming up with ideas   ARTMAKING PRACTICE

Take a series of photographs of tall buildings, interesting architecture and suburban houses, or make a photomontage.

Discussion, research and planning in your visual arts diary

Student worksheet

CONCEPTUAL FRAMEWORK	PRACTICE	FRAMES
Artist Artwork World Audience	Ideas and actions	Structural—methods and materials, visual qualities, planned composition Subjective—imaginative and expressive qualities

Ezra Stoller (1915–2004), USA, *Fallingwater* (Architect: Frank Lloyd Wright), 1963. Colour transparency, 10.16 × 12.7 cm. Photographer: Ezra Stoller/Esto.

Justin Mackintosh (1971–), Australia, *Rose Seidler House* (Architect: Harry Seidler & Associates), 2006. C print photograph. © Justin Mackintosh. Macintosh Photography.

Sheila Smart (1945–), UK/Australia, *Opera House and Sydney Harbour Bridge early morning* (Opera House designed by Jørn Utzon), 2004. Digital photograph. Image: Sheila Smart Photography.

Look at the works of the artists on page 208 as well as those of **Peter Hill** and **Dave Bowman** further ahead in the chapter.

In your visual arts diary:

- discuss the ideas of each photographer, and relate these to the ideas of the architects of the buildings photographed, using the Artmaking Practice table in the Introduction to help you
- list two important actions each photographer and each architect takes to take a photograph or design the building, using the Artmaking Practice table in the Introduction to help you
- write which Frame each artist is working in (using the Frames table in the Introduction to help you) and describe the qualities of that Frame you can see in the artworks
- list and sketch some ideas for photographs you will take of buildings on an excursion.

TEACHER NOTE

Have a class discussion about the ways each photographer and each architect sets out to interest the audience. Refer to the Conceptual Framework table in the Introduction.

Taking action   ARTMAKING PRACTICE

Option 1   Photography

TEACHER NOTE

Organise an excursion so students can photograph distinctive groups of buildings (e.g. a shopping centre, rows of houses or apartments) or architecturally interesting buildings (e.g. churches, mosques, shearing sheds or factories).

- Share school cameras, or use your own camera or your mobile phone camera.
- Work in small groups to take a series of digital photographs of buildings. Look back at the photographs by Ezra Stoller, Justin Mackintosh and Sheila Smart on page 208, and look at the artworks of Peter Hill and Dave Bowman on pages 210 and 212 for inspiration.
- Make use of aspects of the Structural Frame when making decisions about visual qualities, symbols, images and composition.
- Use of a variety of different viewpoints and angles from which to take your shots; for example, looking up, looking across, looking down, silhouetted against the sky, reflected in glass windows and so on.
- Download the images onto a school or home computer and choose a series of six photos.
- Use photographic editing software to make the photos as clear and crisp as possible, and experiment with editing some images using the Subjective Frame (imagination, expressive colour and fantasy, for example). Exaggerate colour and texture, crop, enhance, adjust or add effects to capture a particular mood or atmosphere in your photographs.

Option 2

Photomontage

- Collect photographic images from magazines, as well as some of the photos you have taken on your class excursion.

- Make a large photomontage using a planned, structured approach. Choose a theme for your photomontage, such as 'Glass and Steel', 'Cool City' or 'Disintegration', depending on the type of architecture and building images you can access.
- Download your photos onto a school or home computer and scan your collected images into the computer. Use photographic editing software to arrange the images into a photomontage.

Low-tech alternative
- Print the photos from your excursion.
- Cut the collected images out of the magazines and cut and paste them with your photos to create your photomontage.

In-depth study

Peter Hill

CRITICAL AND HISTORICAL INTERPRETATIONS

Peter Hill, *The Grace Hotel—Sydney*, 2009. Digital photograph, 4800 dpi. © Peter Hill.
1961–, Australia

CONCEPTUAL FRAMEWORK: WORLD

Peter Hill's world is that of contemporary photography. Although he is based in Sydney, his work can be viewed on the website RedBubble, making it international.

ONLINE RESOURCES

Peter Hill

ARTIST FRAMES: STRUCTURAL

Hill is mostly interested in the visual qualities of his subjects. He visits a site or subject again and again to really get to know what he wants to capture with his camera. He then looks at formal elements, such as the linear qualities, and at positive and negative space, and decides on the composition and what he wants to emphasise.

ARTWORK FRAMES: STRUCTURAL

The Grace Hotel in the city of Sydney is a striking building in the inter-war skyscraper Gothic style, designed by the architecture firm Morrow & Gordon. It opened in 1930 and was modelled on the Tribune Tower in Chicago, USA. Hill's photograph captures the soaring vertical lines of the building and its monumental facade, which resembles a vertical stone cliff. To add to the dynamism of the image, the clouds above look as though they are streaming out of the top of the building.

PRACTICE: IDEAS

The artist had been looking at this building continually as he drove through the city. The Grace Hotel dominates the area with an imposing stone presence that is in marked contrast to the newer buildings that surround it. He had an idea that he most wanted to capture the vastness of the building and its vertical lines

PRACTICE: ACTIONS

The Grace Hotel—Sydney was shot on the spur of the moment on a Sunday when there was no traffic and the early morning light was just right. Hill used a Canon EOS 5D Mark II digital SLR camera.

> *I was able to take my time in getting the right angle, perspective, and distance to maximise the effect of the building's presence and lines. The light was just right. Dawn and early morning light is the best time to shoot outdoors, and the building was facing the sun as it arose from below the line of buildings in front across the intersection. Right time. Right place.*
> Peter Hill

When Hill photographed the Grace Hotel, the sky was cloudless and offered no contrast to bring out the lines and strength of the building. However, he had some sky shots he had taken several days previously, and he used his Photoshop software to merge the two images to create the finished work.

AUDIENCE

Hill is planning for his first exhibition in Sydney, but currently exhibits his photography online only. His audience is mainly other photographers. However, this is changing, as his audience broadens to include anyone with an appreciation of photography as art.

WWW www.redbubble.com/people/peterh111
www.sydneyarchitecture.com

In-depth study
Dave Bowman
CRITICAL AND HISTORICAL INTERPRETATIONS

Dave Bowman, *Empire State Building*, 2006. Photograph. © DaveBowmanPhotography.com
1965–, UK

monochrome: one
colour and tones of
that colour

CONCEPTUAL FRAMEWORK: WORLD

Dave Bowman's world is that of international photography. Although he trained initially in the UK as an illustrator, he became increasingly drawn to photography as a fine art form. He is influenced by the street photography of John Deakin, the humour of Elliott Erwitt, and the honesty of Richard Avedon's *In the American West* portraiture.

ARTIST FRAMES: STRUCTURAL

The photographs of Dave Bowman show his interest in visual qualities and the formal elements of design and composition, especially at the moment he actually captures an image with his camera. However, as he processes the photographs on the computer, he uses symbolism to give his images meaning on a deeper level. In *Empire State Building,* 2006, his use of the colour blue is symbolic of mystery and imagination rather than the everyday qualities we usually associate with city buildings.

ARTWORK FRAMES: STRUCTURAL

The Empire State Building is, in Bowman's photograph, tilted on a diagonal to emphasise its dynamic height. It is framed on either side by darker, **monochrome** structures to further emphasise its soaring qualities. A cool blue haze envelops the Empire State, suggesting unearthly, detached, distant qualities, turning what is in reality an office block into an object of mystery.

PRACTICE: IDEAS

The Empire State Building is an **Art Deco** skyscraper designed and built between 1929 and 1931 and is the tallest building in New York. As such, it is a popular attraction for anyone who visits New York and the subject of countless photographs. Bowman's idea was to photograph one of the world's most well-known buildings in such a way that the elements of shape, form and light would together achieve new levels of interest in this icon. He doesn't set out to convey a specific message at the time he takes the photograph but is more interested in the visual qualities and composition.

PRACTICE: ACTIONS

Bowman uses Canon and Leica digital cameras and lenses. This photograph was shot using available light and was then digitally manipulated using a Mac Pro computer. During this process, Bowman made decisions about the mood he wanted to convey. He uses photographic editing software to crop and give the image a diagonal viewpoint. He deepens tones in the foreground and lightens them on the main building. He makes the lower buildings become monochromatic, and to contrast with this, turns the Empire State Building blue.

AUDIENCE

Bowman's photography has featured in a number of books and publications and is accessible to a wide audience on the internet, on his own site and others. He does not set out to take photographs for an audience but believes that if he thinks it's interesting, the chances are that others will too.

www www.davebowmanphotography.com
www.redbubble.com/people/davebowman

Art Deco: an art, design and architecture style popular from the 1920s to the 1940s, using geometric designs and bold colours

ONLINE RESOURCES

Dave Bowman

Let's make an artwork 2
Suburbana

Coming up with ideas ARTMAKING PRACTICE

Draw, paint and print images of the city or of the suburban home.

Discussion, research and planning in your visual arts diary

CONCEPTUAL FRAMEWORK	PRACTICE	FRAMES
Artist	Ideas and actions	Structural—methods and materials, visual qualities, planned composition
Artwork		
World		Subjective—imaginative and expressive qualities
Audience		

Student worksheet

Jonathan Farr, contemporary artist, UK, *Tottenham Court Road from Centrepoint 2*, 2007. Charcoal on paper, 100 × 150 cm. © Jonathan Farr.

Peter O'Doherty (1958–), NZ/Australia, *Steep Drive Maroubra*, 2007. Acrylic on canvas, 61 × 61 cm. © Peter O'Doherty. Photo courtesy of King Street Gallery on William.

Anne Starling (1967–), Australia, *Home Beautiful*, 2009. Lino block, etching, chine collé, 56 × 60 cm. Photograph by Joseph Harb.

Look at the works of the three artists above, as well as the work by **Paul Balmer** further ahead in the chapter.

In your visual arts diary:

- list two important actions each artist takes to make their artwork, using the Artmaking Practice table in the Introduction to help you
- write which Frame each artist is working in (using the Frames table in the Introduction to help you) and describe the qualities of that Frame you can see in the artworks
- explore some aspects of the world of the artist whose work most appeals to you, and describe how these have influenced their artmaking, using the Conceptual Framework table in the Introduction to help you
- collect photographs and images and make some notes on the ideas of the artists you have studied to help you come up with some ideas about your own artworks of buildings.

Taking action   ARTMAKING PRACTICE
Option 1   Drawing

- Use photographs of modern-looking buildings that you took for 'Let's make an artwork 1', or find suitable photographic images in books, magazines or the internet.
- Make a drawing of a partial view of a modern house or apartment using the Structural Frame, for example, modern visual qualities such as straight edges, geometric shapes, repeated lines and a planned composition. Look at the painting by Peter O'Doherty above for inspiration.

- Use drawing materials such as soft pastels, and methods such as perspective, tonal modelling, a dynamic viewpoint and cool, modern colours.
- Keep looking at the photograph and work carefully to keep your drawing crisp and modern.

Option 2 Painting

- Use the Subjective Frame to paint images of some aspects of your city or town. Look at the painting by Paul Balmer on page 216 for inspiration.
- Use imagination, expressive brushstrokes, textured paint, exaggerated colour, and some distortion or abstraction to create a particular mood or atmosphere.
- Use a variety of viewpoints, diagonal angles, patterns of light and shade, textures, details of architecture and repetition to enhance the mood.

Option 3 Printmaking

- Use the Structural Frame to design a hand-coloured lino print based on a suburban house.
- Look back at the print by Anne Starling and the painting by Peter O'Doherty on page 214.
- Use the photographs you took for 'Let's make an artwork 1', or, if these aren't suitable, collect images of suburban houses from magazines or the internet as visual reference.
- Carefully compose the design, making use of the qualities of the lino to give crisp edges as well as pattern and texture.
- Cut and print lino in black on white paper.
- Hand-colour your print carefully with coloured inks or acrylic paint.

In-depth study
Paul Balmer

CRITICAL AND HISTORICAL INTERPRETATIONS

CONCEPTUAL FRAMEWORK: WORLD

Paul Balmer's world is that of contemporary art in New York City, one of the great art centres of the world. His art education began in Australia where he studied visual arts and graphic design. He initially worked in illustration and advertising but now works solely as an artist. Although his subject matter is New York cityscapes, the colours, shapes, simplicity and originality of his work is influenced by his background in South Africa and Australia.

Paul Balmer, *Summer Shadow*, 2008. Oil on canvas, 163 × 163 cm.
1964–, South Africa/USA

ARTIST FRAMES: SUBJECTIVE

Balmer works in an imaginative and expressive way. He doesn't want to draw or paint realistically. He wants to produce artworks that are imaginative images, expressing his delight in the city of New York.

ARTWORK FRAMES: SUBJECTIVE

In *Summer Shadow*, 2008, Balmer depicts the tall buildings of New York, including the iconic Chrysler Building, against a backdrop of the Hudson River as the sun is setting. We recognise the images but they are simplified, abstracted, richly textured and warmly coloured versions, made into a rich evocation of a city that the artist obviously loves.

PRACTICE: IDEAS

Balmer lives in New York and imagines the multitude of its tall buildings bisected by streets as a landscape of majestic peaks, deep ravines and canyons lit by the setting sun. In his painting, the city has become a painted, urban equivalent of the Grand Canyon. His idea is to paint the essence of the city as a majestic landscape, not to depict it realistically.

PRACTICE: ACTIONS

Balmer has made many sketches of the city, but his paintings are done from memory and imagination rather than from direct observation. He paints on canvas using layers of thick oil paint. When this is dry he carefully sands it back so that the under-painted colours begin to show through. The distinctive Art Deco roof of the Chrysler Building, and the patterns created by buildings with many windows, are simplified forms painted as rich textures and intricate details. He creates a sense of depth by painting the buildings brightly lit and emerging from the shadowed streets below. The buildings are depicted as solid towers silhouetted against an orange background that is like the flat backdrop on a theatre stage.

AUDIENCE

Paul Balmer's paintings are increasingly being shown in art galleries all over the world. His paintings work on an emotional level to engage the interest of his audience and to communicate to them the artist's feelings about his new home city.

WWW www.paulbalmer.com

Glossary

abstract:
not representing reality

action drawing:
a style of drawing where the process of drawing is itself the main subject of the work; the drawing can be scribbles, fast scratches or slow squiggles

action painting:
a style of painting in which the main idea is the movement and action of splashing, dribbling or dragging the paint across the surface in a random and energetic way

aerial:
a perspective of the landscape as seen from high in the air, such as the view from an aircraft, crane or high building

Art Deco:
an art, design and architecture style popular from the 1920s to the 1940s, using geometric designs and bold colours

assemblage:
in sculpture, the joining of individual pieces or objects into an arrangement using any suitable equipment, such as PVA glue to join wood, or a soldering iron to join metal

atelier:
artist's studio

binder:
a substance added to an artwork to form a protective coating

cabinet of curiosities:
a room or a display cupboard in which are kept collections of objects of natural history, such as plant specimens

critique:
comment on something's good and bad qualities

Cubism:
a style of modern painting begun in France in the early 20th century that featured flat, fragmented and geometric representations of objects, shown from more than one view point

deity:
a god, goddess, or other divine being

diptych:
a pair of paintings that together make one work of art

discordant:
clashing, unmatching

draughtsman:
someone who draws with skill

ephemeral:
existing for only a short period of time

exposure:
the total amount of light the shutter of a camera lets in when it is open

Expressionism:
an art movement of the early 20th century that emphasised the inner feelings of the artist

Fauves:
artists (in French, 'wild beasts') who belonged to an early 20th-century art movement that used pure, bright colours and simplified form

figurative:
representing or portraying things so they are recognisable

foamcore:
lightweight board with a styrofoam centre often used to mount artworks or in architectural model construction

framing device:
a way of drawing attention to the subject of your image by blocking other parts of the image with something in the scene, leading the eye to the focal point

Futurism:
an Italian art movement from 1910 to the 1920s that embraced everything new and modern and rejected the past

gesso:
a paint made from a mixture of plaster and glue that is used for the background of paintings

herbarium:
collection of dried plants

icon:
an object or image of devotion

impasto medium:
an additive put into paint to make it very thick

Impressionists:
artists who made work that responded directly to the world as they saw it, by capturing its changing qualities, such as movement, as they happened

incidental:
occurring by chance

interactive:
involving a collaboration between the artist, the artwork and the audience

intricate:
detailed

irony:
when a meaning is given that is opposite to the real meaning

kinetic:
describing art in which moving parts are a key element, either involving audience participation (for example, with buttons to push), or using motors or natural forces like wind for power

kitsch:
art considered to be in poor taste

light box:
a glass-topped table or box lit from underneath the glass by fluorescent lights, usually used to view slides or transparencies such as X-rays

MDF board:
multi-density fibreboard, a manufactured wood product made by breaking down wood into fibres, combining it with glues and compressing it to form dense, strong wooden panels

microcosm:
small version of something larger

monochrome:
one colour and tones of that colour

motifs:
designs

mummified:
preserved and wrapped in cloth, as was the custom in ancient Egyptian times

mundane:
ordinary

paradox:
something that contradicts itself

parody:
imitation of something else in a humorous way

photomontage:
an image made by combining photographs or parts of photographs, either by hand or using computer software

Photorealistic:
belonging to a style of painting and drawing in which the artist tries to produce images as clear as photographs, even reproducing photographic flaws such as lens flares, distortions and reduced depths of field

poly clay:
a bendable sculpting clay made from plastic polymers that does not dry out and can be fired to hardness at temperatures low enough to use a normal kitchen oven

Post-Impressionists:
artists who belong to an early 20th-century art movement that used bright colour, broken and expressive brushstrokes and more structured composition than Impressionist artists

recontextualise:
take something from where it belongs and use it in a new way

Renaissance:
a historical period in which artists became fascinated with the Classic age of Rome and Greece, and adopted the styles and subjects of many Classical artworks

rendered:
shaded or depicted

replica:
copy or imitation

scanograph
a digital image captured by scanning objects on a scanner rather than using a digital camera

seamlessly:
without seams or visible joins

shutter speed:
the length of time a camera's shutter is open when taking a photo, affecting the amount of light exposed through the lens to light-sensitive paper or a digital image sensor

sidewalk chalk:
a special sort of chalk for drawing on footpaths

site-specific installation:
a work of art designed for a specific place and relating in some way to that place

SLR camera:
single-lens reflex camera, which uses an automatic moving mirror system that allows the photographer to see exactly what will be captured on film

stencil:
pattern with a cut-out design

stop-motion:
a form of animation where objects are photographed and moved slightly between each shot, giving the appearance, when the photographs are viewed quickly in succession, that the object is moving on its own

Surrealist:
an artist who uses dreamlike images relying on imagination and fantasy

unify:
bring two or more things together to make one

vanitas:
a still-life painting with objects symbolising the fleeting nature of life and its vain, pointless ambitions ('vanitas' is Latin for vanity), such as skulls, unlit candles, dying flowers and hourglasses

Victorian:
describing a style of design from the early 1800s to the beginning of the 20th century, with a focus on elaborate decoration

votive:
an image or sculpture dedicated to a god

Credits

This information is in addition to that provided in the captions on the pages for some images. Numbers given here are page numbers.

Front cover

Banksy (1974–), UK, Street Cleaner, date unknown. Spray-paint stencilled graffiti. **Graffiti painting depicting worker removing prehistoric cave paintings.** The Cans Festival Graffiti Exhibition in Leake Street takes place in an unused London Underground tunnel. It was organised by the graffiti artist known as Banksy. This painting is one of his contributions to the exhibit. © Picture Hooked/LOOP IMAGES/Loop Images/Corbis

Chapter 1

3 Vincent Van Gogh (1853–1890), Netherlands, *Self-Portrait 12*, 1889. Oil on canvas, 65.5 × 50.5 cm. Photo: Corbis. Attributed to Vincent Van Gogh.

5 Jason Mecier (1969–), USA, *Pink*. 3-D mosaic, mixed media, 61 × 89 cm. © Jason Mecier/munrocampagna.com

6 Hercilia Lopes, contemporary artist, Brazil, *Universo-Feminino-X*, 2008. Scanograph, discarded jewellery. © Hercilia Lopes scannography.org

7 Bert Simons, contemporary artist, Netherlands, *Self Portrait*. Laser scan 3-D portrait, paper, life-size.© Bert Simons. www.bertsimons.nl

Chapter 3

29 Marcel Duchamp (1834–1917), France, *Nude Descending a Staircase, No. 2*, 1912. Oil on canvas, 146 × 89 cm. The Louise and Walter Arensberg Collection, 1950. Philadelphia Museum of Art, Philadelphia, Pennsylvania, USA. © The Philadelphia Museum of Art/Art Resource, NY. Photo: Philadelphia Museum of Art/licensed by Viscopy.

Chapter 4

34 Narelle Autio (1969–), Australia, *Untitled (cat#15)*, 2002 from series *Not of this Earth*. Photograph, archival inkjet prints on canvas 66 × 100 cm, edition of 4. © Narelle Autio, image courtesy Stills Gallery.

37 Shoichi Aoki (1955–), Japan, Untitled 1998. Digital photograph originally published in *FRUiTS* magazine no. 11. Tokyo, Japan. Collection: Powerhouse Museum, Sydney.

38 Grace Cossington Smith (1892–1984), Australia, *The Lacquer Room*, 1935–1936. Oil on paperboard on plywood, 74 × 90.8 cm. Purchased 1967. Collection: Art Gallery of New South Wales, Sydney. © Estate of Grace Cossington Smith.

38 Charles Conder (1868–1909), England/Australia, *Departure of the Orient—Circular Quay*, 1888. Oil on canvas 45.1 × 50 cm. Purchased 1888. Collection: Art Gallery of New South Wales. Photograph by Jenni Cater.

Chapter 5

53 Ross Sparks (1965–), Australia, *Tokyo Restaurant*, 2007. Digital photograph, 3457 × 2267 pixels. Photography by Ross Sparks, Copyright Sparrowhawk Consulting, www.sparrowhawk.com.au. This image may not be reproduced without specific consent from the copyright holder.

56 Russell Drysdale (1912–1981), Australia, *The Drover's Wife*, 1945. Oil painting on canvas, 51.5 × 61.5 cm. National Gallery of Australia, Canberra. A gift to the people of Australia by Mr and Mrs Benno Schmidt of New York and Esperance, Western Australia through the American Friends of the Australian National Gallery 1987. © Estate of Russell Drysdale.

58 Ali Yanya (1963–), Turkey/UK, *Crowds I*, 2009. Oil painting on canvas, 40 × 50 cm. Photograph © Sandra Daniel. Artist at www.aliyanya.com

Chapter 6

63 Ando Hiroshige (1797–1858), Japan, *Horse-Mackerel and Prawns*, 1832, from the series *A Shoal of Fish*. Colour woodcut print on paper, 25.6 × 35 cm. http://www.conncoll.edu/visual/Japanese-prints/index-2.html

63 Helle Jorgensen (1958–), Denmark/Australia, *Spotty Fish*, 2005. Hand-coloured lino print, Japanese paper, 30 × 30 cm. © Helle Jorgensen. http://hellejorgensen.typepad.com

66 Wassily Kandinsky (1866–1944), Russia, *Black Lines*, 1913. Oil on canvas, 129.4 × 131.1 cm. Solomon R. Guggenheim Museum, New York. © 2009 Artists Rights Society (ARS), New York/ADAGP, Paris. Solomon R. Guggenheim Founding Collection, by gift 37.241.

70 Katherine Taylor (1974–), USA, *Weebotts*, 2006. Sculpture, sticks, leaves, cardboard, paint, 100 × 100 × 130 cm. © the artist Katherine C Taylor, ktcreature.com

Chapter 7

73 Olive Cotton (1911–2003), Australia, *Skeleton leaf*, 1964. Gelatin silver photograph, 24.7 × 19.6 cm. Olive Cotton Estate, Art Gallery of New South Wales, Sydney.

75 Christian Staebler (1958–), France, *Bryony*, 2005. Digital scanograph, 3543 × 4961 pixels. © Christian Staebler. www.chris-staebler.com

81 Emily Kame Kngwarreye (c. 1910–1996), Australia, *Anwerlarr angerr, Big yam*, 1996. Synthetic polymer paint on canvas, 401 × 245 cm. National Gallery of Victoria, Melbourne. Purchased by the National Gallery Women's Association to mark the directorship of Dr Timothy Potts, 1998.

81 Xia Chang (1388–1470), China, *Bamboo in Wind*, Qingfeng gaojie, Ming Dynasty c. 1460. Hanging scroll, ink on paper, 203.4 × 59.7 cm; overall with mounting 299.7 × 74.6 cm; overall with knobs 299.7 × 83.3 cm. Edward Elliot Family Collection, Gift of Douglas Dillon, 1989 (1989.235.1), The Metropolitan Museum of Art, New York, NY, USA. © The Metropolitan Museum of Art/Art Resource, NY.

84 Mark Dixon (1971–), Canada, *Untitled*, 2005. Acrylic on canvas, 60 × 60 cm. © Mark Dixon. www.markdixon.ca

84 Mark Dixon (1971–), Canada, *Untitled*, 2005. Acrylic on board, 20 × 20 cm. © Mark Dixon. www.markdixon.ca

Chapter 8

91 Artist unknown (Ptolemaic period, c 400–30 BC), 330–30 BCE, Egypt, *Cat*. Bronze cast sculpture, H: 28 cm. Harris Brisbane Dick Fund, 1956 (56.16.1), The Metropolitan Museum of Art, New York, NY, USA. © The Metropolitan Museum of Art/Art Resource, New York.

Chapter 11

128 Juan Gris (1887–1927), Spain, *Still Life with Guitar*, 1912–1913. Drawing, pencil and gouache on paper. Awesome Art.

Chapter 13

146 Richard 'Doc' Nagy (Datamancer), contemporary artist, *Steampunk Laptop*, 2007. Refitted Hewlett-Packard ZT1000 laptop, mixed media. Image: Datamancer. www.datamancer.net.

Chapter 14

156 Jason Salavon (1970–), USA, *Still Life II (Glassware)*, 2007. Custom software and industrial LCD panel, played on a continuous loop. Photo: courtesy of the artist. www.salavon.com

Chapter 16

184 Denise Litchfield contemporary artist, Australia, *The Knitted Tree*, 2009. Knitted yarn, dimensions variable. © Denise Litchfield. www.grrlandog.com

193 Margarita Sampson, *Big Mumma and the Kittens*, 2006. Variable-sized installation, PVC textiles, beading, polystyrene beads. Image courtesy of Adrian Tan. www.philosophyblog.com.au

194 Crop circles, UK. Image: Steve Alexander. www.temporarytemples.com.uk

Chapter 18

208 Ezra Stoller (1915–2004), USA, *Fallingwater*, location: Bear Run PA, (Architect: Frank Lloyd Wright), 1963. Colour transparency, 10.16 × 12.7 cm. Release: not released. Photographer: Ezra Stoller/Esto.

214 Jonathan Farr, contemporary artist, UK, *Tottenham Court Road from Centrepoint 2*, 2007. Charcoal on paper, 100 × 150 cm. © Jonathan Farr. www.jonathanfarr.com

Index